Roger Vergé's
Vegetables in the
French Style

With Martine Anglade

*

Roger Vergé's Vegetables in the French Style

*

Photographs by

Bernard Touillon

Assisted by

Françoise Le fébure

Translated by

Edward Schneider

ARTISAN

New York

*To my father,
an amateur gardener, but a caring one,
who raised his vegetables with
passionate dedication.*

Text and photographs
copyright © 1992 Flammarion, Paris
U. S. translation copyright © 1994 Artisan

Translated by Edward Schneider

Published in 1994 by Artisan,
a division of Workman Publishing Company, Inc.
708 Broadway
New York, NY 10003

Originally published as *Les légumes de mon moulin*
Designed by Marc Walter
Editorial direction by Ghislaine Bavoillot
Color separations by Colourscan France

Vergé, Roger, 1930–
[Légumes de mon moulin. English]
Roger Vergé's vegetables in the French style /
with Martine
Anglade ; photographs by Bernard Touillon,
assisted by Françoise Le fébure ; translated by
Edward Schneider.
Translation of: Les légumes de mon moulin
Includes index.
ISBN 1-885183-04-6
1. Cookery (Vegetables)   2. Cookery, French.
I. Anglade, Martine.   II. Title.
III. Title: Vegetables in the French style.
TX801.V4813 1994
641.6'5—dc20   94-11420

Printed in Germany
First Printing 1994
10 9 8 7 6 5 4 3 2 1

A Passion for Vegetables

MY EARLIEST MEMORIES taste of the little springtime vegetables my father lovingly grew in our garden in central France. As winter came to an end, and as the sun began to warm the soil he had carefully prepared the previous autumn, he would take up his spade and turn over the earth.

The narcissi were beginning to show; the cherry trees were in bud. The birds were wildly chattering in the trees as they waited for his mossy spade to turn up a clod of earth richly larded with worms.

With his rake, my father broke up and pulverized the soil, then divided it into broad beds ready for the seeds, the plants, the tiny bulbs that would soon grow into hardy vegetables.

I take great pleasure in choosing my vegetables in my garden, situated above the village of Mougins.

I remember myself as a child contentedly, gravely supervising my father's patient work as he protected his seedlings from the morning cold and the afternoon sun, and as he sprinkled the beds from the great, bulbous head of a zinc watering can, moistening them with a warm, gentle shower. But more work lay ahead.

I can see him later on, bent double as he weeded, eliminating anything that did not belong, digging out the white roots of the weeds that sapped and depleted his soil. Then he took up his hoe and aerated the earth, in little strokes carefully calculated not to sever a stem or mutilate a plant.

When the shoots sprouted leaves and turned skyward, it was time to weave and set the trellises or the hazel boughs onto which the beans, the peas, the snowpeas would train themselves. The pods swelled; the lettuces formed; the carrots raised their feathery leaves to the sun; the onion greens thrust upward. Beneath the foliage of the potato plants, we knew the earth was hoarding tiny treasures.

My father waited for the cool of the evening to pick his first vegetables, and I often had the treat of joining him. How proud I was to be filling the great wicker baskets with bunches of fresh vegetables and loading them on to the big kitchen table!

And I remember my mother and my aunt working delicately, deftly, scraping young carrots, rubbing the skins from new potatoes, extracting peas from their succulent pods, cleaning the opalescent onions, and more. With love and conscientiousness equal to my father's, they arranged these tiny vegetables in a black iron casserole, topped them with lettuces, and briefly, gently cooked them with pink batons of unsmoked bacon. Suffused with the water of spring showers

Small-scale growers in the Grasse countryside are the trusted purveyors of vegetables for my restaurant, le Moulin de Mougins.

and morning dew, these vegetables needed no more elaborate treatment; they quickly yielded up their aromas and flavors. The women coated them in fresh butter (with its own hazelnut perfume) to create the finest fricassee in the world—a fricassee that, for me, still represents all the happiness that life can afford us.

Many years later I rediscovered that happiness in a mill deep in the heart of Provence, now home to my restaurant. Can any place in the world be more headily aromatic than the Provençal hills? How could a food lover like myself resist the scents of rosemary, sage, savory, wild thyme, and lavender? Here, the flowers and fruits taste of honey and the sun-drenched vegetables have a bolder flavor than elsewhere.

You need only stroll through a Provence marketplace to recognize the diversity and quality of our southern French vegetables. The multicolored displays are magnificent. Gleaming eggplants share the limelight with vivid peppers, bright tomatoes, marbled zucchini as tender as butter, big red onions, pyramids of tiny violet artichokes, young turnips, plump sweet fennel, and braids of perfect garlic. And what a festival of greenery! Chard, its broad stems agleam; silvery cardoons; little heart-shaped cabbages tinged with violet; broccoli—green, yellow, and purple. And herbs by the dozen: bunches of dill, wild fennel, chervil, coriander, and thyme; branches of savory (known locally as *pebre d'ail*) and bay; and first and foremost, the king of the Provençal garden, basil—*pistou*—looking like nothing special growing in its little clay pot but still the envy of the rest of the world.

And just consider this: all those wonders stand side by side with tubs of olives; bouquets of golden lupines; sacks of almonds and pine nuts; torrid spices; fragrant oils; and wines tasting of the sun. How could anyone not adopt Provence, as I did? How could anyone not settle his heart and his life there?

But all markets have a charm of their own, and if you love vegetables as I do, you should always buy them at the farmers' market, where you are far more likely to find a local truck farmer. Maybe the vegetables will be smaller than at the supermarket; perhaps they will still have earth clinging to them or will be damp with dew. But they will definitely have that one essential element without which you might as well not bother cooking vegetables: freshness.

Freshness. You can feel it; you can taste it; you can smell it—but first and foremost, you can see it.

If a vegetable is supposed to be glossy—like eggplants, cucumbers, peppers, and zucchini—keep away if it looks dull. Also keep away from any vegetables with brown or black stains, mold, or holes that could harbor insects. And don't bother with carrots, potatoes, turnips, or beans that have become soft; or with potatoes, peas, beans, garlic, or onions that have begun to sprout.

In the gardens of Le Moulin de Mougins, I carefully monitor the burgeoning herbs and ripening vegetables.

With leafy-topped vegetables like fennel, celery, leeks, and radishes, examine the leaves. They should be green and smooth, not rotting, crushed, or dried out. That is especially true for green vegetables. Some of them, like spinach, rot very quickly, so do not buy the greens if you see the tiniest sign of rot, because it will spread rapidly. Nor should you buy any leafy vegetables on which you can see bugs of any kind (aphids, beetles, or caterpillars, for example); even though the vegetable may look fine outside, its core could harbor unwanted guests.

Firmness is another good indication of freshness in many vegetables, such as green beans, peas, fava beans, eggplants, zucchini, and bell peppers.

The second criterion is season. True, we can buy green beans year-round. Generally they look nice and are of a perfectly calibrated size, but they are next to tasteless. Tomatoes, which are so delicious  when sun ripened, are mediocre when raised in a greenhouse. The same is true for all salad greens and for most other summer vegetables, such as eggplants, zucchini, and bell peppers. They are tastier in season, and cheaper, too.

Recently I was wandering through the wonderful market in Isle-sur-la-Sorgue, about twelve miles outside Avignon. There I saw lovely fresh eggs displayed right next to some bunches of tiny wild asparagus, and it suddenly occurred to me to combine them in a scrambled-egg dish. The same kind of thing happens every day. I love vegetables so much that I am always thinking of new ways to cook them.

Unlike other ingredients such as poultry, meat, and fish—which look radically different when they are cooked—vegetables more or less retain the appearance bestowed upon them by nature: the appearance of life itself. As a cook, I find this a tremendous asset that enables me to visualize the way a new dish will look.

The very appearance of vegetables fascinates me. I almost always munch on a piece as I peel them—or even before, in the garden, when I walk past a ripening tomato, or when I think the radish beds need thinning, or when I have to check on how the peas are doing.

I am eternally amazed by the elegance and intensity of their flavors and by the variety of their textures. What a difference there is between a crunchy carrot and a tender cucumber, between the bitterness of a little green bell pepper and the sweetness of a pea, between an acidic green tomato and the same tomato a few days later when it has had some time to ripen!

The treasure trove of vegetables is indeed infinite, so I am always surprised to recall that chefs have generally given short shrift to these noble ingredients—which could hardly grow without the patience and passionate commitment of gardeners. For the longest time they were used only as an accompaniment for meat or fish. For instance, to set off a saddle of lamb, chefs would prepare little mounds of poached, glazed carrots, green beans, and turnips, with little regard for their flavor or their texture.

But those flavors and textures deserve respect and care. One of my goals in writing this book is to help you bring out the best in these vegetables.

It is certainly true that good vegetables need very little adornment: a dollop of fresh butter, a drizzle of fruity olive oil (perhaps from near les Baux-de-Provence), a few grains of salt, and a little freshly ground pepper. But why not give them more lavish treatment? I can assure you that this book would never have come into being if I didn't deeply believe that the vegetables deserved it!

As a small child I knew the floral flavor of butter melting on a young braised lettuce, the taste of walnut oil permeating a tender heart of celery. These delicate fats (so decried nowadays) are perfectly digestible if used properly and with moderation—and above all, if they are not cooked, but added only at the end of the cooking process.

They are the basis of the sauces I like to serve with vegetables (see the chapter "Sauces and *Coulis*"). To this base I add various spices and aromatics in combinations and quantities chosen carefully so as to bring out each vegetable's flavor.

Garden herbs have a place of honor among these aromatics; in all their diversity, they let you give infinite variety to your sauces. I cannot stress this too much. Even if you have only a tiny handkerchief of land or a few flower pots on your balcony, do grow as many different herbs as you possibly can. They will give you the wherewithal to create original, personal sauces that will shed an entirely new light on your vegetable cooking. Try it. Starting today, add a sprinkling of chopped mint to your peas and a few chervil leaves to your carrots, and lend a subtle garlic note to your cucumbers with some freshly snipped chives. Let me know how it goes!

Spices and other seasonings are also valuable allies, but again they must be employed cannily—especially salt, which we have a tendency to overuse. Vegetables already contain mineral salts whose flavors can all too easily be masked by too much salt. Similarly, some vegetables—radishes, for example—have a natural pepper flavor, so you should avoid adding additional pepper.

On the other hand, sugar is a natural with inherently sweet vegetables such as carrots, turnips, beets, fennel, peas, winter squash, and pumpkin. Traditional French cooking had it right, sprinkling sugar on *carottes Vichy*, adding caramelized sugar to peas, and glazing turnips. These traditions have fallen somewhat out of favor in France—perhaps because we (wrongly) associate food combinations of sweet and salty with Britain and America. In several of the recipes in this book I have tried to revive this approach; to me, these naturally sweet vegetables are a real treat when combined with

I prefer the little black olives of Nice or Nyons. But big or small, olives yield delicous oils—strong-tasting, peppery, or mild, each with its own flavor.

Olive oils from the les Baux Valley, from Opio, from the Haut Var, from Tuscany, and from Umbria. I love to sample their varied aromas.

sugar, honey, almonds, dried currants, or fresh fruit. This was also the inspiration for the vegetable desserts I've suggested as a suitably delectable finish for all-vegetable dinners (see "All-Vegetable Menus," page 237).

Vegetable dishes are all the better for being served on an appropriately set table. At official, formal dinners, for example, I arrange asparagus on special rectangular dishes with silver tongs, and serve it on extremely fine Limoge or Sèvres porcelain.

But when I am entertaining close friends who share my taste for interesting tableware, I like to use one of those charming, colorful, highly decorated 1920s asparagus services. (There are lovely ones for artichokes, too.)

A sprig of thyme can change everything.

Sometimes the recipes themselves are the center of attention. It is best, for instance, to serve a gratin in its own baking dish and choose dinner plates that will go well with this. With homey dishes like vegetable casseroles, I have no hesitation in bringing them to the table in the iron, earthenware, or china casserole in which they cooked, and I select appropriately rustic dinner plates.

When serving a dish that is characteristic of a particular region of France, I always try to find table settings that reflect its regional origins. It seems to me that local handicrafts have a way of making the most of the produce and specialties of the area.

You can create a wonderful Provençal table setting with traditionally patterned tablecloths and ceramics from Uzès—with their sparkling turquoises, peony reds, greens, and ochers—or from Moustiers, with their delicately drawn and colored patterns. They will show off summer vegetables, eggplant molds, *tians*, *pastillas*, and so forth as though displayed in a jewel box. At a summer dinner you can also add a few glass candleholders from Biot.

When you are serving an *aïoli* or an *anchoïade*, make an attractive arrangement of the vegetables on a chestnut-bark or cork tray; these noble rustic materials are a good match for the natural simplicity of the vegetables.

In central France, where I grew up, I like to serve sophisticated vegetable dishes in Gien or Nevers pottery and more countrified ones in rustic stoneware. A pumpkin tart, for example, is perfectly at home on a big stoneware platter from Sologne in soft yellow with brown accents.

When I travel I am always finding traditional crockery so beautiful that it sometimes inspires new recipes—or sends me in search of local dishes.

Don't be timid about doing as I do and trying to match a regional recipe and its local crockery. It makes for an elegant, warm, and exotic atmosphere that will charm your guests.

My passion for vegetables made it inevitable that this book should not be a mere collection of recipes, so I have put a lot of myself into this volume: memories of childhood, of Provence, of my journeys. There is no end to vegetable recipes, but I had to choose only 150. Soups and salads alone deserve one or more books, and I have just hinted at them here, offering a few simple, tasty suggestions. There is nothing to say, however, that I will not go into the subject in greater detail in the future.

The stars of this book are the vegetables nearest my heart: the ones my father grew and my mother and aunt cooked. But even among these, I have highlighted fresh, light vegetables. I am saving for another occasion the pleasure of sharing more recipes for starches—of which I am no less fond.

Yet the irresistible attraction that vegetables exert on me is not limited by my father's garden walls, even though those walls demarcated a whole world for me as a child. Wherever I travel I roam the markets, and that is why I wanted to present recipes for vegetables that are not traditionally grown in France, but that are readily available in ethnic markets both here in France and in the United States.

Did you know that there can be a subtle relationship between vegetables and wine? Take asparagus. It has the bad reputation of altering the flavor of wine, while the problem is really the sauces with which it is often served. Not long ago, I had occasion to try two very different wines with asparagus. With steamed asparagus with *sauce mousseline*—a hollandaise lightened with whipped cream—I drank a sweet Barsac, and it was a perfect marriage. Then I shared a plate of asparagus *en barigoule* (see page 228 for a description) with a friend, and we drank an Amontillado sherry: another great success.

A mélange of tiny, meltingly tender vegetables served with a fresh, fruity Crozes Hermitage from the Rhône Valley is a real treat.

And big red bell peppers, peeled and dressed with fruity olive oil and fresh thyme, are simply marvelous with white Condrieu, also from the Rhône. White Vouvray from the Loire Valley is perfect with white of leek poached and served with a sauce made of walnut oil sparked with a little wine vinegar and fresh tarragon. Provençal red wine from the Coteaux des Baux (a three- or four-year-old Trevallon, for example) is ideal with an eggplant gratin. And, white Châteauneuf-du-Pape drunk with winter squash roasted with a little cinnamon would make for a genuine feast.

Those few examples are just a hint of the joys that await you—joys you can share with your food-loving friends and family.

Rosy red radishes and a rosé wine produced by les vignerons de Saint-Tropez.

PAGES 14–15: *There are so many herbs in Provence! This photograph pictures only a few.*

Sauces and Coulis

I THINK THAT the worldwide renown of French cooking owes a great deal to the variety and quality of the sauces with which it enhances meat, shellfish, and fish. And I agree with the notion that sauces are like the signature of a great chef. But I have never understood—and never shall—why vegetables should be deemed unworthy of these wonderful sauces.

Some people claim that vegetables need nothing beyond their innate flavors, textures, and colors to entice us; these people prefer to eat them plain, crunching them with salt or serving them steamed with a little olive oil or a touch of butter. I like this treatment too, especially when the vegetables are freshly picked and at the height of their season. But I am also sure they merit more elaborate accompaniment, and that is why I love to coat them with sauces based on herbs and vegetables.

Small or large, purple or green, basil is the basis of Provençal pistou.

A sauce can be considered a success when it not only mates well with the vegetable it is served with but also helps bring out its distinctive qualities. It should, therefore, be subtle and delicate so as not to obscure the flavor of the vegetable; but it should also have enough substance to coat the vegetable and give it the body it can lack. Most vegetables contain a great deal of water, so their texture needs to be enhanced. For years I have worked toward this, and I am happy now to pass on these flavorful, easy-to-make sauces.

Although they were developed especially for vegetables, you can use these sauces to add variety to other dishes, depending on your menu or your mood. They can be served with meat, variety meats, fish, or shellfish. I leave it to your appetite and your imagination to find new combinations to enjoy.

A Fruit Sauce

A dressing for summer salads. Don't hesitate to make a little extra. Refrigerated in a bottle or jar it will keep for several days. It is easy to make.

In a saucepan, lightly toast a teaspoon each of fennel and coriander seeds. Add $\frac{1}{2}$ cup of wine vinegar and reduce by one-third. Then add a teaspoon of honey and $\frac{1}{2}$ cup of raspberries. Bring the mixture to the boil, take it off the heat, let it cool completely, and strain it through a fine sieve. Mix with a tablespoon of Dijon mustard and two cups of your favorite oil (personally, I prefer extra-virgin olive oil). Add salt and pepper to taste, and pour into a bottle or jar.

Basic Potato-Cream Sauce

Sauce de Base à la Crème

✳

This basic sauce will provide delicate support for your vegetables. Easy to make and inexpensive, it can be varied in a thousand delicious ways depending on what you add to it—herbs, spices, aromatics, or vegetable purées—and can thus be adapted to the flavor of any vegetable. You will use this potato purée in many of my sauce recipes.

FOR 4 SERVINGS

Preparation: 20 minutes
Cooking time: 25 minutes

1 medium waxy potato,
   such as a red-skinned
4 tablespoons butter or
   fruity olive, walnut, or
   hazelnut oil
¾ cup heavy cream
Salt and freshly ground
   black pepper

First make a potato purée. Peel, quarter, and boil the potato, starting it in cold, lightly salted water. When water comes to the boil, lower the heat and cook potato gently for about 20 minutes, or until it is tender but not falling apart. Drain and put it through the fine disk of a food mill into a bowl.

Add the butter in little pieces, or the oil a little at a time. Beat the mixture with a wooden spoon until smooth. (This purée will keep a day or more in the refrigerator, covered with plastic wrap to prevent the formation of a skin.)

To finish the sauce, bring the cream to the boil, let it boil for 30 seconds or so, then pour it into a blender. Add enough of the potato purée to give it the consistency you want. Blend thoroughly. Season with salt and pepper.

Preferably, serve immediately. But this basic sauce and all its herb variations reheat nicely in the microwave.

Note: The texture of the sauce depends on the amount of potato. If it is too thick for you, you can add a little chicken stock or boiled cream. (If your stock is already salted, do not add too much additional salt.)

Green Sauce

Sauce Verte

✳

This herb sauce goes well with any poached or steamed vegetable. Depending on your mood, you can give prominence to any flavor you like. The sauce is also delicious with white-meat dishes such as chicken fricassée or veal escallops sautéed in butter, with steamed fish such as salmon fillets or strips of sole, or with calves' sweetbreads or calves' or lambs' brains. With a hint of garlic and a pinch of Italian parsley, it is perfect for frogs' legs, snails, shellfish, and more.

Season the cream with salt and pepper and bring to the boil. As soon as it boils, add the herbs. Immediately pour the mixture into a blender and blend until a smooth liquid. Gradually add the potato purée until the sauce is as thick as you want it. Serve immediately; if you let the sauce boil after you have added the herbs, it will lose its lovely color.

Note: If you have no blender, you can use a knife to chop the herbs to a purée and a whisk to prepare the mixture. The method is the same, but you will need a little less than ¹/₂ cup of cream because a sauce made in the blender is thirstier for liquid.

If you want a darker green sauce, drop the herbs into boiling water for a second or two (but not the sorrel, which would disintegrate). Then plunge them into ice water, and dry them by squeezing them in your hand before adding them to the cream. A few spinach leaves will also deepen the color.

For 4 servings

Preparation: 15 minutes
Cooking time: 5 minutes

³/₄ cup heavy cream
Salt and freshly ground
 black pepper
A handful of herbs
 (watercress, nasturtium
 leaves, sorrel, or chervil;
 or a mixture of parsley,
 chives, and tarragon; or
 Italian parsley and garlic
 with a touch of saffron),
 stemmed, washed,
 and dried
¹/₃ cup potato purée,
 prepared with butter
 (page 18)

Six-Herb Sauce

Sauce aux Six Herbes

✳

You will relish this pretty, fresh-tasting sauce with poached or steamed cauliflower, broccoli, salsify, turnips, or carrots. But it also mates well with fish—fillets of sole, turbot, or other delicate white-fleshed fish—with shellfish, with poached white meats such as veal shank or chicken, or with variety meats such as brains or sweetbreads.

Bring the cream to the boil and pour it into a blender. Add the herbs and blend until you have a smooth pistachio-colored sauce. Gradually add potato purée until the sauce reaches the consistency you prefer. Season to taste with salt and pepper, and serve immediately.

For 4 servings

Preparation: 15 minutes
Cooking time: 5 minutes

³/₄ cup heavy cream
¹/₃ cup chopped parsley
¹/₃ cup chopped chervil
3 tablespoons chopped
 chives
About 10 basil leaves
1 heaping tablespoon
 chopped tarragon
1 heaping tablespoon
 chopped dill
¹/₃ cup potato purée,
 prepared with olive oil
 (page 18)
Salt and freshly ground
 black pepper

OPPOSITE PAGE:
Red Bell Pepper Coulis

Red Bell Pepper Coulis
Coulis de Poivrons Doux

✳

FOR 8 TO 10 SERVINGS

Preparation: 15 minutes
Cooking time: 25 minutes

2¼ pounds red bell
   peppers
2 medium white onions
2 tablespoons butter or
   10 tablespoons olive oil
2 medium ripe tomatoes
3 to 4 garlic cloves
   (1 optional)
A large sprig of thyme
2 bay leaves
Salt and freshly ground
   black pepper
Generous ¾ cup water or
   chicken stock
A few leaves of an herb
   such as basil, fresh
   coriander, savory, dill,
   parsley, sage, or rosemary; or a star anise; or
   black Niçoise or Nyons
   olives (optional)

You will find a thousand uses for this coulis, hot or cold: with sun-drenched vegetables such as tomatoes, eggplant, and zucchini or with other fried or grilled vegetables. But don't stop there. How about fillets of red snapper browned in a skillet, then roasted in this coulis along with tiny capers, pitted black Niçoise olives, and a slice of lemon? It's a treat served with rice pilaf.

Seed the peppers and discard the stems and internal ribs. Slice peppers.

Peel the onions and slice them.

Put the peppers and onions into a heavy saucepan with the butter or oil, cover the pan, and let them sweat over very low heat until they are very soft, about 10 to 15 minutes.

Stem the tomatoes and cut them into large chunks; do not seed or juice them.

Peel and lightly crush 3 garlic cloves.

Add the garlic, tomatoes, thyme, and bay leaves to the cooked onions and peppers. Season with salt and pepper and add water or, better, chicken stock.

Cook over medium heat for 15 minutes, then put through the fine disk of a food mill or purée in a blender. If desired, add any of the optional items to vary the flavor. Chop the herbs and remaining clove garlic. Pit the olives and chop. Add the star anise, which you remove before serving. Be inventive and try other additions, too, for nothing is more satisfying than making your own discoveries.

Basil Sauce
Sauce au Basilic

✳

There are many versions of the traditional Provençal sauce, pistou. Its two basic ingredients are basil and olive oil, but depending on local custom, it can also contain garlic, tomatoes, pine nuts, Italian parsley, almonds, anchovies, and so forth. Whatever the ingredients, they are crushed in a marble or wooden mortar to extract all their juices; olive oil is then beaten into the sauce, to end up with a thick cream.

This variation is for sun-drenched vegetables such as tomatoes, bell peppers, and eggplant, either steamed or grilled. But it will also enliven a plain roasted

FOR 4 SERVINGS

Preparation: 10 minutes
Cooking time: 5 minutes

¹/₂ cup heavy cream
About 20 basil leaves,
  chopped
²/₃ cup chopped Italian
  parsley
¹/₂ small garlic clove,
  minced
1 teaspoon hazelnut oil
¹/₃ cup potato purée, made
  with olive oil (page 18)
Salt and freshly ground
  black pepper

fish or a dish of snails and mushrooms sautéed in butter. I personally like it a lot with sea scallops seared in a skillet and garnished with a diced tomato and some peas. And it is even good with large pasta such as ziti, cooked al dente and sprinkled with grated Comté or Swiss Gruyère cheese.

Bring the cream to the boil and pour into a blender. Add the basil, parsley, garlic, and hazelnut oil; blend.

Gradually add potato purée until the sauce reaches the consistency you prefer.

Season with salt and pepper to taste, and serve immediately.

Asparagus Sauce
Sauce aux Asperges

✳

This sauce will bring out the absolute best in poached or steamed potatoes, salsify, leeks, zucchini, or artichoke hearts, or asparagus tips gently cooked in olive oil or butter. And don't be afraid to use it over sautéed chicken breasts or fish fillets. It is very good with risottos, too.

In this recipe you can use only the stalks of the asparagus if you like, saving the tips for another recipe such as a quiche or a salad. But this will result in a paler-colored sauce.

FOR 4 SERVINGS

Preparation: 15 minutes
Cooking time: 25 minutes

2¹/₄ pounds asparagus
1/2 cup olive oil, or
  6 tablespoons butter
A sprig of fresh savory
¹/₂ cup chicken stock
Salt and freshly ground
  black pepper

Peel, wash, and drain the asparagus, then cut into ¹/₂-inch pieces.

Heat 2 tablespoons of the olive oil or butter in a heavy saucepan. When it is hot, add the asparagus and savory. Salt and cook, covered, for 10 minutes over medium heat. Uncover the pan and cook over medium-low heat until the juices are completely reduced, less than 10 minutes.

Remove the savory and purée the asparagus in a blender. Strain the purée through a fine sieve to remove any remaining fibers. Return to the blender and add the chicken stock, remaining oil or butter, and salt and pepper to taste. Blend at high speed until the sauce is creamy. Keep warm in a hot-water bath or double boiler until ready to serve.

If you are not going to use the sauce right away, keep it in the refrigerator. To serve, reheat and blend again to restore the smooth emulsion.

Note: Making this sauce with butter rather than olive oil will result in a more neutral flavor.

Chervil Sauce
Sauce au Cerfeuil

✳

An elegant, delicate sauce for steamed or poached vegetables, or for a white-fleshed fish, such as turbot, poached in a mixture of one part milk to two parts water, served on a bed of steamed baby carrots and sprinkled with coarse sea salt. You could replace the Chartreuse with Izara or any other herbal liqueur of monastic origins (for the monks were great epicures in the old days).

FOR 4 SERVINGS

Preparation: 10 minutes
Cooking time: 5 minutes

³/₄ cup heavy cream
²/₃ cup finely chopped chervil
1 teaspoon green Chartreuse liqueur
¹/₃ cup potato purée, made with butter (page 18)
Salt and freshly ground black pepper
A pinch of freshly grated nutmeg

Bring the cream to the boil, let it boil for 30 seconds or so, then pour it into a blender.

Add the chervil and Chartreuse, then gradually thicken the mixture with potato purée.

Blend well. Add salt and pepper to taste, and finish with a pinch of nutmeg.

Chive Sauce
Sauce à la Ciboulette

✳

Choose this chive sauce to enrich steamed or grilled vegetables, steamed fish, sautéed veal chops, or veal escallops—or even mussels, sea scallops, or bay scallops. Make it at the last minute to preserve its flavor and bright color.

FOR 4 SERVINGS

Preparation: 10 minutes
Cooking time: 5 minutes

³/₄ cup heavy cream
6 tablespoons finely chopped chives
¹/₃ cup potato purée, made with butter (page 18)
Salt and freshly ground black pepper
A pinch of ground ginger

Bring the cream to the boil, let it boil for 30 seconds or so, then pour it into a blender.

Add the chives, blend, then gradually thicken the mixture with the potato purée.

Blend well. Add salt and pepper to taste, and finish with a pinch of ginger.

Watercress Sauce

Sauce au Cresson

✷

FOR 4 SERVINGS

Preparation: 10 minutes
Cooking time: 10 minutes

Leaves from 1 bunch
watercress
3/4 cup heavy cream
1/3 cup potato purée,
made with walnut oil
(page 18)
Salt and freshly ground
black pepper
A pinch of freshly grated
nutmeg

How well watercress and walnut oil go together! They enhance but do not over-power vegetables with a robust flavor, such as steamed or poached celeriac (celery root), celery, broccoli, or cauliflower. A good free-range chicken, poached in stock, carved, and coated with this sauce, would be a real feast. Decorate it with purs-lane leaves or with nasturtium leaves and flowers for a lovely country lunch.

Wash and drain the watercress leaves.

Bring a quart of salted water to the boil, and add the watercress. Drain it immediately, plunge into cold water, and, with your hands, squeeze out as much water as possible.

Bring the cream to the boil; when it has boiled for half a minute or so, pour it into a blender. Thicken with the potato purée and add the water-cress. Blend until smooth.

Season with salt, pepper, and a pinch of nutmeg.

Italian Parsley Sauce

Sauce au Persil Plat

✷

FOR 4 SERVINGS

Preparation: 10 minutes
Cooking time: 5 minutes

2/3 cup finely chopped
Italian parsley
3/4 cup heavy cream
1/2 small garlic clove,
minced
1/3 cup potato purée, made
with butter or olive oil
(page 18)
Salt and freshly ground
black pepper
A few drops of *pastis*
(anise-flavored liqueur),
such as Pernod or Ricard

Flat-leaf parsley is also known as Italian parsley—don't ask me why. The leaves have more body and, more important, have much better taste than curly parsley. Use it and no other in this sauce, which will add even more flavor to poached or steamed carrots, turnips, leeks, asparagus, or cauliflower—and which could hardly be improved upon for lambs' brains poached in water acidulated with lemon juice.

Stem, wash, and dry the parsley. Chop it so finely that it becomes a purée.

Bring the cream to the boil, let it boil for 30 seconds or so, then pour it into a blender. Add the parsley and garlic.

Blend, then add the potato purée. Blend well. Add salt and pepper to taste, and finish with a few drops of *pastis*.

Serve immediately. Do not reheat, as this would change the flavor and the color.

White Bean and Basil Sauce

Sauce aux Cocos Frais et au Pistou

✳

I've been to a Tuscan inn where they brown the hindquarters of a rabbit in olive oil, then simmer it in this sauce, which I loved so much that I wanted to duplicate it for you. It is perfection with any nonstarchy vegetable, and also with sautéed chicken or rabbit. I also recommend it with al dente spaghetti or with baked tuna, swordfish, or sturgeon steaks. And if there is any left, you can add some chicken stock and you'll have a good soup.

You'll need only ⅔ cup of beans, but you may as well buy more because you can make them into an excellent salad by adding thinly sliced raw fennel bulb and a vinaigrette made of wine vinegar and olive oil.

First, make a bean purée. If the beans are fresh, shell them; if dried, soak them overnight in warm water, then drain them. Peel and coarsely chop the onion; heat olive oil in a heavy saucepan and cook the onion until lightly golden. Peel and chop the garlic, and add it to the onion along with the beans, chicken stock, water, a little salt, and the *bouquet garni*. Bring to the boil, then lower the heat and simmer until the beans are very soft, 30 to 40 minutes for fresh beans, 1 hour for dried.

Make the *pistou*. Drop the tomatoes into boiling water for 20 seconds to make it possible to peel them. Peel and seed the tomatoes and place them into a blender along with the olive oil, garlic clove, basil, parsley, and salt and pepper to taste.

Blend until you have a thin, homogeneous paste. If you like Parmesan cheese, you can add it now. Scrape the mixture into a bowl and set aside.

When the beans are cooked, remove the *bouquet garni* and place beans in the blender along with their cooking liquid. Blend until you have a loose purée.

When ready to serve, reheat the bean purée and, off the heat, whisk in the *pistou*.

Adjust seasoning to taste.

For 4 to 6 servings

Preparation: 15 minutes
Cooking time: 45 minutes to 1 hour

⅔ cup large white beans, such as cannellini or great northern, either fresh or dried
1 small onion
1 tablespoon olive oil
½ garlic clove
1 cup chicken stock
1 cup water
Salt and freshly ground black pepper

For the Bouquet Garni
A sprig of fresh thyme
½ bay leaf
A sprig of fresh sage
A few parsley stems

For the Pistou
2 medium tomatoes
¼ cup olive oil
1 small garlic clove, peeled
20 fresh basil leaves
5 parsley sprigs
Salt and freshly ground black pepper
2 tablespoons finely grated Parmesan cheese (optional)

Anise-Scented Beet Sauce

Sauce Rose à l'Anis

✳

FOR 6 TO 8 SERVINGS

Preparation: 10 minutes
Cooking time: 15 minutes

2 medium beets, either
   roasted or boiled
   (page 159)
¼ cup red wine vinegar
1 teaspoon sugar (if the
   beets were boiled)
¾ cup plus 2 tablespoons
   heavy cream
1 whole star anise or
   1 tablespoon *pastis*
   (anise-flavored liqueur),
   such as Pernod or Ricard
½ cup chicken stock
Salt and freshly ground
   black pepper
1 tablespoon Dijon
   mustard (optional)
Chervil, basil, or sage
   leaves, for garnish

What do you think about this? A flavorful, mildly sweet-and-sour sauce to give a pink coating to a poached, steamed, or grilled fillet of white-fleshed fish such as cod or sole anointed with a few drops of lemon juice, or poached vegetables such as asparagus, fennel, or celery. (But add the sauce only at the last minute, as the beets will stain anything they come in contact with.) I also like this sauce with a veal kidney roasted—still cased in its fat, as you can buy them in France—in a casserole; I pour some sauce on to the plate, mix in ½ teaspoonful of Dijon mustard, and put the roasted kidney on top; with mashed potatoes, it's absolutely delicious.

Peel the cooked beets and cut them into small dice.

Pour the vinegar into a saucepan, and add the beets (and the sugar, if they were boiled rather than roasted) and a pinch of salt. Cover and let simmer for about 10 minutes, then remove the lid and let the liquid evaporate completely.

Meanwhile, put the cream into another saucepan; add the star anise, if you are using it, and bring to the boil. Turn off the heat, cover the pan, and let the anise steep for at least 5 minutes. Remove the anise.

When all the beet liquid has evaporated, put the beets into a blender, add the hot cream, and blend at high speed, gradually adding the chicken stock and, if you did not use star anise, the *pastis* until you have a creamy sauce. Do not add too much stock because the sauce could separate.

Season with salt and pepper, and keep warm in a double boiler or hot-water bath.

A nice variation: add the Dijon mustard to the completed sauce.

Decorate the dish with whole chervil leaves, or with deep-fried basil or sage leaves. Serve immediately.

Aïoli

Sauce Aïoli

✳

OPPOSITE PAGE:
Aïoli

This marvelous sauce made of garlic, olive oil, and eggs evokes the sunshine. It lends its name to the famous Provençal dish of poached vegetables and fish, but it has many other uses as well, such as thickening the fish soup known as bourride. If you stir some into a cream sauce at the last minute, it will add

smoothness and a vivid perfume. I recommend it with any raw, poached, or steamed vegetables, and also with snails, braised fennel, baked potatoes, or hard-boiled eggs.

If your breath smells too aggressively of garlic afterwards, crunch a few coffee beans or parsley stems—or better still, share the aïoli with your friends.

FOR 4 SERVINGS

Preparation: 25 minutes
  (including cooking the
  potato)

¹/₂ medium potato
2 garlic cloves
2 egg yolks
Salt and freshly ground
  black pepper
1 cup olive oil

Boil the potato half, unpeeled, starting it in cold, salted water. When it is tender, drain and peel it, then mash it with a fork on a plate.

Peel the garlic and crush in a mortar. Add the egg yolks, mashed potato, and salt and pepper to taste. Work this mixture with the pestle until smooth. Gradually add the oil in a slow stream, mixing thoroughly with the pestle.

If you are not serving your *aïoli* immediately, keep it at room temperature, not in the refrigerator, lest the cold congeal the oil and break the sauce. If this happens accidentally, put a tablespoon of hot water into a bowl and vigorously whisk in the *aïoli* little by little. Plenty of elbow grease will restore your sauce.

Gentle Garlic Sauce with Herbs
Crème d'Ail Doux au Vert

✳

Despite its large proportion of garlic, this sauce is very delicate and gentle because several blanchings tame the garlic. You'll like it with snails (especially the petits gris *that crawl around on stone walls in the French countryside), sautéed in butter with fresh chanterelle mushrooms and little sandwich-bread croûtons. Its pale green color is an added attraction.*

FOR 4 SERVINGS

Preparation: 1 hour
Cooking time: 30 minutes

About 2¹/₂ cups garlic
  cloves
1 cup heavy cream
A sprig of savory
1 bunch watercress
2 tablespoons butter
1²/₃ cups chopped Italian
  parsley
Salt and freshly ground
  black pepper

Peel the garlic and put it into a saucepan with 2 quarts of cold water. Bring to the boil and let boil for 2 or 3 minutes, then drain the garlic in a strainer or colander. Repeat this operation 5 times. On the final repetition, salt the water. Make sure the garlic cloves are completely tender by piercing them with the point of a knife.

Meanwhile, pour the cream into a saucepan with a little salt and the savory, and bring it to the boil. Take

it off the heat, cover the pan, and leave it to steep.

Stem the watercress; wash and drain, then chop finely.

Remove the savory from the cream. Bring the cream back to the boil, then add the cooked garlic. Let it simmer over very low heat for 5 minutes.

Pour the garlic cream into a blender and blend at high speed until smooth and creamy.

Add the butter and chopped parsley and watercress to the blender.

Season with salt and pepper, and blend until you have a delicate, very green sauce.

If you are not going to serve it immediately, keep this sauce warm in a double boiler or hot-water bath; do not boil it again lest the lovely green color fade.

If you think the sauce is too thick (its consistency will depend on the characteristics of the garlic), you can always thin it with some boiled cream.

Tomato Coulis
Coulis de Tomates

✳

This is an excellent keystone for many summer dishes. It is quickly made and will keep for a good week in the refrigerator. Make lots of it; you will be using it constantly with pasta, rice, and most kinds of steamed, grilled, or fried vege-tables. To serve with pork chops, add a tablespoonful of Dijon mustard and a few cornichon pickles, sliced into rounds. If you are going to use this sauce cold, make it with olive oil rather than with butter, which could congeal.

Peel and thinly slice the onions. Put them into a heavy saucepan with the butter or oil and let them cook, covered, over low heat, until they are translucent and tender, about 15 minutes.

Remove the stems from the toma-toes and chop them coarsely; do not discard the juice or seeds.

Peel and lightly crush the garlic cloves.

When the onions are tender, add the tomatoes, garlic, thyme sprig, and salt and pepper to taste. If the tomatoes are too acidic, add some or all of the sugar.

Cook over medium-high heat, uncovered, for 10 to 15 minutes, stir-ring occasionally.

Remove the thyme sprig and put the mixture through the fine disk of a food mill, or purée it in a blender or food processor. Then press it through a fine strainer to remove the remaining seeds.

If desired, transform this sauce in a thousand completely different ways. For example, you can add a few leaves of basil, parsley, or coriander, or some uncooked garlic. Or you can mix it half-and-half with Red Bell Pepper *Coulis* (page 20) or heavy cream, or Six-Herb Sauce (page 19). Mustard and *cornichons* are another natural addition.

Note: It is not always easy in the winter or in big cities to find good, flavorful tomatoes like the ones you grow yourself. If your tomatoes taste pallid, add 2 tablespoons of tomato paste—or even better, 6 or 8 sun-dried tomatoes that have been soaked for 30 minutes in warm water, drained, and coarsely chopped. You can also use sun-dried tomatoes packed in oil; these do not need to be soaked, just drained before use.

FOR 8 TO 10 SERVINGS

Preparation: 15 to 20 minutes
Cooking time: 20 minutes

2 medium young white onions
2 tablespoons butter or 10 tablespoons olive oil
2¼ pounds very ripe tomatoes
3 garlic cloves
A large sprig of thyme
Salt and freshly ground black pepper
1 teaspoon sugar (optional)
A few leaves of basil, parsley, or fresh coriander, or an additional garlic clove (optional)

OPPOSITE PAGE:
Green Pea Sauce

Green Pea Sauce

Sauce aux Petits Pois

✳

This original sauce contrasts the sweetness of peas and the heat of curry powder (do not use more curry powder than I advise, lest you mask the fresh taste of the peas). This sauce is perfect with chicken breasts cooked in cream, fish fillets, or sautéed sea scallops, garnished with a few chervil leaves.

FOR 4 SERVINGS

Preparation: 20 minutes
Cooking time: 30 minutes

About 1⅔ cups shelled
  peas, preferably fresh,
  but frozen if necessary
1 cup heavy cream
A generous pinch of sugar
2 teaspoons mild curry
  powder
Salt and freshly ground
  black pepper
2 tablespoons butter

If you are using fresh peas, shell them, reserving half the pods. Remove the stems, tips, and all strings from the pods.

Put the peas into 1 quart of boiling salted water, and cook them for 5 or 10 minutes, depending on their size and freshness; if they are frozen, boil them for a minute or so. Drain the peas and plunge them into ice water to stop the cooking and cool them off; drain and set aside.

If you are using fresh peas, bring another pot of salted water to the boil and put in the pea pods; cook for 2 or 3 minutes. Cool them in cold water, then drain and set aside.

Put the cream, sugar, and curry powder into a saucepan along with salt to taste. Mix well, then bring to the boil. Let the cream boil for 2 minutes, then add the peas and, if you are using them, the pea pods. Boil for 30 seconds.

Purée the entire mixture in a blender with the butter.

Season to taste with salt and pepper, then strain the sauce through a fine sieve. Keep warm in a double boiler or hot-water bath until served.

PAGES 32–33:
Zucchini blossoms are not only a pretty table decoration; stuffed or deep-fried, they are as delicious as they are beautiful.

Sun-Drenched Vegetables

Artichokes

WHEN YOU SEE an artichoke plant in the garden in full bloom, with lovely purple buds nestled in a bouquet of leaves with their artistic contours, you cannot help but be charmed by its beauty. The artichoke we eat is indeed a flower, and in many countries they use it in bouquets; but in France you will find it more often on your plate than in a vase. Artichokes are delicious from their tender inner leaves and the fleshy base of their outer leaves to their succulent hearts.

There are many varieties, but in France you generally come across only three: the round, slightly flattened *camus breton;* the large but less meaty *vert de Laon* or *tête de chat;* and the little *violet de Provence*—the *artichaut poivrade,* small and tender enough to be eaten raw, which comes to market in the spring and fall.

Each of these varieties is used differently. The *camus* is generally eaten whole, with vinaigrette; in fact, there are special plates with depressions to hold the leaves and the dressing. With the *tête de chat,* we mainly use the hearts. And the *artichaut poivrade* is the central ingredient in a delicious Provençal dish, Baby Artichokes *en Barigoule* (see page 40). It can also be fried, as in Italy, and it is often eaten raw with the Provençal anchovy sauce *anchoïade* or with vinaigrette.

Whatever you plan to do with them, you need to choose your artichokes carefully. Their flavor and texture will be noticeably different only a few days after they are picked. The color must be olive green; the leaves must be crisp, forming a tight globe, and completely blemish-free. The best *artichauts poivrades* have spikefree leaves and a fine violet color.

You can keep artichokes fresh longer by trimming the stems and keeping them immersed in $1/4$ inch of water and covering the artichokes with a damp cloth.

Before cooking the artichokes, soak them for ten minutes in cold water with a few tablespoons of white vinegar added; then wash them in several changes of water to make sure there are no bugs. When you've drained them, trim the tips of the leaves with a stainless-steel paring knife or scissors. If the

Artichoke-Leaf Canapés

Here's a nice way to utilize the leaves of artichokes you have cooked in order to use the hearts: Top them with a tuna and mayonnaise spread, or a blend of roquefort cheese and butter, or—to get a little more elegant—thin slices of smoked salmon, red or black caviar, or *mousse de foie gras.* Arrange the artichoke-leaf canapés in a circle and serve them with drinks before dinner.

stems are long, do not cut them off: break them off, which will pull away the tough fibers from the heart. Then place the artichokes in boiling salted water, a good quart per artichoke. Let them cook, uncovered, for thirty to forty minutes according to size; they are ready when the leaves at the base can be removed easily. Let them drain upside down, and serve them hot with hollandaise sauce, melted butter, or vinaigrette. Do not keep them more than twenty-four hours; any longer than that they will oxidize.

Preparing the smaller *artichauts poivrades* is somewhat different. You need to remove the leaves from the base, and trim the stem down to about an inch in length and peel it with a vegetable peeler (it is very tender and flavorful). You can also sprinkle these trimmed artichoke hearts with lemon juice and slice them into very thin wedges, then sprinkle them over a green salad or a mixed salad including black olives or diced tomatoes.

Artichoke hearts taken from whole cooked artichokes are delicious, but are often overcooked and discolored. Here is how to prepare nice white artichoke hearts that can be cooked to perfection and used any way you like—with thin slices of *foie gras*, for instance, or to garnish roast meat or chicken. Have ready a big bowl of water acidulated with lemon juice. Wash and drain the artichokes, and break off their stems. Then use a sharp stainless-steel paring knife to go all around the artichoke, trimming away the leaves right down to the fleshy base. As soon as you have trimmed one row of leaves, dip the artichoke in the lemon juice and water mixture to keep it from discoloring. When you have removed all the leaves, use a melon baller to scoop out the hairy choke. Finally, cook the hearts in water with lemon juice, salt, and one or two tablespoonfuls of olive oil.

Artichoke hearts are cooked when you can pierce them with the point of a paring knife—about fifteen or twenty minutes after the water comes to the boil.

The wine for the little violet-colored artichokes is a Côtes de Provence or a rosé from Bellet. But a rosé from Touraine will bring out the best in the larger varieties.

Artichokes Stuffed with Eggs
Artichauts Farcis aux Oeufs

✳

In a large pot, bring 4 quarts of water to the boil and add a handful of coarse salt.

Prepare the artichokes. First, break off their stems, then soak them in cold water containing the white vinegar for about 10 minutes. Then wash them under running water and drain in a colander. Cut off the ends of the leaves with a stainless-steel knife or scissors (stainless steel will prevent discoloration).

Put the artichokes in the boiling water and cook them, uncovered, for about 30 minutes. When they are done, drain them upside down in a colander or sieve; do not cool them in cold water.

While the artichokes are cooking, break the eggs into a bowl and beat them vigorously with a fork or a whisk.

Preheat the oven to 250 degrees.

Chop the anchovies, olives, parsley, basil, and garlic.

Using parchment paper or waxed paper, cut 4 strips measuring about 4 × 12 inches.

To the beaten eggs, add 4 tablespoons olive oil, the anchovies, bread crumbs, parsley, basil, garlic, olives, and salt and pepper to taste.

Use the remaining 2 tablespoons of olive oil to grease the strips of parchment or waxed paper, then loosely wrap a strip around each artichoke. Place the paper-wrapped artichokes in a casserole.

Gently spread the leaves of each artichoke, and pour the egg mixture in among the leaves. Pour 6 tablespoons water into the casserole, bring to the boil on top of the range, and bake for about 30 minutes. Remove the paper strips and serve hot. It is a good idea to provide finger bowls containing a mixture of water and lemon juice.

FOR 4 SERVINGS

Preparation: 30 minutes
Cooking time: 1 hour

4 large globe artichokes
5 tablespoons white vinegar
4 eggs
8 anchovy fillets (packed in oil)
20 black Niçoise olives, pitted
2 tablespoons chopped parsley
A few leaves of fresh basil
1 small garlic clove
6 tablespoons olive oil
$\frac{1}{4}$ cup fresh bread crumbs
Salt and freshly ground black pepper

Artichoke Hearts in Anchovy Cream
Coeurs d'Artichauts en Crème d'Anchois

✳

Break off the stems of the artichokes, thus removing the tough fibers, and wash them in warm water. (If you see any bugs, soak the artichokes for 10 minutes in water acidulated with lemon juice and drain.)

In a big pot, bring about 8 quarts of water to the boil and add 2 handfuls of salt. When the water boils again, put in the artichokes and cover the pan with a cloth. Occasionally push the artichokes under the water with a wooden spoon and cook for 20 to 30 minutes, according to the size and quality of the artichokes. They are cooked when you can easily pull off a leaf.

Remove the pot from the heat and let the artichokes cool in their cooking liquid for about 30 minutes, then drain them upside down in a colander.

FOR 4 SERVINGS

Preparation: 1½ hours
Cooking time: 40 minutes

8 large globe artichokes
1 cup small black Niçoise olives (5 ounces)
1 medium ripe tomato
1½ cups shelled tiny fava beans (about 2¼ pounds unshelled)

(continued on page 39)

While the artichokes are cooking, pit the olives.

Peel the tomato. Remove the stem and place tomato in boiling water for 15 seconds (or a little longer if it is not ripe). Cool it in a bowl of cold water; the skin should slip off easily. Cut the tomato in half crosswise and squeeze out the seeds and liquid. Cut the flesh into large dice and set aside.

Gently remove the artichoke leaves; try not to damage the heart. Set aside 24 of the most presentable leaves. With a spoon, scrape away the hairy choke, and cut each heart into 10 wedges.

Remove the tough skin from the fava beans. This is most easily done by putting the shelled beans into boiling water for 30 seconds, then placing them in cold water to cool; it will then be a fairly simple, though time-consuming, matter to pop them out of their skins.

Peel and finely chop the garlic.

Put 2 tablespoons of cream into a large, heavy saucepan; heat it over medium heat, then add the anchovy fillets. Mash them into the cream with a fork, then add the remaining 2 tablespoons of cream along with the artichoke hearts, fava beans, and chopped garlic.

As soon as it boils, remove the pan from the heat and add the chopped olives and diced tomato.

Season carefully with salt and pepper; remember that both the anchovies and the olives are already salty.

Divide into 4 portions, mounding each portion on a warm plate. Garnish with parsley leaves, and arrange 6 of the reserved artichoke leaves around the outside of each plate, points outward.

You might also save a few fava beans for a final garnish.

(continued from page 37)

1 small garlic clove
4 tablespoons heavy cream
8 anchovy fillets (packed in oil)
4 sprigs of Italian parsley
Salt and freshly ground black pepper

Artichokes with Asparagus Stuffing
Artichauts Violets Farcis d'Asperges

✱

Bring 4 quarts of water to the boil and add a handful of coarse salt.

Break off the stems of the artichokes and remove the largest outside leaves. Place the artichokes in the boiling water and cook for about 20 minutes, or until a leaf can be removed easily.

Put another 2 cups of salted water on to boil.

Peel the asparagus and cut off the tips so they are about 1½ inches long. Boil the tips in the salted water until tender but still slightly firm, about 12 minutes. Place them in cold water to cool, drain thoroughly, then cut them in half lengthwise; set the asparagus tips aside.

Cut the peeled stalks of the asparagus into ¼-inch pieces. Melt the butter in a saucepan and add the asparagus pieces along with a pinch each of salt and sugar. Cook over low heat, covered, for about 5 minutes. Now add the peas and a pinch of nutmeg. Cover the pan again and, still over low heat, cook for another 10 minutes. If you are using frozen peas, add them after 10 minutes and cook for 5 minutes. Remove from the heat and keep warm.

When the artichokes are cooked,

FOR 4 SERVINGS

Preparation: 1¼ hours
Cooking time: 1 hour

4 medium artichokes
8 medium asparagus spears
2 tablespoons butter
A pinch of sugar
¾ cup very small peas, shelled (a generous pound unshelled)
A pinch of freshly grated nutmeg
½ cup heavy cream, very cold
Salt and freshly ground black pepper
1 egg yolk
Chervil leaves for garnish

OPPOSITE PAGE:
Artichokes with Asparagus Stuffing

put them in cold water, but do not cool them completely—only enough so that you can handle them comfortably. Cut each artichoke in half lengthwise, using a serrated or very sharp, thin-bladed knife to avoid crushing them. Remove the hairy choke and the little central leaves, then put the artichoke halves into a baking dish, cut side up. Fill the hollowed out artichoke halves with the asparagus-pea mixture.

Preheat the broiler and put 2 cups of salted water on to boil.

Beat the chilled cream with a whisk; when it begins to stiffen, add salt and pepper to taste, then the egg yolk. Continue to beat until soft peaks form.

Cover the stuffing in each artichoke half with the cream mixture, and put the baking dish under the broiler until the topping turns golden, 5 to 10 minutes.

Meanwhile, reheat the 16 asparagus tip halves in boiling salted water. Drain them well, and arrange 2 pieces on each stuffed artichoke half.

Serve on hot plates, garnished with chervil leaves.

Baby Artichokes en Barigoule

Petits Artichauts Violets en Barigoule

✳

FOR 2 SERVINGS

Preparation: 25 minutes
Cooking time: 20 minutes

1 young carrot
1 medium white onion
4 garlic cloves
5 basil leaves
2 tablespoons chopped parsley
8 baby artichokes
1 lemon, cut in half
5 tablespoons olive oil
½ bay leaf
A sprig of fresh thyme
Salt and freshly ground black pepper
½ cup dry white wine

OPPOSITE PAGE:
Baby Artichokes en Barigoule

In the eighteenth century, the term barigoule *referred first to a kind of wild mushroom (Lactarius deliciosus or saffron milkcap), and then to a dish combining Provençal artichokes with wild mushrooms, all perfumed with herbs from our hillsides—a venerable southern French recipe that is used to this day. This version has been simplified, but you can always give it a hint of the woodlands by adding a few wild mushrooms.*

Peel the carrot and the onion, and cut them into thin slices. Peel the garlic; put 2 cloves aside, and mince the other 2 with the basil and parsley.

Cut the stems of the artichokes to about 1½ inches. Cut about ⅜ inch off the artichoke tops, then break off 2 or 3 rows of leaves from the base. Peel the artichoke bottoms and stems, and rub each with half a lemon as you finish trimming it. Place them in cold water acidulated with the juice from the remaining lemon half. Gently spread the leaves of each artichoke, and use a small spoon or melon baller to remove the choke; return the artichokes to the lemon water.

In a heavy nonreactive casserole, warm the olive oil over low heat. Slowly cook the onion and carrot until they begin to turn golden, then arrange the artichokes in the casserole in a single layer. Add the bay leaf half, thyme, the 2 whole peeled cloves of garlic, and salt and pepper to taste.

Pour the wine into the casserole; add water until the artichokes are just covered. Cook over medium heat for 15 minutes, covered, then remove the lid and reduce the cooking liquid over high heat to thicken the sauce.

Off the heat, add the minced garlic mixture, and check for seasoning. Stir well and serve immediately.

Eggplant

GLEAMING SKIN; a plump, elongated shape: the eggplant is a vegetable you'd want to caress with eyes and fingers, even if you didn't know its luscious flavor.

Suspended as if by a miracle amid its tangle of leaves and its little mauve blossoms, the almost luminescent eggplant seems to be a magnet for sunlight—even piled up in the market or in your shopping basket. Only cooking can dull its glow.

There are many varieties of eggplant: long, round, violet streaked with black, even blue or white. I like them all, although I think the little white ones are less flavorful.

When shopping, avoid eggplants that have lost their luster or have brown blemishes. Your eggplant should be firm but supple. Too hard and it will be unripe and, perhaps, unpleasantly acidic. Too soft and overripe, and its texture will be grainy and its flavor sharp.

Some people use coarse salt to draw out the eggplant's sharpness, but why try and change the nature of a vegetable that has some personality?

I am ambivalent about the skin; although it is thin, it always seems to stay with you long after dinner. So apart from recipes where I stuff the eggplant, I generally peel it after cutting off the spiky stem end.

The flesh of the eggplant oxidizes and discolors when it comes in contact with iron, so when trimming and cooking eggplant be sure to use only stainless steel or other nonreactive equipment.

Eggplant works well sautéed, deep-fried, or stewed with other vegetables. But it should be kept away from water, because it will soak it up like a sponge. So, don't try poaching it; you'll have a disaster on your hands. It acts like a sponge with oil as well, and that is why I prefer to cook eggplant in a hot oven, either on a cookie sheet or in a baking dish.

Its intense flavor goes well with all the other sun-drenched vegetables, and especially with tomatoes and bell peppers. But its best ally is olive oil, which brings out its unctuousness.

With this formidable vegetable you can drink Barbaresco from Italy's Piedmont region or a red Châteauneuf-du-Pape—two robust wines born under the sun.

My Eggplant Caviar

Eggplant caviar can be banal; it can verge on the disgusting if not well prepared. But a good version is delicious spread on grilled country bread and sprinkled with olive oil and lemon juice or wine vinegar.

Cut a big eggplant in half lengthwise. Cut through the flesh in a grid pattern, but do not pierce the skin. Sprinkle on olive oil and salt, and place skin side down in a sheet pan in a preheated 425 degree oven for about thirty-five minutes, or until the flesh is very tender.

Using a stainless steel spoon, scoop out all the flesh and place it in a food processor or blender with two tablespoons chopped tomatoes, half a minced garlic clove, and either a pinch of cayenne pepper or a few chopped basil leaves. Blend well, then add olive oil as though you were making mayonnaise (between $^1/_2$ cup and 1 cup, depending on the size of the eggplant).

When it is completely smooth and homogenized, it is ready to serve.

Crisp Eggplant Fritters
Beignets d'Aubergines Croustillants

✳

This is unquestionably one of my favorite dishes. The eggplant's sharpness is abated by the batter: mild-tasting yet ever so slightly bitter. Very simple, but very good—and even better with a coulis of tomatoes or red bell peppers (see pages 29 and 20).

Peel the eggplants and cut them lengthwise into slices a scant 1/4 inch thick.

If you are using fresh marjoram, chop it. Sprinkle the eggplant slices with marjoram and stack them until you are ready to fry them.

With a whisk, blend the flour and chilled beer in a mixing bowl; the consistency should be fairly thin, like crêpe batter.

Heat the oil to 360 degrees. If you have neither an electric fryer with thermostat nor a deep-fat thermometer, you can check the temperature by dipping the end of a wooden chopstick or skewer in cold water, then putting it into the oil. The oil has reached the proper temperature when it begins to bubble up vigorously around the tip of the chopstick. Don't forget to remove the chopstick before you fry your fritters.

Dip each slice of eggplant into the batter, let it drain over the bowl for a moment, then immediately place it in the hot oil. Turn the fritters with one chopstick or the handle of a wooden spoon; using tongs could damage the batter. When the fritters are nicely browned on both sides, about 5 minutes, take them out of the oil and let them drain on paper towels.

Serve them arranged on a folded napkin. Do not salt them until the moment you place them on the table: as it melts, the salt will generate moisture that will make the crust soggy.

FOR 4 SERVINGS

Preparation: 15 minutes
Cooking time: 15 minutes

2 medium eggplants (1 to 1 1/4 pounds total)
1 teaspoon fresh marjoram, or 1/2 teaspoon dried
2/3 cup all-purpose flour
2/3 cup cold beer
2 quarts neutral vegetable oil (such as corn or peanut) for deep-frying
Salt

Eggplant with Black-Olive Stuffing
Aubergines Farcies aux Olives Noires

✳

You can replace the Niçoise olives in this recipe with other black olives such as those from Nyons. The important thing is that they be preserved in oil, not brine, which would change the texture of the dish; brined olives, especially the big ones, are full of water.

PAGE 44:
Eggplant with Black-Olive Stuffing

Preheat the oven to 400 degrees. Cut the stems off the eggplants and cut them in half lengthwise. With a knife, cut through the flesh in a grid pattern, but do not pierce the skin. Sprinkle olive oil and salt on each half, place on a sheet pan or cookie sheet, and bake for about 30 minutes or until tender.

Meanwhile, clean the mushrooms by trimming the ends of the stems and rinsing briefly. Immediately chop them coarsely.

Heat 2 tablespoons olive oil in a large skillet over medium heat; add the mushrooms and stir with a wooden spoon until they have rendered all their liquid.

Wash the parsley and mint, then drain it; peel the garlic. Chop the mint, parsley, and garlic medium-fine.

Beat the eggs in a bowl.

When the eggplants are tender, remove them and lower the oven temperature to 350 degrees. Use a stainless-steel spoon to scrape the eggplant flesh out onto a cutting board, without damaging the skins. Chop the flesh using a stainless-steel knife. Add eggplant to the skillet containing the mushrooms, turn the heat to high, and let the juices evaporate from the mixture, stirring constantly with a wooden spoon. Try to get the mixture as dry as possible without burning.

Remove skillet from the heat, then add the herb-garlic mixture, 2 tablespoons of bread crumbs, the olives, and the eggs. Add pepper and a little salt to taste (remember that the olives are salty).

Stuff the eggplant skins with this mixture; try to keep the original form of the eggplants, tamping down the stuffing with a fork. Sprinkle with the remaining bread crumbs and arrange the eggplant halves in an ovenproof dish greased with 1 tablespoon of olive oil.

Sprinkle with the remaining 3 tablespoons of olive oil and bake for about 15 minutes. Serve very hot.

FOR 4 SERVINGS

Preparation: 40 minutes
Cooking time: 45 minutes

4 small eggplants
 (2¼ pounds total)
8 tablespoons olive oil
7 ounces white
 mushrooms
⅔ cup chopped parsley
4 fresh mint leaves
1 garlic clove
2 eggs
½ cup fresh bread crumbs
½ cup (3 ounces) black
 Niçoise olives, pitted
Salt and freshly ground
 black pepper

Eggplant Gratin with Béchamel Sauce

Gratin d'Aubergines à la Béchamel

✴

I got this recipe from my friend Raymond Vidal, who made the famous Club de Cavalière hotel near Saint-Tropez what it was in its heyday. It was a household recipe given to him by a wonderful old nanny, la mère Berthet. Like all the old-time cooks, she was a great one for keeping everyone happy with dishes based on béchamel sauce. We adored béchamel when I was a child, and I'm sad to see it condemned nowadays by the followers of nouvelle cuisine—which has always inspired more journalism than appetite. Incidentally, I like to make béchamel sauce with olive oil rather than with butter, even though that is not the standard recipe. Try it—it's delicious with eggplant.

PAGES 46–47:
Most French eggplants are long and very deep purple, but I prefer them less ripe, firmer, and a lovely violet color. There are white eggplants as well.

FOR 4 SERVINGS

Preparation: 35 minutes
Cooking time: 65 minutes

3 medium eggplants
   (about 1 3/4 pounds total)
1 garlic clove
7 tablespoons olive oil
2 tablespoons flour
1 cup whole milk
1 cup heavy cream, cold
Salt and freshly ground
   black pepper
A pinch of freshly grated
   nutmeg
3 1/2 ounces Swiss Gruyère
   cheese, grated (about
   3/4 cup)

Peel the eggplants. Peel and finely mince the garlic.

In a saucepan, heat 3 tablespoons of olive oil over low heat, then add the flour. Blend well with a whisk and cook for 2 minutes, making sure the flour does not brown. Add the cold milk, continuing to mix with the whisk to prevent lumps from forming.

Continue to whisk the mixture as you bring it to the boil over low heat. When it boils, add the cold cream. Season with salt, pepper, and nutmeg, and return to the boil. Remove from the heat and add the minced garlic. Keep this béchamel warm without letting it boil again.

Preheat the oven to 550 degrees.

Cut the eggplant into rounds a scant 1/4 inch thick. Oil 1 or 2 sheet

pans or cookie sheets with a tablespoon of olive oil, sprinkle them with salt, and arrange on the sheets as many eggplant slices as will fit in a single layer. Put them into the very hot oven long enough to soften the eggplant without drying it out—about 10 minutes. Repeat until you have cooked all the eggplant. Reduce the oven temperature to 350 degrees.

Pour the béchamel sauce into a baking dish or gratin dish, then arrange the eggplant slices on top of the sauce. Sprinkle with grated cheese. Place the baking dish into a larger baking pan containing enough hot water to come half way up the side of the dish. Bake for about 45 minutes. Bring to the table in the baking dish.

FOR 4 SERVINGS

Preparation: 35 minutes
Cooking time: 50 minutes

2 medium eggplants
   (about 14 ounces total)
8 large stalks of broad-
   stemmed Swiss chard,
   both leaves and stems
   (16 if they are small or
   the narrow-stemmed
   variety)
1 tablespoon flour
7 tablespoons olive oil
1 tablespoon coriander
   seeds or ground
   coriander
2 garlic cloves
2/3 cup fresh bread crumbs
Salt and freshly ground
   black pepper
1 cup Tomato Coulis
   (page 29)

OPPOSITE PAGE:
Eggplant Bundles with
Tomato Coulis

Eggplant Bundles with Tomato Coulis
Ballotins d'Aubergines au Coulis de Tomates

✳

Peel the eggplants and cut them into 3/8-inch dice.

With a paring knife, carefully cut the leaves of the Swiss chard from the stalks without damaging them; save the leaves. Peel the stalks with a vegetable peeler if you are using the broad-stemmed variety, and cut them into small dice.

The stalks should be cooked in a flour-and-water mixture known as a *blanc*. Put the tablespoon of flour in a strainer, hold the strainer over a pan and pour cold water through the flour into the pan until all the flour has dispersed in the water. To cook

the chard stalks you will need about 2 quarts of water in all. Salt the water, bring to the boil, and put in the chard stalks. Cook for about 20 minutes, or less if you are using the narrow-stemmed variety. Drain the stalks and place them in cold water to cool. Drain and reserve.

Bring to the boil another 2 quarts of water with a handful of coarse salt. When it boils, dip in the chard leaves to make them supple. Remove them immediately and plunge them into ice water. When cold, take them out of the water, drain them, and spread them out on a clean cloth.

Heat half the olive oil in a skillet over medium heat; do not let it smoke. Add the diced eggplant, season with salt, and sauté, stirring frequently with a wooden spoon, until tender. Drain in a strainer. Put the skillet back on the heat with another tablespoon of olive oil and sauté the cooked chard stalks until lightly golden.

Preheat the oven to 275 degrees.

If you are using whole coriander seeds, toast them for a few minutes in a dry skillet, then pulverize them in a spice grinder, blender, or mortar and pestle; sift this powder through a fine strainer.

Mince the garlic finely.

In a large bowl, combine the eggplant, chard stalks, minced garlic, coriander, and bread crumbs.

Season with pepper and taste for salt; mix well.

If your chard leaves were large, cut them in half lengthwise. To form each bundle, take 2 pieces of chard leaf and overlap them crosswise on your work surface. Put a ball of the eggplant mixture in the center and fold the leaves over to form a little package. Put the 8 bundles into a baking pan, smooth side up.

Sprinkle them with the remaining olive oil, loosely cover with aluminum foil, and cook in the oven for about 20 minutes.

Heat the tomato *coulis* over low heat. Spoon ¼ cup of *coulis* onto each of 4 plates, and serve 2 eggplant bundles per person. Baste with a little of the juices from the baking pan before serving.

Eggplant Gratin Vieux Peygros
Gratin d'Aubergines du Vieux Peygros

✳

Vieux Peygros, in Mougins, is where they used to grow flowers for the perfume industry, especially violets and jasmine blossoms. I've given its name to this eggplant gratin because it is so fragrant and so evocative of the aromas of the Mougins countryside.

Peel the onions, slice them thin, and cook over low heat with 2 tablespoons olive oil in a heavy saucepan; do not let them brown.

Preheat the oven to 550 degrees.

Peel the eggplants and cut them into slices about ⅛ inch thick.

Peel the garlic. In a food processor or blender, or by hand, very finely chop the savory (reserving a sprig for garnish, if desired), parsley, and garlic. Set aside.

Oil 2 sheet pans with 2 tablespoons olive oil each and sprinkle lightly with salt. Arrange the eggplant slices on the pans in a single layer and bake until tender, about 10 minutes. If necessary, repeat until you have cooked all the eggplant. Set aside.

Reduce the oven temperature to 350 degrees.

Cut the tomatoes into thin slices.

Lightly oil a large gratin dish or baking dish with olive oil and

FOR 4 SERVINGS

Preparation: 30 minutes
Cooking time: 65 minutes

2 medium onions,
 preferably white
About 10 tablespoons
 olive oil
4 medium eggplants
 (2¼ pounds total)
2 garlic cloves
A few sprigs of savory
¼ cup chopped parsley
4 ripe medium tomatoes
Salt and freshly ground
 black pepper
2 tablespoons bread
 crumbs
2 tablespoons grated
 Parmesan cheese

OPPOSITE PAGE:
*Eggplant Gratin Vieux
Peygros*

arrange on it half the eggplant slices, then the cooked onions. Salt lightly. Top this with half the sliced tomatoes and sprinkle with the chopped herb-garlic mixture. Now comes the remaining eggplant, then the rest of the tomatoes. Season with salt and pepper.

Mix the bread crumbs and the Parmesan cheese and sprinkle on top of the tomatoes. Drizzle with 2 tablespoons of olive oil.

Bake the gratin for 45 minutes; if it looks as if it is drying out, reduce the temperature to 325 degrees or lower.

Bring to the table in its baking dish; you can decorate it with a sprig of savory.

Note: When the gratin is cooked, you can try this variation: make 4 depressions in it with a small ladle and break a very fresh egg into each depression. Put it back into the oven for about 10 minutes, or until the eggs are set but still soft, then sprinkle the eggs with salt and freshly ground pepper before serving.

FOR 4 SERVINGS

Preparation: 50 minutes
Cooking time: 1 hour
Cooling time: 15 minutes

2 medium eggplants (a little over 1 pound total)
5 tablespoons olive oil
1 red bell pepper
1½ ounces French bread or sandwich bread, crusts removed (equivalent to about 2 slices of sandwich bread)
½ cup plus 2 tablespoons milk
3 eggs
1 teaspoon ground cardamom
2 or 3 drops Tabasco sauce
¾ cup plus 2 tablespoons heavy cream
Salt and freshly ground black pepper
Tomato or Red Bell Pepper Coulis (pages 29, 20) (optional)

OPPOSITE PAGE:
Eggplant Cake

Eggplant Cake
Gâteau d'Aubergines

✳

Within the firm, gleaming exterior of this "cake" lies a delicate vegetable purée. You can serve it hot or cold, possibly with a salad of mixed young greens, with a rice pilaf, or with baby lamb chops. By all means, save the leftovers—they'll reheat very well.

Preheat the oven to 350 degrees.

Cut the stems off the eggplants and cut them in half lengthwise. With a knife, cut through the flesh in a grid pattern, but do not pierce the skin. Sprinkle olive oil and salt on each half, and bake skin side down on a sheet pan or cookie sheet for 20 or 30 minutes, depending on the size of the eggplants.

Lower the oven temperature to 300 degrees.

Carefully scrape the flesh out of the eggplants and put it into a food processor or blender; cut the skin into long 1-inch-wide strips.

With a pair of tongs, hold the red pepper over the open flame of a gas burner, turning it until it is charred and blistered on all sides. (This may also be done under the broiler.) Put the pepper into a paper bag and set aside for a few minutes until it is cool enough to handle. Pull the skin off, then cut off the stem and remove the seeds and fibrous ribs. Cut 6 diamond shapes from the pepper for decoration; coarsely dice the remainder and set aside.

Lightly oil a 7- or 8-inch round cake pan, or a ring mold. Line the bottom and sides with the strips of eggplant skin, shiny black side down; if you like, you can make a lattice of these strips. Soak the bread in the milk for a few minutes, then

squeeze out the liquid. Set the soaked bread aside. Lightly beat the eggs.

In the food processor or blender, purée the eggplant flesh. Add the cardamom, Tabasco, eggs, soaked bread, and cream. Season to taste with salt and pepper and continue to process or blend until very smooth. Add the diced pepper and process or blend once more.

Fill the cake pan with the purée, taking care not to disturb the eggplant-skin lining. Cover with a sheet of aluminum foil and bake at 300 degrees for 30 minutes. Remove from the oven and let cake cool for 15 minutes before unmolding it onto a serving platter. Decorate with the bell-pepper diamonds.

Serve with Tomato or Red Pepper *Coulis*.

Tian of Eggplant, Bell Peppers, and Savory

Tian d'Aubergines aux Poivrons Doux et à la Sariette

✳

Originally the Provençal word tian *meant a broad, deep earthenware platter for cooking certain traditional vegetable or fish recipes. It has gradually come to be the name of the preparation itself.*

FOR 6 SERVINGS

Preparation: 25 minutes
Cooking time: 1 hour
    15 minutes

2 medium white onions
7 tablespoons olive oil
3 garlic cloves
4 medium eggplants
    (2¼ pounds total)
4 red bell peppers
5 savory sprigs
Salt and freshly ground
    black pepper

Peel the onions, slice them thin, and cook them over low heat in a small, heavy-bottomed saucepan with 2 tablespoons olive oil for 10 minutes. They should be tender but not browned. Peel and mince the garlic and add it to the onions.

Preheat the oven to 350 degrees.

Peel the eggplants and slice them into circles about ¼ inch thick.

Quarter the red peppers and remove the stems, seeds, and internal ribs. Stem and chop the savory.

Spread the onion-garlic mixture in the bottom of a large, shallow baking dish or roasting pan with a lid. Ideally, it should be of glazed earthenware, but enameled iron, glass, or ovenproof china will do. Sprinkle the onions with the savory, then arrange a layer of peppers and eggplant in alternating rows. Season to taste with salt and pepper. Drizzle with the remaining 5 tablespoons of olive oil. Cover the pan and bake for about 1 hour. Occasionally, press the vegetables down with a wooden spoon to make sure they are well permeated by the oil. Cook until all the liquid has evaporated and the vegetables have begun to caramelize.

Serve in the baking dish, either hot or at room temperature.

Cucumbers, Squash, and Zucchini

THE CUCURBITS ARE a huge and rather odd family, with spherical or ovoid members such as pumpkins and melons as well as long, cylindrical ones such as cucumbers and zucchini, all encompassing a vast diversity of flavor, texture, and color.

In France, two varieties of cucumber come to market year-round: one is smooth-skinned and long, and the other is shorter, with a nubby skin. The American equivalent of the first is the so-called English, or "burpless," cucumber and is often sold shrink-wrapped in plastic; the second is closer to the standard American cucumber. Both taste good, and you can judge them by the same criteria: they should look bright in color and should be firm to the touch. On the other hand, they require different preparation. The English cucumber has fewer seeds and can be eaten without peeling. The other kind should be peeled first, because its skin is thick and can be bitter. You should also seed it by cutting it in half lengthwise and scraping the seeds out with a teaspoon. After slicing, it can be made more digestible by salting it and letting it stand in a colander or strainer for an hour.

We generally eat cucumbers in salads, which is very nice, but be aware that they are also delicious hot, just dipped for a moment in boiling water and served with a spicy herb butter, or briefly sautéed and seasoned with mustard and chives. Some white wines are perfect with cucumber—for example, dry Jurançon from the foothills of the Pyrenees.

Then there are the little *cornichons*, which are more of a condiment because they are eaten pickled in brine or vinegar. I buy tiny ones, still in their infancy, with their little crinkled yellow flowers still attached.

Winter squash or pumpkins, yellow, green, orange, or red: these epitomize the vegetables I ate as a child—the ones so common both in the garden and in fairy tales. Every fall my father saved some room for them in the garden shed, next to the bunches of onions and the braids of garlic and shallots. I'll never forget those magnificent still lifes.

Yet however beautiful they are, their flavor is beyond description. They have a gentle flavor, slightly sweet, deliciously soft—soft and warm, like my mother's hands, hands that transformed them into silken purées, luscious gratins, and sweet, creamy soups.

And in late spring she sometimes picked their huge apricot-yellow blossoms to make succulent fritters or to stuff, like zucchini blossoms.

Different varieties

Cucumber Salad

One of the best ways of eating cucumbers is still to dress them with a vinaigrette made of wine vinegar and a neutral oil such as peanut, corn, or sunflower; salt and pepper; and snipped herbs such as chives, parsley, chervil, dill—or, even better, mint, which brings out their freshness. You can also replace the oil with cream or, like the Turks and the Greeks, with plain yogurt made from either cow's or sheep's milk.

of pumpkins and squash have different flavors. I like the big, round, red-fleshed pumpkin like Cinderella's carriage. (Maybe I am still under the fairy-godmother's spell.) When they first appear in the market, their flesh is still suffused with water and they are blander than after they have spent the winter maturing on a bed of straw. The pumpkin's soft flavor and texture seem to cry out for sugar, boiled milk, butter, and cream. But for cold purées served in summer I recommend olive oil. And for soups, croûtons of bread browned in the oven or sautéed in olive oil are obligatory.

The raspberry and violet notes of red Loire Valley wines using the Cabernet Franc grape (Bourgueil, Chinon, Saumur, and Touraine) are a good accompaniment to the fruity richness of this vegetable.

Unless the gardener has taken the trouble to let them grow on a nice flat stone, pumpkins will have soil adhering to them, and they should be washed in plenty of water. When they have been washed and dried, they should be peeled with a stainless-steel knife so as not to discolor their flesh. Then remove the seeds from the cavity. To eat these delicious seeds, free them from their network of fibers, wash them, and let them dry on a screen or rack before toasting them in the oven. Rinse the peeled pumpkin, then cut it into large cubes;

Pickling *Cornichons*

To make a jar of pickled *cornichons*, begin by brushing away any mud with a nail brush; washing the *cornichons* would soften them. Put them into a clean kitchen towel with a handful of coarse salt, and rub away the fine down on their skin. Then arrange them in a preserving jar that has been sterilized with boiling water, along with a sprig of tarragon; twenty small white pearl onions, peeled; a few black peppercorns; and a small dried chili pepper. Fill the jar with white vinegar. And that's that!

you can either boil them (starting with cold water) or bake them in the oven, wrapped in aluminum foil.

Here is another way that yields delicious results; it is my method of choice for somewhat smaller pumpkins. When I've washed the pumpkin, I simply cut a six- or eight-inch "lid" from the top and scoop out the seeds and fibers with a spoon. I salt the inside, and the underside of the lid, and put the whole pumpkin in a very hot oven for about half an hour. I then remove all the cooked flesh to make a soup, a purée, or a gratin—to be served in the pumpkin itself. Try it; it is a spectacular presentation for a dinner party.

In France, zucchini are without doubt the stepchildren of our sun-drenched vegetables. Here, they are unjustly viewed as a diet vegetable and are ignominiously cooked in boiling water, from which they emerge soft, insipid, and stripped of all character. They deserve better—*much* better—because they are wonderfully delicate and tender.

New varieties of summer squash have appeared here over the years, including round ones, which are perfect for stuffing (see page 216), and several long varieties, either dark green, or marbled with white, or bright yellow. They all have about the same flavor and texture.

If you cannot go out at dawn and pick

your own zucchini, try to get to the farmers' market early in the morning before they have spent hours in the heat, crammed into crates. Choose bright-colored, unblemished zucchini, and keep them cool, but not cold, until you wash and slice them. And what a pleasure they are to slice! The knife goes through them like butter as you watch droplets appear on the flesh: droplets of an oil deemed most delicate. If your zucchini are not too large, there is no need to peel them or to remove their seeds, but always cut off the two ends.

They lend themselves to a wide variety of preparations. I like them a lot raw, sliced very thin, in salads; or cubed or cut into slices, dredged in flour, and sautéed in olive oil. They always go with olive oil—indeed, who would ever think of sautéing them in butter? They are also delicious deep-fried, grilled, or slowly simmered in a ratatouille along with their eternal partners: tomatoes, eggplant, onions, and thyme. But they contain a great deal of water, so don't poach them.

A Cool Summer Salad

Squeeze the juice of a lemon into a salad bowl; take another lemon, remove all its peel and white pith, cut it into segments between its membranes, and add these to the bowl, discarding the pits. Add three small zucchini cut into $^1/_8$-inch slices, some diced tomato, and a little sea salt. Leave to macerate.

Then add some black olives, fresh coriander, and fresh mint. Dress with olive oil and season with plenty of pepper. Serve immediately.

Because of their delicacy, they need to be exalted—for example, by stuffing them. And that brings back more fond memories of childhood, of the family dinner table. I can still see zucchini in the garden, grown fat on rain and sunshine, a good foot or more in length.

My mother and my aunt Célestine would pick them, wash them, and cut an inch-wide trench all the way down each one. They would scoop out all the seeds (and there were plenty of them in these massive specimens), then prepare a stuffing with sausage meat, leftover cooked meat, parboiled rice, salt, and pepper. Then they would stuff the zucchini, dot them with butter, sprinkle them with thyme, and cook them in a baking dish with a little water for about two hours.

With zucchini you can drink a supple, harmonious wine from the Midi made from the Cinsault grape (such as Côtes de Provence or Coteaux du Languedoc).

58

Sautéed Cucumbers with Chives
Concombres Sautés à la Ciboulette

✳

Hot cucumber dishes are rare, but I've found that quick cooking brings out the flavor without spoiling the crunchy texture. This recipe won't disappoint you as long as you choose very firm cucumbers and do not exceed the cooking time.

FOR 4 SERVINGS

Preparation: 15 minutes
Cooking time: 8 minutes

2¼ pounds large
  cucumbers
A bunch of chives
4 teaspoons butter
¼ cup heavy cream
1 tablespoon Dijon
  mustard
⅓ cup chopped parsley
Salt and freshly ground
  black pepper

Peel the cucumbers with a vegetable peeler, cut them in half lengthwise, and scoop out the seeds with a teaspoon. Cut them into julienne about 1½ inches long.

Wash the chives and cut them into ½-inch lengths.

Warm a serving platter in a cool oven (about 200 degrees).

Melt the butter in a large skillet, add the cucumbers, and raise the heat to high. Salt, and toss the cucumbers in the pan for 2 minutes—not a moment more. Add the cream and bring to the boil.

Remove from the heat, add the mustard, chives, and parsley, and season to taste with salt and pepper. Serve immediately in the hot serving platter.

This dish can also be served cold, but not icy.

Winter Squash and Tapioca Flan
Flan de Courge au Tapioca

✳

This very elegant end to a meal, which depends for almost all its sweetness on the natural sugars in the squash, should be served in its cooking dish, so choose a pretty ovenproof glazed earthenware or porcelain dish in colors that harmonize with your table setting. You can serve it hot or cold—and if you flavor it with vanilla, you will suddenly find your children enjoying tapioca.

FOR 4 SERVINGS

Preparation: 30 minutes
Cooking time: 1 hour
  40 minutes

3¼-pound winter squash
  or pumpkin (weight
  including skin and
  seeds)
2 teaspoons sugar
Scant 1 cup milk
1 vanilla bean, or
  1 teaspoon pure vanilla
  extract
1 tablespoon fine tapioca
4 eggs
3 tablespoons butter
A pinch of freshly grated
  nutmeg
Salt

Preheat the oven to 350 degrees.

Peel the squash and remove the seeds and fibers.

Cut the flesh into ¾-inch chunks and place them on a double sheet of aluminum foil about 20 inches long. Sprinkle with the sugar, add salt, and wrap the foil around the squash, making a sealed package. Place on a baking sheet and bake for 45 minutes to 1 hour.

In the meantime, pour the milk into a saucepan, add the vanilla bean, if using, and a pinch of salt, and bring to the boil. Sprinkle the tapioca into the boiling milk, stirring with a whisk; lower the heat and cook for 5 minutes. Remove from the heat and add vanilla extract, if using.

Remove the squash from the oven, open the foil package, and put the squash through a sieve, potato ricer, or the fine disk of a food mill into a large bowl.

Lower the oven temperature to 275 degrees.

Remove the vanilla bean (if you've used it), and mix the tapioca into the squash purée.

Beat the eggs in a small bowl.

Cut 2 tablespoons of the butter into small pieces and add to squash mixture, mixing well, then add the beaten eggs and a pinch of nutmeg.

Season to taste with salt and mix well. Butter a bak-ing dish or gratin dish, scrape the mixture into the dish, and smooth the surface.

Bake in a hot-water bath deep enough to half-immerse the bak-ing dish. Bake for 10 minutes at 275 degrees, then lower the temper-ature to 250 degrees, and bake for another 30 minutes, or until set.

Put the baking dish on a tray, and serve.

Pumpkin Purée with Olive Oil
Purée de Potiron à l'Huile d'Olive

✳

Pumpkins ripen in the late summer and the fall; they keep throughout the winter as their juices and their flavor grow more and more concentrated. They are eaten nearly year-round. In fall and winter you can make soups, gratins, and hot purées; in summer, there are cold purées enhanced with aromatic herbs or vegetables.

FOR 4 SERVINGS

Preparation: 10 minutes
Cooking time: 40 to
   50 minutes

1 small pumpkin (about
   4½ pounds)
2 tablespoons semolina
   (optional)
4 garlic cloves
7 tablespoons olive oil
A few drops of Tabasco
   sauce
Salt
4 slices country bread,
   toasted or grilled
   (optional)

Preheat the oven to 475 degrees. Cut a 6-inch lid from the top of the pumpkin and scoop out all the seeds and fibers with a large spoon.

Salt the inside of the pumpkin and its lid, and put into the oven. After about 30 minutes, the flesh should be cooked and no liquid should remain inside the pumpkin. If liquid remains, put in the semolina and cook for another 10 or 15 min-utes. If the pumpkin flesh is still not tender, continue cooking until it is, checking often.

Peel and mince the garlic.

Remove all the cooked flesh from the pumpkin with a large spoon.

Heat 2 tablespoons of olive oil in a skillet, and when it begins to smoke add the pumpkin. Cook over high heat, stirring and pressing with a wooden spoon to evaporate the pumpkin juices, for 5 minutes. When the pumpkin has broken into a thick purée, turn it into a bowl and gradually mix in the remain-ing 5 tablespoons of olive oil, then the minced garlic, Tabasco sauce, and some salt. Mix well with a wooden spoon.

Keep warm over hot water, but serve fairly quickly—if you like, with pieces of toasted or grilled country bread brushed with olive oil.

Note: For a wonderful summer variation, assemble the following ingredients:

1 6 1/2-ounce can tuna packed in oil, drained and flaked
1/2 cup black Niçoise olives
4 hard-boiled eggs

10 slices red bell pepper
10 slices green bell pepper
A sprig of mint, stemmed
A sprig of basil, stemmed

Let the pumpkin purée cool, place it on a large serving platter, and garnish with the above ingredients.

Winter Squash Soup

Soupe à la Courge

✳

Here is another dish that reminds me of childhood flavors. Its texture is a caress, its flavor sweet, its color soft—it is a true delicacy. In my parents' house, this soup was often an entire winter dinner—but what a dinner! I still remember it with emotion.

If your children have irreconcilable differences with soup, I am sure this one will bring them together.

Peel and chop the onion. Peel the squash, remove the seeds and fibers, and cut it into chunks. Peel and wash the optional sweet potato, and cut it into chunks. In a heavy saucepan or casserole, cook the onion in olive oil until golden.

Add the squash and sweet potato. Cook over very low heat, stirring frequently with a wooden spoon to prevent sticking, for 5 minutes. Add

1 cup of water and the milk; this should just cover the vegetables. Add salt, pepper, and the sugar.

Cook for 30 minutes over low heat, then purée in a food mill, food processor, or blender.

Return the purée to the heat. Add the butter and the cream, and bring to the boil for a moment. Serve immediately, garnished with thick slices of toasted country bread.

FOR 4 SERVINGS

Preparation: 15 minutes
Cooking time: 50 minutes

1 large onion
2 1/4-pound winter squash or pumpkin (weight including seeds and fibers)
1 sweet potato (optional)
2 tablespoons olive oil
1 cup milk
Salt and freshly ground black pepper
2 teaspoons sugar
4 teaspoons butter
1/4 cup heavy cream
4 thick slices country bread, toasted or grilled

See photograph on page 62.

Pumpkin Tart
Tarte à la Citrouille

✳

This tart is from central France, specifically the town of Millançay, in Sologne. It is traditionally served on All Saint's Day—the day after Halloween. You can eat it warm or cold and with or without whipped cream.

Make the *pâte brisée.* Cream the butter, softening it if necessary in a warm place or in the microwave oven, but not allowing it to melt. Put the flour onto a work surface and make a well in the middle. Add the water, salt, softened butter, and sugar. Mix with your fingertips until a dough forms. Roll it into a ball, wrap it in plastic wrap or a towel, and let it rest for 1 hour in the refrigerator.

While the dough is resting, peel the pumpkin and remove the seeds and fibers. Cut the flesh into small dice and cook in the oven, or in a heavy saucepan with a little water, for about 20 minutes. The liquid should evaporate completely, resulting in a very dry purée of pumpkin. Leave to cool.

Preheat the oven to 425 degrees. Generously butter a 10-inch tart pan with high sides. Roll out the pastry and line the pan. Prick the bottom with a fork and line the pastry with aluminum foil or parchment paper, then pour in dried beans, lentils, pie weights, or clean pebbles to keep the pastry from blistering. Bake for 10 to 15 minutes; the pastry should begin to set but should not brown.

Remove the beans and the foil; do not turn off the oven.

When the pumpkin purée is cool, add the eggs, salt, semolina, cinnamon, nutmeg, ginger, brown sugar, and evaporated milk or cream. Mix well.

Turn this mixture into the partially baked tart shell and return to the oven. Bake for 15 minutes, then lower the heat to 350 degrees and bake for another 30 minutes.

FOR 8 SERVINGS

Preparation: 1 hour 45 minutes (including resting time for the pastry dough)
Cooking time: 65 minutes

For the Pastry (pâte brisée)
10 tablespoons butter, at room temperature
1⅔ cups all-purpose flour
¼ cup ice water
A pinch of salt
1 tablespoon sugar

1 small pumpkin (3¼ pounds)
3 eggs, lightly beaten
½ teaspoon salt
4 tablespoons semolina
1 teaspoon ground cinnamon
A pinch of freshly grated nutmeg
½ teaspoon ground ginger
½ cup light brown sugar
⅔ cup evaporated milk or ¾ cup heavy cream

OPPOSITE PAGE:
Winter Squash Soup (*see page 61*).

Zucchini Pound Cake with Pine Nuts
Cake de Courgettes aux Pignons

✳

OPPOSITE PAGE:
*Zucchini Pound Cake with
Pine Nuts*

An original cake, delightfully aromatic; it will keep for several days in the refrigerator wrapped in aluminum foil.

FOR 1 LOAF CAKE

Preparation: 25 minutes
Cooking time: 1 hour
15 minutes

Melt the butter over low heat. Peel, wash, and dry the zucchini and grate them coarsely.

Preheat the oven to 425 degrees.

In a food processor, blend the eggs, melted butter, sugar, and vanilla.

In a bowl, mix the flour, salt, baking powder, and cumin, then add this to the butter mixture in the food processor. Process until smooth. Return to the bowl and add the grated zucchini and the pine nuts.

Butter and flour a 6-cup loaf pan and scrape the batter into it. Smooth the top, bake for 10 minutes, then lower the oven temperature to 350 degrees and bake for another hour.

Unmold onto a cooling rack.

10 tablespoons butter
3 small zucchini
(10 ounces total)
4 eggs
1¼ cups sugar
1 teaspoon pure vanilla
extract
2 cups all-purpose flour
1 teaspoon salt
1½ teaspoons baking
powder
⅔ cup pine nuts
A pinch of ground
caraway

Monsieur Jourdan's Zucchini Galette
Galette de Monsieur Jourdan

✳

This galette is named not after the Alphonse Daudet character, but after a restaurateur near Manosque (about thirty miles northeast of Aix-en-Provence). I have pleasant memories of this thin, crisp pastry topped with slices of zucchini, and I wanted to share them with you.

FOR 4 SERVINGS

Preparation: 1 hour
35 minutes (including
resting time for the
pastry dough)
Cooking time: 15 minutes

Put the flour and salt on your work surface and make a well in the middle. Add the oil and warm water and knead until smooth. Form the dough into a ball, wrap it in plastic wrap or a towel, and refrigerate for at least 1 hour.

Preheat the oven to 425 degrees.

Wash and dry the zucchini and cut them into thin rounds.

Remove the dough from the refrigerator and roll it into a thin circle, about ⅛ inch thick. Place it on a cookie sheet. Prick the dough circle with a fork, then arrange the zucchini slices on top. Do not overlap them; you should see pastry between the slices. Press the zucchini slices into the pastry, sprinkle with sea salt and thyme, and bake for 15 minutes. The crust should be very crisp.

Serve very hot.

1⅔ cups all-purpose flour
A pinch of salt
½ cup olive oil
6 tablespoons warm water
2 firm medium zucchini
(12 ounces total)
A pinch of coarse sea salt
A pinch of thyme leaves

Zucchini and Pearl Onions with Cardamom

Courgettes et Petits Oignons à la Cardamome

✳

FOR 4 SERVINGS

Preparation: 30 minutes
Cooking time: 25 minutes

7 ounces white pearl
  onions
4 tablespoons olive oil
1 teaspoon cardamom
  seeds
3 bay leaves
Salt and freshly ground
  black pepper
1/2 dried chili pepper
8 small firm zucchini
  (1 1/4 pounds total)
4 ounces dried figs
1 teaspoon tomato paste
2 juicy lemons
2 tablespoons fresh
  peppermint or other
  mint leaves
2 tablespoons fresh
  coriander leaves

Peel the pearl onions and put them into a heavy saucepan with 2 tablespoons of olive oil, the cardamom,

and bay leaves. Add water to cover, salt, pepper, and the chili pepper. Cook over high heat, covered, for 10 minutes.

Meanwhile, trim the ends of the zucchini, and cut them into 2-inch lengths; cut each piece in half lengthwise, or into quarters if your zucchini are on the large side.

Cut the figs into small dice, put them into a sieve, and rinse under warm running water for a few minutes. Drain the figs.

Add the zucchini and the tomato paste to the onions. Make sure that there is enough liquid; if not, add a little water. Cover the saucepan and return to high heat for 5 minutes.

Meanwhile, remove the peel and white pith from the lemons and cut the flesh into small dice, being careful to discard the membranes and the seeds. Chop the mint and the coriander.

Uncover the saucepan, add the remaining 2 tablespoons of olive oil, and let it boil fiercely to emulsify the oil and the cooking juices.

Remove from the heat and add the figs and lemon. Do not reheat.

When you are ready to serve, remove the bay leaves and the chili pepper, and add the chopped mint and coriander. Check for seasoning, and mix well. Serve warm.

Fennel

AN INEVITABLE FIXTURE of a French country walk, fennel stands tall in the scrubland, topped with wispy leaves and yellow parasols of blossom. It is very much a part of the Provençal landscape, and all country children munch its anise-flavored stalks. Since time immemorial, its seeds have been used to flavor the little local Christmas cakes, its stalks to scent grilled bass, and its leaves (which look very much like dill) to garnish platters of fish. But it is its fleshy, pearly bulb that makes it popular as a vegetable, especially in the Midi; it is less well known elsewhere in France.

You should choose big, white, tight fennel bulbs, and avoid those whose skin has been gnawed by bugs. Whatever leaves remain should be bright green.

Like celery, fennel must be stripped down to reach its tender heart. Its tough bottom and most of the stalks should be trimmed away; this will give you a regular, rounded shape.

You can cook fennel in boiling salted water or in a *blanc*—cold water containing flour and lemon juice—which will fix its color.

What I like best is to cut the bulbs in half lengthwise and gently braise them in a casserole, on top of the stove or in the oven, with olive oil, a pinch of sugar, and the juice of a lemon. They become meltingly tender and make you think you are eating candied anise.

The powerful flavor of fennel is enhanced by sugar, by fruits such as apricots; by sweet vegetables such as onions, bell peppers, and tomatoes; and by lemon, which adds a pleasant acidic note and also tenderizes the flesh. Coriander seeds and bay leaves are a good match, too.

It is customary to serve fennel with grilled or steamed fish, with which it goes very well, or with *aïoli*. But how about mating it with grilled lamb, duck with figs or olives, or a chicken with lemon?

I suggest serving a chilled rosé from Bandol—a wonderful complement to fennel's anise flavor.

Fennel Trimmings Soup

How many of you know that the outer skin of fennel—too fibrous to be enjoyed as a vegetable—makes a delicious, very delicate soup that is a perfect prelude to a fish dinner?

Take the peelings and stalks of the fennel, plus the white part of one or two leeks. Cut everything into thin strips and sweat over low heat in a covered pan with 3 tablespoons of olive oil and a lightly crushed clove of garlic.

After fifteen minutes, add a quart of hot chicken stock and let it cook another fifteen minutes. Purée in a food processor or blender, then put through a fine strainer to eliminate all the fibers.

Put four egg yolks, two tablespoons of olive oil, and a few tablespoons of the fennel soup in a blender; blend to emulsify to a thick, creamy consistency.

Bring the soup back to the boil, remove it from the fire, and pour the egg yolk mixture into the soup, whisking constantly.

Season with salt and plenty of pepper and serve immediately.

Hearts of Fennel
Braised in Vegetable Coulis

Coeurs de Fenouil Braisés dans leur Coulis

✳

Trim the fennel by cutting off the stalks and the bottom. Remove the fibrous outer skin with a vegetable peeler, and cut each bulb in half lengthwise.

Preheat the oven to 300 degrees.

Peel the onion and cut it into thin slices. Wash the red pepper, remove the stem, seeds, and internal membranes, and cut into thin circles. Peel and lightly crush the garlic.

Put the olive oil into a heavy casserole over low heat. Add the onion and red pepper and cook gently, stirring frequently, for about 10 minutes; do not let the vegetables brown.

When the onion and pepper are growing tender, add the garlic and arrange the fennel halves in the casse-role. Add the chicken stock and salt to taste. Bring to the boil, then cover and put in the oven for 30 minutes.

Meanwhile, peel the tomatoes. Remove their stems and place them in boiling water for 15 seconds (or a little longer if they are not ripe). Cool them in a bowl of cold water. The skins should slip off easily. Cut them in half crosswise and squeeze out the seeds and liquid. Cut the flesh into coarse dice. Add the tomatoes and the sugar to the fennel, and return to the oven for another 20 minutes.

When they are done, remove the fennel halves from the casserole with a slotted spoon and arrange them in an oven-proof gratin dish or baking dish; keep warm. Put the remaining

FOR 4 SERVINGS

Preparation: 30 minutes
Cooking time: 90 minutes

4 fennel bulbs (2 pounds total)
1 large onion
1 red bell pepper
1 garlic clove
2 tablespoons olive oil
2/3 cup to 1 cup chicken stock
2 medium tomatoes
1/2 teaspoon sugar
Salt and freshly ground black pepper
24 black Niçoise olives, pitted
2 tablespoons fresh coriander leaves

vegetables and juices from the casserole into a blender or food processor and purée them. Season to taste with salt and plenty of pepper, then strain over the fennel. Spread the pitted olives over the fennel and return to the oven for 10 minutes.

Chop the fresh coriander coarsely and sprinkle it over the fennel when you are ready to serve.

Fennel with Figs Scented with Bay Leaves
Cocotte de Fenouil aux Figues et au Laurier

✳

FOR 4 SERVINGS

Preparation: 10 minutes
Cooking time: 1 hour

8 young fennel bulbs
Juice of $\frac{1}{2}$ lemon
1 tablespoon flour
4 tablespoons butter
6 fresh black figs
2 bay leaves
2-inch cinnamon stick
Salt and freshly ground
   black pepper
2 or 3 fig leaves, if possible

Remove the outer layer from the fennel, and trim the base and the stalks, leaving neat bulbs. Wash and dry the fennel, and cook it for 30 minutes in boiling water with coarse salt and the lemon juice. Let the fennel cool in the cooking liquid. When it is cool enough to handle but still warm, drain and pat dry with a towel. Dredge lightly in flour.

Preheat the oven to 250 degrees

Melt half of the butter in a skillet. When it is just beginning to color, add the fennel and cook on all sides until golden, about 15 minutes. Then arrange the fennel in a single layer in a casserole. Cut the figs in half lengthwise and slip the pieces between the fennel bulbs.

Add the bay leaves and cinnamon, and season to taste with salt and plenty of pepper. Dot with the remaining 2 tablespoons butter and lay the fig leaves on top, covering completely. (Lacking fig leaves, cover with a piece of waxed paper.) Put the lid on the casserole and bake for 20 to 30 minutes.

Serve in the casserole after removing the fig leaves, cinnamon stick, and bay leaves.

OPPOSITE PAGE:
*Fennel with Figs Scented
with Bay Leaves*

Peppers

Bursting with color—yellows, reds, oranges, greens, violets—peppers are beautiful, simply beautiful. In fact, they are so beautiful they might have been molded in shiny plastic. But luckily they only look and feel like plastic. Their flavor—slightly sharp, slightly bitter—is strong and striking, but can be very sweet in the yellow and red varieties.

Choose firm, very smooth, heavy, thick-fleshed peppers. For *coulis* and ratatouilles and other long-cooked vegetable stews, you can opt for the small, thin-fleshed varieties; their skins will disappear in the cooking. For salads and stuffed peppers, I recommend the longer green frying peppers, whose skin will not be a nuisance to eat. The most common bell varieties are fatter and shorter; they have plenty of flesh, but thick skins that can be indigestible.

If you are going to eat them raw, and if they are fresh and firm, the easiest way to peel them is with a vegetable peeler. If you are going to cook them, there are several ways you can get the skins off. Some people drop them into very hot oil for a couple of minutes; others blanch them in boiling water. My choice is to rub them with oil and put them into the embers of a fireplace, under the broiler, or directly on the hot element of an electric range or over the burner of a gas range.

When their skin is completely blackened and blistered, put the peppers in a tightly closed plastic or paper bag or wrap them tightly in newspaper. In fifteen minutes they will have softened and you will easily be able to pull the skin off under running water. Always remove the stem, the seeds, and the pulpy ribs.

As with most other sun-drenched vegetables, the best cooking fat is olive oil—in which they can also be preserved very nicely.

Any aromatic herb or any other ingredient that evokes the Mediterranean will be a good match for peppers: thyme, savory, black olives, garlic, eggplant, or tomatoes. They also mate well with fish, especially brined anchovies.

Their bright colors make them decorative—for instance, in omelettes or to garnish dishes like the eggplant cake on page 52, which would otherwise look a little stark.

Young red wines such as Spanish Riojas or light Médocs from Bordeaux blend with their warm flavor, their crunch, and their sweetness.

Whether they are green, yellow, red, or even purple, fleshy, shiny, firm peppers are so sweet that they seem to have sugar added. But be careful of their cousins, the chili peppers, which can be diabolical.

Another César's Salad

My friend, the sculptor and excellent cook César, has attuned this Spanish pepper and anchovy salad to Provence.

You'll need elongated, somewhat twisted green peppers, known as frying peppers in the United States; a few anchovy fillets, preferably preserved in brine rather than oil (found in some Italian markets); 1/2 teaspoon of young savory leaves; a finely minced clove of garlic; a handful of little black Niçoise olives (either pitted or not); wine vinegar; good fruity extra-virgin olive oil; and salt and pepper.

Wash and dry the peppers, remove the stems and seeds, and cut them lengthwise into thin strips.

Mix all the ingredients, and lightly crush the anchovies into the dressing. Let the salad marinate for 30 minutes before serving.

Marinated Red Bell Peppers with Anchovies

Poivrons Rouges Marinées aux Anchois

✳

I generally serve this typically Mediterranean dish warm, with thick slabs of grilled country bread.

Place the peppers under the broiler, over a gas flame, or in the embers of the fireplace until the skins blacken. Put them in a plastic bag to steam off the charred skins.

Peel and finely mince the garlic.

Remove the peppers from the bag and peel them with your fingers. Remove the stems, cut the peppers in half lengthwise, and remove all seeds and membranes. Dry the peppers with paper towels, then cut them into ¾-inch strips.

Preheat the oven to 225 degrees.

Lightly oil a gratin dish or baking dish with about 1 tablespoon of the olive oil. Arrange a layer of pepper strips in the dish, then arrange on top the garlic, the savory, the anchovy fillets, and the olives. Season to taste with freshly ground pepper.

Top with the remaining peppers and add salt—only a little because the anchovies and olives are already salty. Sprinkle with the remaining 3 tablespoons olive oil and heat in oven for about 10 minutes, or until warm.

OPPOSITE PAGE:
Marinated Red Bell Peppers with Anchovies

FOR 4 SERVINGS

Preparation: 30 minutes
Cooking time: 30 minutes

4 fleshy red bell peppers
4 garlic cloves
4 tablespoons olive oil
2 tablespoons chopped fresh savory
8 anchovy fillets (packed in oil)
30 black Niçoise olives, pitted
Salt and freshly ground black pepper

Bell Peppers Sautéed with Wine Vinegar

Sauté de Poivrons Doux au Vinaigre de Vin

✳

Remove the stems, seeds, and ribs from the peppers. Cut them in half lengthwise, then into strips ⅜ inch wide.

Peel and crush the garlic.

Heat 3 tablespoons olive oil in a skillet and add the peppers, garlic, and chili pepper.

Add salt, and sauté the ingredients for a minute uncovered; then cover

the skillet and cook 5 minutes over medium heat.

Uncover the skillet, raise the heat and reduce the juices until the oil sizzles, then add the wine vinegar and let it reduce.

Remove the chili pepper.

Turn out into a serving dish and drizzle with the remaining 2 tablespoons olive oil.

FOR 4 SERVINGS

Preparation: 5 minutes
Cooking time: 10 minutes

3 fleshy bell peppers, either all the same color or 1 red, 1 yellow, and 1 green
3 garlic cloves
5 tablespoons fruity extra-virgin olive oil
1 small chili pepper, either fresh or dried, whole
Salt
2 teaspoons wine vinegar

75

Tomatoes

THE TOMATO is the fruit of the sun, the Queen of Summer. I used to (and would still prefer to) believe that the tomato was born in our Provençal soil beneath the blue-green olive trees and the flowering fig trees. But it came to us from the New World and, in fact, met with considerable resistance in Europe when it was brought over by the Spanish explorers. This is a fruit with roundness, brilliance, juiciness, acidity, and sugar —indeed, its overall allure has connections with love, which may be why it was once called the love-apple.

People who grow and understand their own tomatoes know that many factors need to be judged before you can bite into one. First, its color. Green means fritters, pickles, and jams; pink means salads; red means *coulis*, purées, ratatouille, or soup. Then you must touch it, handle it; and be sure to rub the leaves, because it would be a pity to miss their good smell. Cradle the tomato in the palm of your hand; consider its perfect shape. With your fingernail, cleanly sever the stem. Now, shut your eyes and inhale deeply before you finally take a bite—lest voracity get the better of respect.

Nature is no miser, and she is particularly generous with tomatoes. There are a thousand and one varieties: tiny cherry tomatoes, plum (or Roma) tomatoes, slicing tomatoes, big beefsteak tomatoes, and more. Most of them are good in all recipes, but for sauces or vegetable stews I recommend plum tomatoes.

When shopping it is most important that you know how to assess their quality, although there are so many kinds that it is difficult to be a good judge of them all. Tomatoes generally look fine in the market, but don't trust their appearance. The best criterion is fragrance, so do not hesitate to pick one up and smell it. The stem should retain the garden aroma of the plant itself; if it doesn't, your tomato will lack flavor and will be good only for decoration, or perhaps as a container for something like a little seafood salad. To be sure, tomatoes will grow in a hothouse, but they need the sun if they are going to be any good.

So if you want tomatoes in the winter, forget the tasteless ones you'll find in the supermarket. Use dried tomatoes, or the tomato sauce you put up in jars at the height of the season, when the tomatoes were bursting with juice and sunlight (see the recipe on page 80).

Here is how to make your own dried tomatoes: use moderately ripe, perfectly smooth-skinned, unblemished plum tomatoes. Wipe them with a towel, cut them in half crosswise, then put them cut side

Simple Salads

It is strange that tomatoes taste different depending on how you cut them. When they are ripe, cut them into thin slices with a sharp knife (a tomato-slicing gadget could crush them). Green tomatoes are tastier in thick, crisp wedges. But always douse them generously with olive oil and a little wine vinegar, or lemon juice if they are not completely ripe.

The flavor of tomatoes is so enticing and rich that all you need to add are a few grains of coarse sea salt and some basil or mint leaves. But on the other hand, they do not shun the company of cucumbers, green peppers, little black olives, anchovies, hard-boiled eggs, garlic, scallions, or celery.

down on a wicker or bamboo—or stainless metal—screen, either outdoors or in any dry, well-lit, and very airy place. After a few weeks, the tomatoes will have curled up on themselves without losing any of their wonderful fragrance. To use them, all you need to do is soak them for ten minutes in warm water.

Whether you are going to eat them cooked or raw, you must always clean the earth from your tomatoes and remove the stems, including where they are anchored in the core of the tomato.

Tomatoes should sometimes be peeled, especially for *coulis* and in hot dishes where they must melt away into the sauce. This is child's play once the tomatoes have been dipped in boiling water for ten or fifteen seconds.

It can also be unpleasant to come across the seeds while you are eating; just cut the tomatoes in half and squeeze out the seeds with your hand. (In Provence we even have a special verb for this: *esquicher.*) If the tomatoes are not too ripe, you can cut them into rounds for salad using a tomato slicer with parallel serrated blades set into a frame (you'll find these gadgets in some housewares and fancy kitchenware stores), but I prefer using a sharp knife to cut them into thick wedges.

Owing to its beauty and shape, the tomato cries out to be stuffed and baked, or filled with well-seasoned combinations such as tuna salad, shrimp with anchovy butter and olives, the salt cod and garlic mixture known as *brandade*, tabouleh (cracked wheat, garlic, and parsley salad), and so forth. To hollow out your tomatoes, use a small spoon or, if you need little balls of tomato flesh for garnishing, a melon baller.

I don't think there is any vegetable for which it is easier to find combinations. Tomatoes are delicious with all the sundrenched vegetables—eggplants, peppers, and zucchini—and go well with starchy vegetables such as potatoes, dried beans, and chickpeas. Grilled meats, especially lamb, draw out its best qualities, as do fish; you can use tomatoes in just about any sauce for fish.

All herbs, aromatic vegetables, and spices go with tomatoes, especially those that evoke the south of France: thyme, rosemary, savory, oregano, bay leaves, onions, garlic, and sea salt. And you can bring out different characteristics—a pinch of sugar will highlight their sweetness, while a few drops of lemon juice will give prominence to their acidity.

Bandol or rosés from the Côtes de Provence, all rich with sunshine, can contribute their fresh note to this acidic, juicy fruit.

Green Tomato Fritters

Beignets de Tomates Vertes

✳

FOR 2 SERVINGS

Preparation: 10 minutes
Cooking time: 10 to
20 minutes, depending
on the size of your
deep-fryer

For the Batter
1 scant cup all-purpose
flour
2 tablespoons cornstarch
2 teaspoons baking
powder
Ice water

1 large green tomato
Oil for deep-frying
Sea salt

Aren't tomatoes marvelous? You can enjoy them no matter how ripe or unripe they are!

When green, they are extremely clean-tasting, acidic, and refreshing. These crisp fritters can be made only with tomatoes that are completely green. They make a fine appetizer as part of an early summer or autumn country dinner.

Prepare the batter by blending the flour, cornstarch, and baking powder together in a bowl, using a wire whisk. Add ice water, whisking constantly, until you have a thick cream. The thinner the batter, the thinner the crust, but do not make it too thin or it will not coat the tomato slices.

Wash and dry the tomato, remove the stem, and cut it into 3/8-inch slices.

Heat the oil to 350 degrees.

Dip the tomato slices into the batter, then add them to the fryer one by one. Because of their size, you will probably be able to cook only a few of these at a time.

Turn the fritters to make sure they brown on both sides. When they are golden brown and crisp, remove them from the oil and drain on paper towels. Sprinkle with salt and serve immediately.

Green Tomato Jam

Confiture de Tomates Vertes

✳

FOR 6 CUPS

Preparation: 15 minutes
Maceration: 24 hours
Cooking time: 2 hours

4 1/2 pounds large green
tomatoes
4 1/2 cups sugar
3 lemons, preferably not
sprayed or waxed (if
you can get only
ordinary supermarket
lemons, scrub them
well before using)

In Provence they traditionally make this jam in September, when the tomatoes remaining on the vine will never ripen. You can simply spread it on bread, or you can make an excellent tart by spreading it on a pâte brisée *crust. The best recipe I've ever tasted is this one from Guy Gedda, who owns a restaurant in Bormes-les-Mimosas, at the very edge of the Dom Forest. He keeps up a family tradition of flavorful Provençal cooking that radiates honesty and nature.*

See photograph on page 241.

Wash the tomatoes, cut off the stems, and cut them into 8 to 10 wedges each. In a stainless-steel bowl, arrange alternate layers of tomatoes and sugar. Let this macerate in the

refrigerator for 20 to 24 hours; stir 2 or 3 times during this period.

The next day, pour the tomatoes into a preserving pan or large stainless-steel saucepan. Start cooking the jam over high heat, then reduce the heat to very low as soon as it comes to the boil.

Remove the scum with a spoon or skimmer.

Do not peel the lemons, but cut them in half lengthwise, then cut each half into $1/8$-inch slices. After the jam has cooked for 1 hour, add the lemon slices and cook for an additional hour, still over low heat.

Sterilize 6 half-pint canning jars. Fill the jars with the hot jam, then seal. Process in a hot-water bath for 15 minutes. Remove jars from water and let cool. Check seals and then store.

Caramelized Sautéed Tomatoes

Tomates Estrancinnées

✳

In Provençal, the word estrancinner *is used to describe a way of cooking tomatoes in a skillet over high heat until they are caramelized and shriveled.*

If you don't know this authentic Provençal recipe, and if you ever happen to be in Aix-en-Provence, go to the restaurant Chez Gu near the Cours Mirabeau, and tell them I sent you. They serve most of the great traditional Provençal dishes there.

Wash and dry the tomatoes. Remove the stems, cut them in half crosswise, and squeeze out the juice and seeds.

Heat a large skillet and add the olive oil. Put in the tomato halves skin side down, season with salt and pepper, and raise the heat to the highest it will go. Don't be afraid to let the flames lick the sides of the skillet.

Cook until the tomato skins start to brown, about 20 minutes. Sprinkle the cut sides with sugar and turn, still over hellishly high heat. The tomatoes will start to caramelize— and do not be scared if they begin to turn black, too.

Serve by bringing the hot skillet right to the table, along with some anchovy fillets, Niçoise olives, and slices of toasted country bread rubbed with a clove of garlic. Or you can serve the tomatoes ungarnished as an accompaniment to lamb chops that have been generously sprinkled with thyme and then grilled.

FOR 4 SERVINGS

Preparation: 5 minutes
Cooking time: 15 minutes

6 large firm tomatoes
6 tablespoons olive oil
Salt and freshly ground
  black pepper
1 tablespoon sugar
A few anchovy fillets,
  some little black Niçoise
  olives, and 4 slices of
  country bread, toasted
  or grilled and rubbed
  with raw garlic
  (optional)

OPPOSITE PAGE:
*Sautéed Cherry Tomatoes
with Basil*

Sautéed Cherry Tomatoes with Basil

Tomates-Cerises Sautées au Basilic

✳

FOR 4 SERVINGS

Preparation: 10 minutes
Cooking time: 5 or 6
  minutes

1 generous pound cherry
  tomatoes
1 garlic clove, peeled
20 basil leaves
2 tablespoons chopped
  parsley
¼ cup olive oil
1 teaspoon sugar
Salt and freshly ground
  black pepper
½ teaspoon thyme leaves

Cherry tomatoes are so fragrant and fruity that they need very little by way of preparation. This simple recipe will be even more delicious if you make it quickly and at the last minute; delay will sacrifice the firmness of the tomatoes.

Wash the tomatoes, dry them thoroughly with paper towels, and remove their stems.

Chop together the garlic, basil, and parsley.

Warm a serving dish in a 200 degree oven.

Put the oil into a skillet over high heat. When the oil begins to ripple, add the well-dried tomatoes.

Sprinkle with sugar, salt, and pepper and toss briefly. Add the garlic mixture and the thyme and mix well.

Serve immediately in the hot serving dish.

Tomato Sauce

Tomates Concassées

✳

FOR 8 TO 10 SERVINGS

Preparation: 15 minutes
Cooking time: 30 minutes

4½ pounds tomatoes,
  preferably plum
1 large onion
3 garlic cloves
¼ cup olive oil
1 large sprig thyme
2 bay leaves
A pinch of sugar
Salt and freshly ground
  black pepper

Take advantage of the summer's abundant, fragrant, and inexpensive tomatoes to prepare this basic sauce. Serve it with vegetables, pasta, rice, fish, or white meats—or as a filling for omelettes cooked in olive oil and scented with fresh basil.

This tomato sauce can also be turned into a tomato or bell pepper coulis. Or you can scent it with basil, coriander, oregano, garlic, or many other aromatics.

Peel the tomatoes. Remove their stems and place them in 6 or 7 quarts of boiling water for a minute or so, then cool them in a bowl of cold water. The skins should slip off easily. Cut them in half crosswise and squeeze out the seeds and liquid. Chop them coarsely.

Peel and finely chop the onion and garlic. Put the olive oil into a saucepan and warm it over medium-low heat. Add the onion and garlic, stir until lightly golden, then add the tomatoes, thyme, bay leaves, sugar, and salt to taste.

Cook over high heat, stirring occasionally with a wooden spoon until all the juices have boiled away. Season with plenty of pepper.

Tomato-Oregano Tarts

Tartes aux Tomates et à l'Origan

✳

FOR 4 SERVINGS

Preparation: 25 minutes
Cooking time: 30 minutes

1 scant pound very ripe
   tomatoes
2 tablespoons olive oil
Salt and freshly ground
   black pepper
1 slice white bread
½ pound all-butter puff
   pastry (available frozen
   in gourmet shops)
2 tablespoons capers, or
   4 ounces small black
   Niçoise olives
6 oregano or rosemary
   sprigs

Stem the tomatoes, put them in a pot of boiling water for 10 seconds, plunge into cold water, and peel them. Chop them coarsely.

Put the olive oil into a wide saucepan or a skillet over high heat. Add the tomatoes and salt and pepper to taste and sauté for 7 or 8 minutes.

Put a baking sheet into the refrigerator to chill.

Preheat the oven to 425 degrees.

Trim the crusts from the bread and process the crumb until you have fine bread crumbs. Mix with the leaves from the 2 oregano sprigs. Add pepper, mix with the tomatoes, and set aside.

Roll the puff pastry into a generous 12-inch square. Using a tart ring or plate as a template, cut out four 6-inch disks, and place them on the chilled baking sheet. Prick the disks all over, leaving a half-inch border all around, with a fork.

Bake the pastry circles for 10 minutes.

Remove the baking sheet, but do not alter the oven temperature. Spread a layer of tomatoes on each disk and sprinkle with capers or olives. Season to taste with salt and pepper. Return to the oven for another 8 minutes.

Garnish each tart with a sprig of oregano and serve immediately.

OPPOSITE PAGE:
Tomato-Oregano Tarts

PAGES 84–85:
*Cabbages—white, red, Savoy,
napa—there's more to them
than cabbage soup.*

Tomatoes with Mustard-Cheese Topping

Tomate Moutardée en Croûte de Comté

✳

FOR 4 SERVINGS

Preparation: 10 minutes
Cooking time: 20 minutes

8 ripe medium tomatoes
Salt and freshly ground
   black pepper
1 tablespoon Dijon
   mustard
1 tablespoon *tapenade*
   (black olive spread;
   available in jars in
   gourmet shops)
1 teaspoon thyme leaves
4 ounces Comté or Swiss
   Gruyère cheese,
   shredded
1 cup fresh white bread
   crumbs
¼ cup olive oil
16 black Niçoise olives,
   pitted

Preheat the oven to 450 degrees.

Stem the tomatoes, cut them in half crosswise, and squeeze out all the juice and seeds. Arrange them tightly together in a baking dish in a single layer, cut side up. Season with salt and pepper.

Mix the mustard, *tapenade*, and thyme. Brush each tomato half with this mixture, and sprinkle with the cheese and bread crumbs, then with the olive oil. Place a pitted olive on each tomato half.

Bake for 15 to 20 minutes.

Green Vegetables

Swiss Chard

SWISS CHARD IS used in diverse ways across France. In the Midi, for example, they accent the leaves in dazzling Swiss chard pies, sweet or savory. In the north and the east, they favor the fleshy stalks of the broad-stemmed chard common in France in gratins or sauced with béchamel. In the Auvergne, no garden is without Swiss chard. When they make a stuffing for zucchini, a breast of veal, or a chicken—or when they prepare the little chicken, prune, and herb fritters known as *farçous*—chard leaves are always used for their slightly sharp, but never acid, note.

Like spinach, Swiss chard leaves grow limp quickly, so they should be cooked soon after picking. Or make sure they are very fresh when you buy them at the farmers' market. You can tell immediately when chard is fresh: the stalks are uniformly bright and glossy, the dark green leaves are shiny and not withered.

If you intend to use the leaves, choose fully mature chard so there will be as much green as possible. In America, this should present no problem.

If you can get the broad-stemmed chard, remove the fine opalescent outer layer of the broad, fleshy stalks. Just cut crosswise into the flesh and pull back the outer layer. Do this on both sides of the stalk. Cut the peeled stalks into two-inch lengths, then lengthwise into pieces around ³/₈ inch wide. If all you can find is the thin-stemmed variety of chard, all you need do is cut the stems into two-inch lengths unless they are very old and fibrous. To preserve their whiteness until you cook them you can place them into cold water acidulated with a little lemon juice or a few tablespoonfuls of white vinegar. They should be cooked in a *blanc* (see page 244 and individual recipes) for about fifteen minutes (less for the thin-stemmed varieties); then let them cool in their cooking liquid before draining them and finishing your dish. Recipes calling for chard stalks are best made with broad-stemmed chard; you can prepare them using thin-stemmed varieties, but you will need more chard to make up the same quantity of stalks.

Swiss chard stalks have a very subtle flavor, and for wine I recommend a fresh young white Graves from Bordeaux or a more floral white Cassis (from the Provençal village of Cassis near Marseilles —not to be confused with the syrupy black currant liqueur *crème de cassis*). But the sharpness of the chard leaves would go well with a red Bellet from near Nice with its intense fruity bouquet.

Along the Mediterranean coast, people favor the lovely deep-green leaves of Swiss chard, while in other parts of France they prefer the broad white stalks.

Omelette Trucca

In Nice they call this a Niçoise omelette; in Cannes they call it Cannoise. It is a treat whatever its hometown.

Sweat some Swiss chard leaves until their liquid has reduced completely. Meanwhile, over low heat, cook a sliced large onion in olive oil. Beat eight eggs with a pinch of salt, some pepper, and a pinch of thyme leaves; add the cooked onions and chard to the eggs.

Heat some olive oil in a skillet until very hot, then pour in the egg mixture. Add as much grated Parmesan cheese and chopped walnuts as you like. As the omelette sets, lift up its edges from time to time with a fork to let the uncooked eggs flow underneath. When it is fairly well set, sprinkle it with white bread crumbs and some olive oil. Turn the omelette over and let it cook until golden brown. Reverse it onto a serving dish and serve, hot, warm, or cold.

Swiss Chard Pie Niçoise
Tourte de Blettes à la Niçoise

✳

When you are in Nice be sure to visit that local institution, Hélène Barale. Her restaurant is a temple of good eating where the local traditions live on. She will relish explaining every dish to you, and she'll do it in the local dialect—at least until she realizes that your Niçois is a little rusty. But even if you don't understand every word, you will certainly get the drift of this great, warm-hearted, high-spirited lady's gastronomic message.

Here is the recipe for tourta de blea, *as Mme. Barale would call it in Niçois. It is a wonderful dessert that you can enjoy with a nice cold, sweet glass of Muscat de Beaumes de Venise.*

FOR 8 SERVINGS

Preparation: 1 hour
Resting time for the
  pastry: 1 hour
Cooking time: 35 to
  40 minutes

¾ cup dried currants

For the Pastry
¾ cup plus 2 tablespoons
  butter
3½ cups all-purpose flour
2 eggs, beaten
½ cup sugar
¼ cup cold milk
Zest of ½ lemon
¼ cup rum
1 teaspoon salt
1½ teaspoons baking
  powder

For the Filling
2¼ pounds Swiss chard
¼ cup apricot jam
⅔ cup pine nuts
¼ cup rum
¼ cup orange-flower
  water
3 small apples, such as
  McIntosh or Golden
  Delicious
1 egg
2 tablespoons sugar

Soak the currants in a little warm water until plumped, about 15 minutes. Drain.

Make the pastry. Soften the butter in a warm place or by kneading it with your hand. Put the flour on your work surface and make a well in the middle. Into that well, place the butter, eggs, sugar, cold milk, lemon zest, rum, and salt. Mix well with your fingertips. Sprinkle with the baking powder and knead until smooth. Wrap the dough in a towel or plastic wrap and put it in the refrigerator to rest for at least 1 hour.

While the dough is resting, stem the Swiss chard; you will use only the leaves. (Save the stalks, wrapped in a damp towel, for another dish, perhaps a gratin.)

Put 2½ quarts salted water on to boil.

Preheat the oven to 500 degrees.

Wash the leaves in several changes of water to remove every last trace of earth; drain in a colander. Put them into the boiling water. When it returns to the boil, remove the chard leaves and cool them in cold water. With your hands, squeeze out all the

water. Chop the chard coarsely and put it into a bowl along with the currants, apricot jam, pine nuts, rum, and orange-flower water.

Peel, core, and thinly slice the apples. Beat the egg in a cup or a small bowl.

Roll the dough into a rectangle about ⅛ inch thick; cut it in half and place one half on a clean cookie sheet or sheet pan. Top it with a ¾-inch-thick layer of filling, leaving a ¾-inch border of dough at edges. Spread the apple slices on top of the filling. Lightly brush the border of dough with a little of the beaten egg. Cover the filling with the other half of the dough, push edges together to seal the seams well, then fold the edges over and press down to create a tight edge.

Brush the top of the pie with the beaten egg, then use a pair of scissors or a sharp paring knife to make little slits in the top crust, every inch or so.

Bake for about 35 minutes, checking often to make sure the pie doesn't burn.

Remove the pie from the oven, sprinkle it with granulated sugar, and let it cool.

Note: Hélène assures me that this pie is even better the next day. Leftover pastry or filling will keep in the refrigerator for 2 or 3 days, should you want to make another Swiss Chard Pie.

Gratin of Swiss Chard Stalks with Tomatoes
Côtes de Blettes Gratinées aux Tomates

✳

Here are the aromas and flavors of Italy. Fontina is a mild cheese made of whole cow's milk; it melts and browns to perfection. I advise using fontina Val d'Aosta, *which has a particularly fine aroma.*

Cut away the chard leaves without bruising them; you can use them in another dish (such as the Swiss Chard Pie Niçoise on page 88). If you are using broad-stemmed chard, or if the stalks are old and fibrous, use a small knife or vegetable peeler to remove the fine membrane on each side of the stalks. Cut the stalks into pieces 2 inches long by 3/8 inch wide and, to keep them from discoloring, immediately place them into cold water containing the lemon juice.

Prepare a *blanc* by dispersing the flour and a handful of coarse salt in 3 quarts of water (see page 244 for the technique).

Drain the chard stalks and add them to the flour-water mixture. Put the pan over medium heat and bring to the boil; cook over low heat for between 10 and 20 minutes, or until the stalks are tender. Drain in a strainer or colander.

Preheat the oven to 350 degrees.

While the chard is cooking, peel the tomatoes. Remove their stems and place them in boiling water for 15 seconds (or a little longer if they are not ripe). Cool them in a bowl of cold water; the skins should slip off easily.

Cut tomatoes in half crosswise and squeeze out the seeds and liquid. Cut the flesh into coarse chunks.

Peel and finely chop the onion and garlic. Heat half the olive oil in a heavy saucepan and add the chopped onion; when it has turned golden, in about 8 minutes, add the garlic and the tomatoes. Add salt to taste, and raise the heat to high to boil off the tomato juices quickly.

Pour the remaining olive oil into a skillet, heat it over medium heat, and add the chard stalks; raise the heat and sauté until slightly golden, about 5 minutes. Add salt and pepper to taste.

Add the reduced tomato-onion mixture to the chard, mix well, and turn out into a buttered gratin dish.

Mix the Parmesan, fontina, and marjoram, and sprinkle over the chard. Bake for about 15 minutes, or until the top is golden brown.

Serve very hot.

FOR 4 SERVINGS

Preparation: 30 minutes
Cooking time: 50 minutes

2 1/4 pounds Swiss chard (or more, depending on the thickness of the stalks)
Juice of 1 lemon
2 tablespoons flour
4 small tomatoes
1 small onion
1 garlic clove
5 tablespoons olive oil
Salt and freshly ground black pepper
1 tablespoon grated Parmesan cheese
1 1/2 ounces Italian fontina cheese, grated
Pinch of fresh marjoram leaves

Stuffed Swiss Chard
Farcis de Blettes

✳

I hate seeing people throw away the green leaves of Swiss chard—as they often do in France, where the broad, fleshy stalks are often used on their own. Instead, prepare this typically Mediterranean recipe, in which the soft flavor of the leaves is enhanced with a currant and pine nut stuffing. It is a real treat, and you'll be glad you tried it.

Soak the currants in a little warm water for 10 minutes, then drain. Parboil the rice in salted water for 12 minutes, then drain it in a strainer and cool it under cold running water.

Peel the onion and chop it fine; sauté for 1 minute in a skillet with 1 tablespoon of olive oil.

Wash and dry the chard, making sure not to damage the green leaves. Run a knife along the stalks, separating the green from the white. Cut the stalks into 2-inch lengths.

Prepare a *blanc* by dispersing the flour and a handful of coarse salt in 3 quarts of water (see page 244 for the technique). Bring to the boil and add the chard stalks. Cook them for 10 or 15 minutes or until just tender, then drain well and chop coarsely with a knife.

Heat 4 tablespoons olive oil in a skillet over medium heat. Add the boiled chard stalks and sauté them, stirring often, for 5 minutes.

Preheat the oven to 275 degrees.

Put the sautéed stalks into a bowl and add the currants, pine nuts, parboiled rice, chopped onion, and salt and pepper to taste. Form this stuffing into little balls, about 1 tablespoon of stuffing each, and wrap each ball neatly in a Swiss chard leaf.

Arrange the balls tightly in a baking dish, smooth side up. Sprinkle with the remaining 3 tablespoons olive oil, add about 1/4 inch of water, and bake for around 35 minutes.

Serve hot, in the baking dish.

FOR 4 SERVINGS

Preparation: 1 hour
Cooking time: 70 minutes

1 tablespoon dried currants
4 teaspoons rice
1 medium onion
8 tablespoons olive oil
1 bunch leafy Swiss chard with large leaves (about 12 pieces)
1 tablespoon flour
1 tablespoon pine nuts
Salt and freshly ground black pepper

Swiss Chard with White Onions

Fricassée de Blettes et d'Oignons Blancs

✳

FOR 4 SERVINGS

Preparation: 45 minutes
Cooking time: 90 minutes

1¾ pounds Swiss chard
3 tablespoons white
   vinegar or lemon juice
2 medium tomatoes
2 medium white onions
10 tablespoons olive oil
1 heaping tablespoon
   flour
1 teaspoon caraway seeds
1 garlic clove
Salt and freshly ground
   black pepper
1 tablespoon chopped
   fresh coriander leaves

Run a knife along the chard stalks to remove the leaves. Carefully wash and drain the leaves. If you are using broad-stemmed chard, use a vegetable peeler or paring knife to remove the fibrous outer layer of the stalks. Cut the stalks into 2-inch lengths, then if necessary cut each piece lengthwise into ⅜-inch strips. Immediately place these into a bowl of water acidulated with the vinegar or lemon juice.

Peel the tomatoes. Remove their stems and place them in boiling water for 15 seconds (or a little longer if they are not ripe). Cool them in a bowl of cold water. The skins should slip off easily.

Cut tomatoes in half crosswise and squeeze out the seeds and liquid. Cut them into ⅜-inch dice and place them in a strainer to drain.

Peel the onions and cut them into thin slices. Put them into a heavy saucepan with half the olive oil, 3 tablespoons water, and a little sea salt. Cover the pan and cook over very low heat for about 40 minutes; the onions must not brown and should become very tender.

Drain the chard stalks and put them into a large saucepan. Put flour into a fine strainer, hold this over the saucepan, and slowly pour 2 quarts

cold water over the flour. Add a handful of salt and let the chard stalks cook for 10 or 15 minutes over medium heat; the stalks should remain slightly *al dente*. Remove the pan from the heat, but let the stalks sit in their cooking liquid for about 20 minutes before draining them in a colander.

In a small, heavy-bottomed skillet or saucepan, toast the caraway seeds over medium heat until they just begin to take color. Crush them to a powder in a mortar or a spice grinder and sift the powder to remove any fibers.

Peel the garlic and mince finely.

Cut the chard leaves into ¼-inch strips and add to the onions. Mix well with a wooden spoon, raise the heat to high, and let the mixture cook, uncovered, until all the chard's water has evaporated.

Heat the remaining 5 tablespoons olive oil in a skillet and add the chard stalks, thoroughly drained. Sauté until lightly golden, then add the chard leaf mixture, tomatoes, garlic, and caraway. Season to taste with salt and pepper, stir well, and cook for 5 to 10 minutes more.

Sprinkle with chopped fresh coriander leaves before serving.

Swiss Chard Pastilla
Pastilla de Feuilles de Blettes

✳

Phyllo-dough pies are very popular in Greece, Turkey, and Morocco. The delicious Moroccan version, called pastillas, *are traditionally filled with pieces of squab, Málaga raisins, almonds, and so forth. Here is a sweet* pastilla *you could serve as dessert following an all-vegetable dinner. It tastes of the Middle East and balances the warmth of its spices with the sweetness of its currants and sugar.*

FOR 4 SERVINGS

Preparation: 30 minutes
Cooking time: 40 minutes

2 tablespoons dark rum
2 tablespoons dried
   currants
2¼ pounds Swiss chard
   (or less if using very
   leafy thin-stemmed
   chard)
1 small onion
1 garlic clove
3 tablespoons olive oil
Salt and freshly ground
   black pepper
2 tablespoons pine nuts

For the Pastry
5 sheets phyllo dough
1 heaping teaspoon
   confectioners' sugar
½ teaspoon ground
   cinnamon

Carefully warm the rum and soak the currants in it.

Run a knife along the chard stalks to remove the leaves. Wrap the stalks in a damp towel and save them for another dish. Wash the chard leaves in several changes of water to remove every particle of soil. Drain them and cut them roughly into strips.

Preheat the oven to 425 degrees.

Peel and chop the onion. Peel and mince the garlic.

In a skillet, warm the olive oil over high heat. Add the onion; when it is golden, add the garlic and chard leaves. Add salt to taste, and cook over high heat until all the chard's water has evaporated.

Put the pine nuts into a baking dish and toast them in the oven or under the broiler, taking care not to let them burn. You can also do this in the microwave oven.

When the chard is completely dry but has not yet begun to brown, remove the skillet from the heat.

Drain the currants and add them to the chard, along with the pine nuts. Season with salt and pepper. Spread the mixture on a cutting board or tray to cool.

Generously grease an 8-inch cake pan or tart pan with butter.

Lay the sheets of phyllo dough in the pan one by one, putting them in at different angles to make sure you have overhanging flaps of dough you can fold over the filling. Fill with the chard mixture.

Fold the dough over the filling and bake for 15 minutes.

Mix the confectioners' sugar and the cinnamon.

When the *pastilla* comes out of the oven, heat the pan on top of the stove over medium heat for 2 or 3 minutes in order to make sure the bottom is crisp. Unmold, upside down, onto a heatproof serving platter. Using a small strainer, dust the *pastilla* with the sugar-cinnamon mixture, and run it under the broiler to caramelize.

Serve immediately.

Celery and Celeriac

FIRST AMONG ALL the virtues of celery —no matter what the variety—is the powerful aroma that pervades every part of the plant.

There are at least three types of celery for culinary purposes: common celery; celeriac (knob celery or celery root); and the rarer leaf celery, or soup celery.

Only the central heart of a head of celery is really tender. Since it constitutes a small part of the plant, I recommend your buying the biggest heads of celery you can find. Use only five or six inches of the stalks, and remove the very green outer stalks, saving them for the soup pot. Peel the outermost remaining stalks with a vegetable peeler to remove the tough fibers, and place the hearts in acidulated water to keep them from darkening. If you want to boil them, use water in which flour has been dispersed—a *blanc* (see "The Right Way to Cook," page 244). But I prefer to braise them in the oven or cook them in broth. To be completely tender, they will need about an hour of cooking.

The very tender central stalks can be sliced raw into a summer salad—a tomato salad, for example.

You can find celeriac, or celery root, in the market nearly year-round, its big round form sometimes topped with leaves. Be sure to choose firm celeriac; without its leaves it is difficult to know how fresh it is by merely looking at it. A soft celeriac will generally be dried out, hollow, and pulpy—good only to add flavor to a soup.

You can eat celeriac raw (grated and served with rémoulade sauce); cooked in the broth of a *pot-au-feu*; or puréed—delicious with game or roast beef. In all events, wash it carefully before you peel it (either with a vegetable peeler or a sharp paring knife), so the peelings will be nice and clean. You can dry these peelings by stringing them on a thread and hanging them in the open air, or by spreading them out in a dry place; they will be very useful for flavoring sauces, broths, and soups.

Once it has been peeled, celeriac turns brown rapidly, so it must be placed in water acidulated with lemon juice. The best way to boil it is in a *blanc* (see "The Right Way to Cook," page 244).

As for leaf celery (which you are unlikely to find in American markets), we use it in France almost entirely for seasoning soups or the broth for cooking boiled beef or chicken. When very young, the leaves can be snipped into a salad or used along with other herbs for seasoning or in a herb sauce.

Celery's powerful aroma makes choosing wine something of a challenge. For common celery, I choose a tannic country wine from Southwest France, perhaps a Cahors; and for celeriac I opt for a lively Rhône Valley red made from the Grenache grape, such as Gigondas or Châteauneuf-du-Pape.

Celeriac Gratin with Meat Juices

Gratin de Céleri-Rave au Jus

✳

Wash and peel the celeriac and cut into quarters. Place in a deep saucepan. Put the flour into a small strainer and pour cold water through the strainer in order to disperse the flour in the water, creating a lump-free *blanc*. Add additional water to cover the celeriac, then add the milk. Do not add salt.

Bring to the boil, uncovered, over high heat, then reduce the heat to medium-low. Cover the pan and simmer for 30 minutes, then check the celeriac by piercing with a paring knife; it should be tender.

While the celeriac is simmering, preheat the oven to 300 degrees.

Drain the celeriac and cut the quarters into slices $1/4$ inch thick. Arrange the slices in a gratin or baking dish. Bring the meat juices to the boil. If you are using unsalted stock, add salt to taste. Add the butter and stir until it melts, then pour the mixture over the celeriac. Bake for 15 minutes. Remove from the oven, sprinkle with the grated cheese, and bake for 10 minutes more, or until nicely browned.

When done, season with pepper to taste and serve in the gratin dish.

FOR 4 SERVINGS

Preparation: 20 minutes
Cooking time: 1 hour

$2^1/_2$ pounds celeriac
  (2 large celeriacs)
1 tablespoon flour
1 cup milk
4 tablespoons butter
$1/2$ cup juices from a roast chicken, pork, or veal, or rich chicken or veal stock
3 ounces Gruyère cheese, grated
Salt and freshly ground black pepper

Homemade Celery Salt

Celery salt is very useful for seasoning tomato sauces or soups, vegetable broths, and salads, and it couldn't be easier to make at home.

Put some dried celeriac peelings (see page 96) into a blender along with a handful of high-quality coarse sea salt, and blend to a powder. Strain the mixture and keep it in a jar or a tightly sealed canister.

Celery Hearts with Walnut Oil
Coeurs de Céleri à l'Huile de Noix

✳

This is a very simple dish that will be even better if you use a first-class unblended walnut oil. The very best is pressed from toasted walnuts and most often comes from central France.

Strip away the most fibrous exterior stalks of the celery (save them for soup). Cut off the celery tops, leaving each heart about 5 inches long. Save a few pale leaves from the very center for garnish; wrap them in a damp cloth and put them in the refrigerator.

Use a vegetable peeler to strip the external fibers from each celery heart; trim the base until it is white. Wash the celery in lukewarm water, spreading the stalks to make sure there is no sand caught inside the heart.

Skin the walnuts. Put them into boiling water for a few seconds, then use a small, pointed knife to scrape off the brown skin—this is painstaking work, but worth doing. Cut them into thin slices with a sharp, thin-bladed knife rather than merely chopping them.

Preheat the oven to 250 degrees.

Bring the chicken stock to the boil, turn off the heat, and add the butter.

Dry the celery hearts and arrange them in an ovenproof casserole. Salt lightly and pour the hot chicken stock over the celery. Cover the casserole, bring to the boil on top of the stove, then cook in the oven for 30 to 45 minutes. After 30 minutes begin checking the celery; you should be able to pierce it easily with the point of a knife. Continue cooking until it is very tender.

When they are done, remove the celery hearts from the cooking liquid and arrange them on a warmed serving platter. Put the casserole over high heat, uncovered, and reduce the cooking liquid until it thickens to a syrupy consistency. Add the walnut oil and whisk until the sauce emulsifies.

Pour the sauce over the celery hearts, season with pepper, and garnish with the walnuts and celery leaves.

Serve very hot.

FOR 4 SERVINGS

Preparation: 30 minutes
Cooking time: 1 hour

4 large heads of celery,
   pale in color
12 walnuts, shelled
2 cups chicken stock
4 teaspoons butter
Salt and freshly ground
   black pepper
3 tablespoons walnut oil

Potato-Celeriac Pancakes with Cream and Celery

Criquettes de Pommes de Terre et de Céleri à la Crème

✳

A traditional criquette *is a little pancake made of grated potatoes. It is a specialty of the Dauphiné region, although a slightly different version is prepared in Lorraine.*

FOR 4 SERVINGS

Preparation: 15 minutes
Cooking time: 30 minutes

2 large potatoes
1 small celeriac (about 3½ ounces)
Salt
4 tablespoons butter
1 tablespoon peanut oil
1 medium onion, preferably white
The pale heart at the center of a head of celery and a few of its leaves
¼ cup *crème fraîche* or whipped heavy cream
A pinch of freshly grated nutmeg

Peel the potatoes and celeriac and wipe them clean. Grate them finely. Mix and season with salt.

With your hands, divide the grated vegetables into 8 balls, and flatten each one into a pancake about ⅝ inch thick.

Heat the butter and oil in a large skillet over medium heat. Add the pancakes and cook until lightly browned on one side, then turn them over. Press them with your spatula to help them hold together. Cook for a total of 15 to 20 minutes, turning occasionally.

Meanwhile, peel the onion and cut it into thin slices. Salt lightly and place in a strainer to let the salt draw out some of the onion's liquid.

Pluck some of the palest central leaves from the celery heart and set aside. Thinly slice the stalks and set them aside.

When the pancakes are cooked, arrange them, overlapping, around the edge of an ovenproof platter. Spread some *crème fraîche* or whipped cream on each pancake, then sprinkle with nutmeg and top with thinly sliced onion.

Put the platter under the broiler or in a very hot oven for a couple of minutes. Before serving, put the sliced celery heart and leaves in the center of the platter.

Serve immediately.

The Cabbage Family

THE MEMBERS of this enormous family may vary a great deal in their looks, but they all share an assertive flavor that I would call a trifle wild, but not without gentleness. As they cook, they emit a strong odor that many people find unpleasant. It doesn't bother me in the least, for it evokes fond memories of childhood: delicious soups (those succulent *potées*) and plump stuffed cabbages.

There is great diversity among the green cabbages. In France, the first appear in the spring: the *coeurs-de-boeuf*, or oxheart, cabbages named for their somewhat pointed shape. Their broad leaves are not packed into a tight head and are excellent for individual stuffed cabbage rolls. You can retain their delicacy through brief cooking or through very gentle braising in a casserole.

In autumn and winter, market space is shared by small Savoy cabbages; large, smooth, pale-green cabbages often called white cabbages; and big cabbages with nubbly surfaces. The very tasty Savoy cabbages are delicious gently braised with partridge or pheasant, and they are also good stuffed; but their fragility disqualifies them from boiling—in soups such as *potée*, for instance. Heads of white cabbage are very tight, and the ribs of the leaves can be tough. Remove these ribs and slice the leaves thin for a nice salad. Layered into earthenware crocks and fermented in coarse salt, scented with juniper berries or caraway seeds, shredded white cabbage—sauerkraut—takes on a delicious acidic flavor; it can be cooked in an Alsatian *choucroute* with white wine or beer, or with sour cream as in central Europe.

The various other green cabbages work well in soups, stuffed cabbage, and salads.

In France, red cabbage is grown abundantly in Alsace and Lorraine; it is harvested in winter. It has a slightly sweet flavor that can be brought out by cooking in red wine with apples, cranberries, or red currants. It is a good match for game, especially wild boar.

Red cabbage is no less wonderful in a rustic salad: cut the cabbage into strips, put them into a bowl, and pour in some boiling wine vinegar. Let the cabbage steep in the vinegar for a few moments, then drain it and season with oil, salt, and pepper. Sprinkle with a few pork or duck cracklings, or with walnuts or chestnuts. Eaten by the fireside, this is a positively noble salad.

French children adore the tiny size and sweetness of those

Cauliflower-Stalk Soup

As a child, I munched on the stalks of the cauliflower my mother was preparing for dinner, so I've always appreciated their slightly sweet flavor. And my mother made them into delicious soups. She sliced them, sweated them in butter with a little white of leek, then added a quart of water, salt, and a couple of mealy potatoes. When the cauliflower stalks, leeks, and potatoes were all tender, she would put the soup through the fine disk of a food mill, reheat it without returning it to the boil, take it off the heat, and add a few tablespoons of thick *crème fraîche* and a few sprigs of chervil. You can make the same soup from broccoli stalks.

winter pearls, Brussels sprouts. You can boost this appeal by serving them with chestnuts or by puréeing them to make a delicate mousse. I like to steam them, then sauté them in good fat, either browned butter or high-quality lard—enough to coat them well.

When buying cauliflower, look for snow-white heads. Wash the florets in water containing a hint of white vinegar, then drain them and either boil them in salted water or steam them. Check for doneness with the point of a knife; they are done when tender but still somewhat firm. Cool them in cold water, and drain. Some people throw a little bread or garlic into the water to minimize the strong cooking odor, but I don't quite believe in these tricks. I just open the kitchen window.

Broccoli—green, purple, or yellow—is cauliflower's Mediterranean cousin. Preparation and cooking are similar to those for cauliflower, although the two vegetables are somewhat different both in flavor and in texture. Buy them on the small side, with tight florets; avoid broccoli whose flowers have begun to open or to show yellow.

With cauliflower and broccoli, it is normal to eat only the florets, but the stems and flower stalks are good, too.

Let me touch on a few of the less familiar members of the cabbage family.

Napa cabbage (Chinese cabbage) is long and pale green. At a distance, you might mistake it for a romaine lettuce. It lacks the substantial flavor of its Western cousins,

but it has a very nice, slightly sweet taste and a texture that is appealing when the vegetable is sliced and stir-fried for a few moments over very high heat in a wok or skillet (see "The Right Way to Cook," page 247).

In France we no longer see much kohlrabi, a rustic vegetable that was once very common in the countryside and that is still found in the United States. Like the *chou pommé*, which has also just about disappeared from French markets, it adds an inimitable flavor to *pot-au-feu* and broths. When dipped in a coating of wax, kohlrabi will keep for months. I wish more French cooks would buy them when they are available, even though they remind us of the grim years of postwar privation. So don't hold a grudge; give kohlrabi a try.

Recently, French greengrocers have been carrying sea-kale (*crambe maritime*), which comes to market as white shoots topped with barely-sprouted leaves. They are eaten like asparagus—poached and served with vinaigrette or Hollandaise sauce. To my taste, these tender shoots are lacking in flavor.

Wines will vary depending on preparation. The lightly sour taste of central European sauerkraut goes well with a Riesling from Alsace or from Germany (such as those from Mosel-Saar-Ruwer or the Rheingau). But for stuffed cabbage or a hearty *potée*, I would opt for a powerful red, such as a Corbières, a Coteaux d'Aix, or a Gaillac. With red cabbage you'll enjoy a red Bandol or an Alsatian Pinot Noir.

Central European Sauerkraut

Chou Blanc à la Mode d'Europe Centrale

✳

This one recipe will yield two very different results, depending on whether you ferment the cabbage in salt (see Variation). The acidic flavor of the fermented version is particularly nice with the cream.

FOR 4 SERVINGS

Preparation: 15 minutes
  (plus 5 days'
  fermentation)
Cooking time: 45 minutes
  to 1 hour

1 large white cabbage
  (3¼ pounds)
4 generous tablespoons
  coarse sea salt
2 medium onions,
  1 studded with 2 cloves
1 bay leaf
1 garlic clove
½ teaspoon ground
  caraway seeds
6 tablespoons lard, or
  goose or duck fat
½ tablespoon sweet
  Hungarian paprika
1 teaspoon tomato paste
1½ tablespoons heavy
  cream
½ cup plain yogurt
Salt

Wash the cabbage and cut it in half lengthwise. Remove the entire core and the tough ribs of the leaves, then slice into ⅜-inch strips. Put the cabbage into a crock along with the sea salt and mix well. Place the clove-studded onion and the bay leaf in the crock. Put a plate on top of the cabbage and weight it with something weighing at least 1 pound. Keep the crock in a cool place, but do not refrigerate.

After about 24 hours the cabbage will have rendered a great deal of water and will be swimming in brine; let it ferment for 3 or 4 days before using.

Before cooking, rinse the cabbage in cold water, then drain it thoroughly in a strainer, extracting as much liquid as possible by squeezing with your hands.

Peel the remaining onion and slice thin; peel and lightly crush the garlic.

If you cannot get ground caraway, toast some caraway seeds in a dry skillet, then grind them in a mortar or a spice mill.

Melt the fat in a heavy cast-iron casserole. Add the onion slices and cook over low heat until soft, then add the paprika. Mix well with a wooden spoon, then add the tomato paste, ground caraway, and garlic.

Add the cabbage to the casserole and mix well with the other ingredients. Add ¼ cup warm water. Cover the casserole and cook over low heat for 20 minutes. From time to time, stir and add a little water as required to prevent the cabbage from scorching.

When done, uncover the casserole and turn up the heat to boil off the juices. Add the cream and the yogurt. Let this bubble away for 3 or 4 minutes, stirring constantly. Check for seasoning; remove the garlic clove before serving.

Variation: You can also make this dish without fermenting the cabbage. Wash the cabbage and cut out the core and the tough central ribs of the leaves. Bring 3 quarts of water to the boil with 2 handfuls of salt. Add the cabbage and let it boil for 3 minutes. Cool the cabbage in cold water, drain well, and slice into ⅜-inch strips. The remainder of the recipe is unchanged.

Cabbage with Mushroom Stuffing

Chou Farci aux Champignons

✳

Deep inside, everyone in France harbors a memory of the stuffed cabbage our grandmothers simmered in their beautiful black cast-iron casseroles, the aroma pervading the entire house. There are so many versions, from the most rustic—where the cabbage is filled with sausage meat, to the most sumptuous—where the leaves are spread with foie gras and truffles. Here is an elegant, original recipe that will warm your chilly winter or early spring evenings. Serve this dish with steamed new potatoes and drink a white wine from the Savoie, such as a Chignin, a Roussette, or a Seyssel.

Trim the base of each mushroom stem; rinse and dry the mushrooms and cut them into small dice.

In a wide saucepan or a skillet, melt 1½ tablespoons of the butter. When it sizzles, add the diced mushrooms. Season with salt, and cook over high heat until the mushrooms have rendered all their liquid.

Meanwhile, if you are using whole caraway seeds, toast them in a dry skillet, then grind them in a mortar or a spice mill.

When all the mushroom liquid has evaporated, add 2 tablespoons heavy cream and half the caraway. Boil for a minute, then add the cheese, stirring well with a wooden spoon. Season with salt and pepper, then put the mixture on a plate to cool.

Bring 4 quarts of water to the boil with a handful of salt.

Remove the core and the outer leaves from the cabbage, taking care not to let the head come apart. Wash in cold water, spreading the leaves with your fingers. Boil in the salted water for 2 minutes, then remove the cabbage and cool it in cold water. Drain it in a colander, with the hol-lowed-out core down, squeezing gently with your hands. (If you can find only a tight-headed cabbage, boil it for longer, perhaps 8 minutes, until it is possible to spread the leaves for stuffing.)

Put the cabbage on a clean towel and gently spread the leaves with your fingers. Sprinkle the leaves with salt, and stuff small portions of the mushroom mixture between the leaves.

Close the leaves, restoring the cabbage to its original shape.

Peel the onion and cut into thin slices.

Peel the tomatoes. Remove their stems and place them in boiling water for 15 seconds (or a little longer if they are not ripe). Cool them in a bowl of cold water. The skins should slip off easily. Cut them in half crosswise and squeeze out the seeds and liquid. Chop coarsely.

Peel and lightly crush the garlic.

Preheat the oven to 300 degrees.

Choose a heavy casserole a little wider than the cabbage. Over low heat, melt the remaining butter and add the sliced onion. Cook, cov-ered, until the onion is soft but not

FOR 4 SERVINGS

Preparation: 40 minutes
Cooking time: 1½ to 2 hours

12 ounces white mushrooms
5 tablespoons butter
Salt and freshly ground black pepper
½ teaspoon caraway seeds or ground caraway
4 tablespoons heavy cream
2 ounces strong-flavored hard cheese (such as tomme de Savoie or cheddar)
1 loose-headed white cabbage or Savoy cabbage (3¼ pounds)
1 large onion
2 medium tomatoes
1 garlic clove
1 teaspoon sweet Hungarian paprika

See photograph on page 107.

OPPOSITE PAGE:
Cabbage with Mushroom Stuffing

browned, about 5 minutes. Uncover and let any juices evaporate. Add the paprika and mix well with a wooden spoon. Add the tomatoes, the remaining caraway, garlic clove, 2 tablespoons of water, salt, and pepper.

Place the stuffed cabbage in the casserole and cover. Bring to the boil, then place in the oven to cook for 1¹/₂ hours, checking occasionally to make sure that the tomatoes have rendered enough liquid; if the casserole has boiled dry, add a little water and lower the oven temperature.

When done, remove the cabbage with a skimmer or spatula, being careful not to damage it. Put it on a serving platter and keep it warm—for example, in the turned-off oven.

Put the casserole over medium heat. Reduce the juices, then add the remaining cream. Let it boil very briefly; long cooking will change its fresh flavor.

Pour the contents of the casserole into the blender and blend at high speed to create a smooth sauce. Add salt and pepper if necessary.

Pour off any water on the serving platter the cabbage may have given off, then top with the sauce.

Cauliflower with Mustard Cream
Blanc de Chou-Fleur en Crème de Moutarde

✳

For 4 servings

Preparation: 30 minutes
Cooking time: 45 minutes

1 large cauliflower or
  2 smaller ones
  (2¹/₄ pounds total)
5 tablespoons butter
1 tablespoon flour
¹/₂ cup milk
³/₄ cup heavy cream
Salt
2 tablespoons Dijon
  mustard
2 tablespoons small capers
2 tablespoons chopped
  parsley

Cut the base and the green leaves away from the cauliflower. Wash and drain the cauliflower, taking care not to break it. Place 2 handfuls of coarse salt in a large pot containing 6 or 7 quarts of water and bring to the boil. Add the cauliflower and cook, uncovered, for about 15 minutes (10 minutes if you are using 2 smaller heads).

Meanwhile, melt 1¹/₂ tablespoons of butter in a heavy saucepan; add the flour and blend well with a wire whisk. Pour in the milk, whisking continuously to prevent lumps. Bring slowly to the boil, then add the cream. Turn off the heat and add salt to taste. Keep the sauce warm.

When the cauliflower is tender but not too soft, remove it and cool it in a bowl of cold water. When cool, drain in a colander or strainer.

With a small knife, cut the cauliflower into florets and dry them in a towel.

Heat the remaining 3¹/₂ tablespoons butter in a skillet. Just when it is beginning to color, add the cauliflower florets. Salt lightly and sauté until just golden. Arrange the florets upright in a deep serving dish.

Reheat the cream sauce, but do not boil. Add the mustard to the sauce and whisk to blend thoroughly.

Coat the cauliflower with the mustard-cream sauce and sprinkle with the capers and parsley before serving.

OPPOSITE PAGE:
Cauliflower Soup with Chervil

Cauliflower Soup with Chervil
Crème de Chou-Fleur au Cerfeuil

✳

FOR 4 SERVINGS

Preparation: 25 minutes
Cooking time: 35 minutes

1 large cauliflower or
  2 smaller ones
  (2¼ pounds total)
1 large white onion
1½ tablespoons butter
Salt
A pinch of freshly grated
  nutmeg
4 egg yolks
3 tablespoons heavy
  cream
Chervil sprigs, for garnish

Cut the base and the green leaves away from the cauliflower, and wash it carefully in cold water.

Peel the onion and cut it into thin slices. Put it into a heavy saucepan with the butter and 3 tablespoons of water. Cover and cook over medium heat for 10 minutes; do not let the onion brown.

Cut 2 small bouquets of florets away from the cauliflower and set them aside. Chop the remainder coarsely and add to the onion. Cover the pan and let the cauliflower render its juice. Add 1½ quarts water, salt to taste, and a pinch of freshly grated nutmeg. Cook over medium heat, covered, for about 25 minutes.

Meanwhile, bring 2 cups of salted water to the boil, then add the reserved florets. Cook until *al dente*, about 6 minutes. Cool them in cold water, and drain well.

In a small bowl, whisk together the egg yolks and the cream.

Purée the cauliflower soup in a blender or food processor. Return it to the saucepan and bring to the boil. Add about ½ cup of hot soup to the egg yolk mixture, stir well, and return this to the soup. Heat over low heat, whisking constantly, until the yolks have thickened the soup; do not let it come to the boil.

Check for seasoning and pour the soup into a hot tureen or into individual bowls. Garnish with the reserved cauliflower florets and sprigs of chervil. Serve hot.

Smothered Red Cabbage
Fondue de Chou Rouge

✳

FOR 4 SERVINGS

Preparation: 20 minutes
Cooking time: 25 minutes
Resting time: 15 minutes

1 large red cabbage
  (2¼ pounds)
½ cup plus 2 tablespoons
  red wine vinegar
1 medium onion, studded
  with 2 cloves
2 bay leaves
4 tablespoons good lard
Salt and freshly ground
  black pepper
2 small apples, such as
  McIntosh or Golden
  Delicious

Remove the outside leaves of the cabbage; cut out the core and tough ribs. Wash the cabbage, cut it into thin strips, and place it in a bowl. Bring the vinegar to the boil and pour it over the cabbage. Let it stand for 10 minutes, then drain thoroughly in a colander, squeezing well with your hands to eliminate most of the vinegar.

Put the cabbage, onion, bay leaves, and lard into a casserole with a little water. Add salt to taste, cover the casserole, and cook over very low heat for about 20 minutes.

Meanwhile, peel and core the apples and cut them into ⅜-inch cubes. When the cabbage has cooked for 20 minutes, add the apples and cook for another 3 or 4 minutes, covered. Turn off the heat and let rest, still covered, for about 15 minutes. Remove the onion and bay leaves and season with salt and pepper before serving.

See photograph on page 163.

Cauliflower Flans
Flan de Chou-Fleur

✳

FOR 4 SERVINGS

Preparation: 15 minutes
Cooking time: 40 minutes

1 small cauliflower, or
  6 ounces cauliflower
  florets
½ cup plus 2 tablespoons
  heavy cream
2 eggs
1 heaping teaspoon finely
  grated Comté or Swiss
  Gruyère cheese
Salt and freshly ground
  black pepper
A pinch of freshly grated
  nutmeg

Choose a very white cauliflower. Remove the core and the surrounding leaves, and separate into very small florets. Wash thoroughly in cold water. You need only 6 ounces for this recipe, but you should cook them all; set aside what you need and use remainder for another recipe.

Place a tablespoon of salt in a pan with a quart of water and bring to the boil. Add the cauliflower florets and cook them until tender but still firm (less than 10 minutes). Cool them in cold water and drain in a colander.

Preheat the oven to 300 degrees.
Bring a kettle of water to the boil.

Add half the florets to a blender or food processor, along with the cream, eggs, grated cheese, salt, pepper, and nutmeg. Purée thoroughly.

Butter four 3-inch soufflé molds or custard cups. Divide the reserved florets among the molds, and fill with the cream mixture.

Put the molds in a baking dish and add enough boiling water to come half way up the sides of the molds. Bake for about 30 minutes, until set.

Let the flans rest for 10 minutes after you remove them from the oven. Unmold and serve with Red Bell Pepper *Coulis* (see page 20).

Brussels Sprouts with Chestnuts
Choux de Bruxelles aux Châtaignes

✳

FOR 4 SERVINGS

Preparation: 30 minutes
Cooking time: 1 hour

7 ounces chestnuts
5 tablespoons butter
A pinch of celery salt
  (page 97)
1 teaspoon sugar
½ cup chicken stock
1¼ pounds Brussels
  sprouts
Salt and freshly ground
  black pepper

OPPOSITE PAGE:
*Brussels Sprouts
with Chestnuts*

Preheat the oven to 550 degrees. Make an incision on the flat side of each chestnut. Put the chestnuts on a baking sheet and place in the hot oven.

After about 15 minutes, remove the chestnuts. Soak a heavy towel in ice water and wring it out very well. Spread the towel over the chestnuts; the sudden contrast between hot and cold will make it easy to remove the outer and inner layers of the chestnuts.

Put the peeled chestnuts in a small, heavy saucepan and add 1½ tablespoons butter, a pinch of celery salt, the sugar, and a little salt. Add the chicken stock. Cook over medium heat, uncovered, for 10 minutes. Keep warm.

Bring 3 quarts of salted water to the boil.

Trim the Brussels sprouts. Wash and drain in a colander. Cook in the salted water, uncovered, for 15 minutes over high heat. Check that the sprouts are tender by piercing them with a knife. Drain in a colander.

Melt the remaining 3½ tablespoons butter in a casserole; add the sprouts along with the cooking liquid from the chestnuts. Simmer over medium heat for 10 minutes. Season to taste with salt and pepper.

Turn the Brussels sprouts into a deep, warmed serving dish and sprinkle with the chestnuts.

Belgian Endive

THIS CRISP, JUICY winter vegetable is so prized by our neighbors in Belgium that they have organized an Endive League, which counts the most eminent personalities among its proud members. I understand their fervor; I like the idea that there is at least one fresh young vegetable to crunch in the middle of winter.

Endives are best when very fresh, but they will keep for two days in the refrigerator, wrapped in a damp cloth to keep any light from getting to them and turning the tips of their leaves green. Choose very white, tight, and above all, unblemished endives.

Before cooking, I cut away any brown parts at the base and trim the pointed end by about ³/₈ inch. I place them in a tight-fitting casserole and add salted water to cover, plus a little lemon juice, a pinch of sugar, and a sprinkling of neutral-tasting oil. I weight them with a plate, then put the lid on the casserole and braise in the oven for about forty-five minutes. Finally, I let them cool in their cooking liquid. That way they never become slimy, as they can if poached too long.

And such kid-glove handling gives them no cause for bitterness!

When cooked, endive is meltingly delicious, but when raw it is crisp and refreshing. It makes delectable salads, from the classic endive with Gruyère and walnuts to such unusual versions as endive with apples, walnuts, mayonnaise, and paprika, or with Comté cheese, walnuts, and caraway. But you can also leave the beaten track by combining endive with other cheeses, especially blues such as Roquefort, bleu de Bresse, bleu des Causses, or fourme d'Ambert.

Choose a wine that will counterbalance the endive's bitterness, such as a spicy red Minervois. Or, for salads with walnuts, a white Côtes de Jura with its own walnutty notes. For salads with Roquefort, serve Port.

Try this unusual but simple method if you have a wood or charcoal grill: put some medium-size endives on the grill covered with a plate to weight them, and grill them for about five minutes on each side. Serve immediately, sprinkled with salt and drizzled with a not too fruity olive oil or a knob of butter.

Endive Salad
with Walnut Cream

Share this original salad huddled around the fire with friends, with an icy north wind blowing outside.

Wash some medium-size endives, trim the pointed ends, and cut them into quarters lengthwise. Dip the leaf ends in a little paprika, and arrange the endives in a ring on a serving platter, ends outward. Mash a slice of Roquefort with enough good-quality walnut oil to make a thick cream. Spoon the cream over the root ends of the endive quarters, garnish with a few shelled walnuts, and serve with brown bread.

PAGE 113:
Endives with Almond Cream

Endives with Almond Cream
Endives au Lait d'Amandes Douces

✳

FOR 4 SERVINGS

Preparation: 10 minutes
Cooking time: 50 minutes

8 very white medium
  endives
2 tablespoons corn or
  peanut oil
1 teaspoon sugar
Juice of ½ lemon
Salt
½ cup blanched slivered
  almonds
1¼ cups heavy cream
1½ tablespoons butter

Preheat the oven to 325 degrees.

Cut away the brown base of the endives and trim about ⅛ inch from the pointed end. Wash in cold water and drain in a colander. Arrange them tightly in a casserole with the oil, sugar, lemon juice, and a teaspoon of salt. Add cold water to cover.

Put a plate on top of the endives to weight them, cover the casserole, and bake for about 30 minutes. Check for doneness by piercing the base with a paring knife; the blade should go in easily.

Meanwhile, put the almonds and the cream in a heavy-bottomed saucepan and bring slowly to the boil. Simmer for 5 to 10 minutes over low heat, making sure the cream does not boil over.

Salt lightly, then purée the almonds and cream in a blender. Strain the purée through a fine sieve, stirring and pressing with a wooden spoon so that as much mixture as possible passes through the strainer. Check for seasoning and keep warm.

Drain the endives in a colander and raise the oven temperature to 400 degrees.

Heat the butter in a skillet until it just begins to color, then add the well-drained endives and cook until light golden on both sides, 5 to 8 minutes. Arrange in a gratin or baking dish and cover with the almond cream. Bake for about 15 minutes, or until the cream has thickened nicely.

Stir-Fried Endive Leaves
Feuilles d'Endives Sautées Minute

✳

FOR 4 SERVINGS

Preparation: 15 minutes
Cooking time: 5 to
  8 minutes

5 medium endives
4 tablespoons butter
1 tablespoon sugar
Salt and freshly ground
  black pepper
2 tablespoons chopped
  parsley

This dish takes but a few minutes to prepare, and will be good only if cooked at the very last moment, guaranteeing fresh taste and crisp texture. So get all the ingredients ready, then wait until your guests are seated before beginning to cook.

Wash the endives and dry them in paper towels. Separate the leaves, saving the little hearts for a salad.

Heat a serving dish in a cool oven (175 degrees).

Melt the butter in a large skillet over high heat. When it begins to color, add the endive leaves, sprinkle with sugar, and season to taste with salt and pepper. Sauté quickly so the endives do not start to render water, 5 to 8 minutes. Sprinkle with parsley and turn out into the warmed serving dish. Serve immediately.

Spinach and Sorrel

Is THERE ANYTHING greener than spinach? Out in the French countryside they still use its cooking liquid to dye their Easter eggs a beautiful, bright green.

The crisp, dark green leaves of spinach are often full of soil, so after removing the stems and ribs, wash them in several changes of cold water. But do not let them soak, because they can begin to rot very quickly; rather, immediately drain them and dry them in a towel.

It is customary to boil or steam the spinach briefly, but I prefer to sauté the leaves in a big skillet filmed with olive oil or lightly browned butter; this preserves the slightly sharp leafy flavor. (If that sharpness bothers you, you can add a pinch of sugar.) I always add a lightly crushed garlic clove to the cooking oil. When the spinach has rendered all its water, I season it to taste.

The bigger and darker colored the leaves, the less acid the flavor, although the greater the sharpness. So I'd advise choosing younger, lighter-green leaves, which are generally fresher and in better condition.

To compensate for excessive acidity or sharpness, add something sweet such as sugar, honey, or fruit—or cream, butter, or béchamel sauce.

Hard- or soft-boiled eggs go especially well with spinach.

Sorrel is very acid-tasting and is rarely eaten by itself. In any event, you'd need a massive quantity, because it melts down to nothing when you cook it. Spinach is its best complement, but mashed potatoes, cream sauces, and eggs are other good choices. Be sure to remove all the ribs from the leaves, because they remain woody even after cooking. Do not cook sorrel in water; it will lose its color and virtually disappear. I recommend sautéing it in a skillet.

A fine, aromatic, fruity chardonnay such as Meursault, Chablis, or Pouilly-Fuissé will help counter the slight sharpness of the spinach and will highlight its good flavor.

Spinach Soup

Spinach soup is delicious, especially enriched with egg "drops" and garnished with butter-fried croûtons.

Slice an onion and cook it gently in butter. When it is very tender, add a teaspoon of curry powder, a pinch of sugar, a little salt and about a quart of chicken stock. Stir well and bring to the boil, then add ¾ pound of spinach leaves that have been stemmed, washed, and drained. Bring to the boil, and purée in a blender or food processor, then put through a fine sieve. Return to the saucepan, reheat, and add ¼ cup of heavy cream. Bring back to the boil and turn off the heat. In a bowl, thoroughly beat two eggs, then slowly pour them into the soup, stirring constantly. Sprinkle with bread cubes fried in butter.

Spinach-Sorrel Purée with Eggs

Fondue d'Epinards et d'Oseille aux Oeufs

✳

This purée is no less delicious for being simple—and simple to make. The butter gives it a delicate hazelnut flavor, and the marbling of egg adds extra appeal. Don't omit the croûtons, which add crunch to this soft, creamy dish.

FOR 4 SERVINGS

Preparation: 40 minutes
Cooking time: 15 minutes

1 pound spinach
6 ounces sorrel
4 eggs
Salt and freshly ground
  black pepper
4 tablespoons heavy cream
12 slices of French bread
  (*baguette*)
8 tablespoons butter
A pinch of freshly grated
  nutmeg

Stem the spinach and sorrel, but keep them separate. Wash each in several changes of cold water and drain well.

Bring 3 or 4 quarts of salted water to the boil. Add the spinach leaves, and as soon as the water returns to the boil, remove the spinach and plunge it into cold water. Drain thoroughly, squeezing in your hands to remove all water. Chop finely in a food processor or meat grinder, or with a knife.

Thoroughly beat the eggs and add salt, pepper, and 2 tablespoons of cream. Blend well, and reserve.

Fry the bread in 4 tablespoons of butter until golden; keep warm.

Put the remaining 4 tablespoons of butter into a casserole and heat until it just begins to turn golden. Add the sorrel leaves, stirring with a wooden spoon; the sorrel will melt down very quickly.

Add the chopped spinach, a pinch of nutmeg, and some salt. Sauté over high heat, stirring constantly with a wooden spoon, for 3 minutes. Add the remaining 2 tablespoons of cream and bring quickly to the boil; do not let it boil for more than an instant, lest the spinach lose color.

Add the beaten eggs, folding them gently into the mixture; you want streaks of yellow amid the green of the spinach and sorrel.

Surround the purée with the croûtons and serve.

OPPOSITE PAGE:
*Tender, young spinach—
a perfect salad with a
sprinkling of olive oil.*

Spinach with Eggs

Feuilles d'Epinards aux Oeufs

✳

FOR 4 SERVINGS

Preparation: 30 minutes
Cooking time: 15 minutes

3¼ pounds spinach
1 garlic clove
7 tablespoons butter
Salt and freshly ground
   black pepper
A pinch of freshly grated
   nutmeg
½ teaspoon sugar
2 eggs
1 tablespoon heavy cream
About 20 small cubes
   of bread

OPPOSITE PAGE:
*Spinach with
Goat Cheese Toasts*

This simple recipe is an original variation on the classic combination of spinach, eggs, and croûtons. Rather than being hard- or soft-boiled, the eggs are poured right into the spinach, forming a colorful, tasty marbling.

Stem the spinach and wash it in several changes of water. Drain well in a colander, then dry in a towel.

Peel and lightly crush the garlic.

In a large skillet, heat 5 tablespoons of butter with the garlic clove. When the butter turns lightly golden, add the spinach and stir over high heat. Add salt, a pinch of nutmeg, and the sugar (to cut the sharpness of the spinach). Stir well with a wooden spoon and cook to evaporate all the water the spinach renders, about 10 minutes.

Meanwhile, thoroughly beat the eggs and the cream in a small bowl. Season with salt.

Melt the remaining 2 tablespoons butter in a small skillet and fry the cubes of bread until golden. Reserve these croûtons.

When the spinach water has boiled away, lower the heat and pour in the eggs in a slow stream, stirring gently with a wooden spoon. Do not completely blend the eggs into the spinach; yellow streaks should remain visible. It is ready to serve as soon as the eggs have set.

Remove the garlic, and serve with the croûtons.

Spinach with Goat Cheese Toasts

Epinards aux Croûtons de Rigotte

✳

FOR 4 SERVINGS

Preparation: 45 minutes
Cooking time: 30 minutes

2¼ pounds spinach
2 garlic cloves
7 tablespoons olive oil
Salt and freshly ground
   black pepper
12 slices of French bread
   (*baguette*), about ¼ inch
   thick
2 small young (but not
   newly made) goat
   cheeses, about 2 inches
   across, French *rigottes*
   or similar, if available
2 tablespoons chopped
   fresh savory

Stem the spinach, wash it thoroughly, and drain. Peel the garlic and lightly crush it.

Put 2 generous tablespoons of olive oil into a large skillet with the garlic cloves. Heat over high heat until the oil begins to smoke, then add the spinach. Add salt to taste and cook, stirring from time to time with a wooden spoon, until the

spinach is tender and all its liquid has boiled away, about 10 minutes. When cooked, turn off the heat and keep warm.

While the spinach is cooking, preheat the broiler. Brush the slices of bread with olive oil and brown them on both sides. Remove these croûtons, but do not turn off the broiler.

Cut each goat cheese horizontally

into 6 slices. Place a slice of cheese on each croûton and sprinkle with some savory and pepper.

Remove the garlic from the spinach and check for seasoning. Divide the spinach among 4 preheated plates.

Drizzle the cheese-topped croûtons with olive oil and run them under the broiler to melt the cheese.

Put 3 croûtons on each plate beside the spinach, and serve immediately.

A nice first course.

Spinach and Mushroom Gratin
Gratin d'Epinards aux Champignons

✳

FOR 4 SERVINGS

Preparation: 1 hour
Cooking time: 20 minutes

2¼ pounds spinach
7 ounces white
  mushrooms
2 garlic cloves
6 tablespoons butter
Salt and freshly ground
  black pepper
A pinch of freshly grated
  nutmeg
3 tablespoons heavy cream
1 egg yolk

Stem the spinach, wash it thoroughly, and drain. Trim the ends of the mushroom stems; rinse the mushrooms quickly, dry them, and cut them into thin slices. Peel the garlic.

Melt 4 tablespoons of butter in a skillet over high heat. When it turns hazelnut brown, add the garlic cloves, then the spinach. Season with salt and a pinch of nutmeg. Cook the spinach over high heat until all its liquid has boiled away, about 10 minutes.

Turn the spinach into a gratin dish, and remove the garlic cloves. Keep warm.

Rinse the skillet and return it to the heat; when dry, add the remaining 2 tablespoons butter; when it turns hazelnut brown, add the mushrooms. Season them with salt and pepper, and cook until their liquid has evaporated and they turn lightly golden. Add 1 tablespoon heavy cream. Bring to the boil and check for seasoning. Spread the mushrooms evenly over the spinach in the gratin dish.

Whip the remaining 2 tablespoons of cream until soft peaks form. Whisk in the egg yolk; pour evenly over the mushrooms.

Run the gratin dish under the broiler (not too close to the heating element) until the top is golden brown.

Spinach-Coconut Flans
Petits Flans d'Epinards à la Noix de Coco

✳

Stem the spinach and wash the leaves in several changes of water. Drain in a colander and dry in a towel.

Bring 1 quart of salted water to the boil. Add the spinach leaves, removing them immediately with a skimmer or tongs. Immediately plunge them into cold water, then drain in a colander.

Place the coconut, a pinch of salt, and the cream in a saucepan and bring to the boil. Immediately turn off the heat, cover the pan, and let steep for 15 minutes. Then strain the liquid through a fine sieve into a measuring cup, stirring with a wooden spoon to press through as much cream as possible. You should have a scant 1/2 cup; if you are short, make up the difference with cream.

Preheat the oven to 300 degrees.

Chop the blanched spinach. Heat butter in a skillet until it begins to turn golden; add the spinach, a pinch of nutmeg, and salt and pepper to taste. Stir to mix well, and let cool.

Bring a kettle of water to the boil.

Butter four 3-inch soufflé molds or custard cups.

Beat the eggs in a bowl and add the coconut cream and the spinach. Mix well and check for salt. Fill the molds three-fourths full with the spinach mixture, place them in a baking dish, and add enough boiling water to the baking dish to come half way up the sides of the molds.

Bake for about 30 minutes or until set. Leave to rest for a few minutes, then unmold onto a serving platter. Serve with a *coulis* of red bell peppers (see page 20).

FOR 4 SERVINGS

Preparation: 20 minutes
Cooking time: 30 minutes

6 ounces spinach
1 teaspoon unsweetened dried coconut
Salt and freshly ground black pepper
1/2 cup plus 1 tablespoon heavy cream
2 teaspoons butter
A pinch of freshly grated nutmeg
2 eggs

See photograph on page 163.

Honey-Crusted Spinach Leaves

Feuilles d'Epinards en Croûte de Miel

*

Like Swiss chard, spinach leaves are a good ingredient for sweet recipes. This crisp, delicious dessert will be a pleasant surprise for your guests, so don't be shy about trying it.

FOR 4 SERVINGS

Preparation: 30 minutes
Cooking time: 20 minutes

1¼ pounds spinach
2 eggs
½ cup all-purpose flour
5 teaspoons honey
1 teaspoon lemon juice
1 cup peanut or corn oil
3 tablespoons cornstarch

Stem the spinach and wash the leaves in several changes of water. Drain in a colander, then dry in a towel.

Add a handful of coarse salt to 4 quarts of water, and bring to the boil. Add the spinach leaves, and remove them immediately with a skimmer or tongs. Immediately plunge into a bowl of cold water, and drain in a colander; avoid crushing the leaves. Spread the leaves on a cloth or paper towels to dry thoroughly.

Beat the eggs in a small bowl. Put the flour on a plate. In a small saucepan, warm the honey; add the lemon juice and mix well. Keep warm.

In a saucepan, heat the oil to 350 degrees.

Divide the spinach leaves into little piles of 3 or 4 leaves each. One by one, dredge these in the flour, dip into beaten egg, and place them in the heated oil to fry until brown, turning once or twice—gently, so as not to break them. Drain on paper towels.

Brush each fritter with the honey-lemon mixture, then, using a small strainer, dust with cornstarch; this will form a crisp crust.

Serve warm, not hot.

Peas, Snowpeas, and Young Fava Beans

I ADORE THESE sweet, delicate vegetables: tender fava beans, hardly bigger than the nail of your little finger and too young even to need skinning; sugary peas, good even raw; snowpeas, a short-lived springtime treat.

Perhaps more than any other vegetable, these will not wait: they are good when freshly picked and very young, their tiny white flowers still clinging to the end of the pod. And they should be cooked immediately after shelling, because they deteriorate on contact with the air. In fact, they are best shelled right into a bowl of cold water.

With young favas, you'll need patience, because to end up with a quarter pound of shelled beans you'll have to start with ten times that weight. But once you've shelled them and slipped them out of their inner skins, they cook very quickly in a little liquid, and they are so delicious with a little butter and fresh savory that you will never regret all the work.

With peas, don't let them swell in their pods before picking them. The bigger they are the more mealy and the less juicy they become. But even large peas make good purées, scented with mint or curry powder, or soups.

We eat snowpeas whole, either steamed or braised in a little butter. Choose nice green ones, not too big; make sure the peas in the pods are not too mature and that there are no tough fibers.

And there is a newer variety on the market, the sugar-snap pea, which falls somewhere in between regular peas and snowpeas. All you need do is nip off the ends, cook them quickly in boiling salted water, and serve them with butter, salt, and pepper.

Make sure you do not overwhelm these tender springtime vegetables with aggressive wines. Choose a pleasant, gentle accompaniment for them. For peas and snowpeas, I recommend a Saint-Amour from Beaujolais or a Bourgueil or a Saint-Nicolas de Bourgueil from the Loire Valley. Since favas have a slight southern accent, you can opt for a red Bellet from near Nice.

When picked at just the right moment, snowpeas are all tenderness.

A Fresh Idea

Try this only if you have your own vegetable garden, because extreme freshness is critical here.

Pick four tiny lettuces that have not yet formed into heads. Rinse them without separating the leaves, then let them drain upside down on a towel. Meanwhile, shell some very young peas—about ¾ cup for four servings. Put one lettuce on each plate, open the leaves flat and drizzle with some heavy cream mixed with a few drops of lemon juice. Sprinkle some peas on each plate and season with sea salt.

To savor the salad's pure flavors, drink nothing more than cold water.

Buttered Young Fava Beans

Févettes au Beurre Frais

✳

Tender young fava beans are a springtime treat you will wholeheartedly enjoy despite the work involved in shelling them. But once they are shelled, it will take you barely a quarter of an hour to finish this recipe—a recipe that, for the sake of freshness, must be prepared at the very last minute.

Shell the beans and slip each bean out of its tough skin.

In a shallow pan, bring the chicken stock to the boil; add a little salt. Add the fava beans, 1 tablespoon of the butter, and the savory. Boil over high heat, uncovered, for 5 minutes.

When no more than 2 tablespoons of cooking liquid remain, the beans are done. Remove the savory, and add the remaining butter and parsley. Let the sauce boil so that the butter will be emulsified into the cooking liquid and become creamy.

Season to taste with salt and pepper, and serve hot.

OPPOSITE PAGE:
Buttered Young Fava Beans

FOR 4 SERVINGS

Preparation: 1 hour
Cooking time: 10 minutes

5 1/2 pounds small fava beans
1 scant cup chicken stock
4 tablespoons butter
A sprig of fresh savory
2 tablespoons chopped parsley
Salt and freshly ground black pepper

Young Fava Beans in Cream

Févettes à la Crème

✳

Shell the beans and slip each bean out of its tough skin.

Pour the cream into a shallow pan; add salt and the savory, and bring to the boil. Add the fava beans and boil, uncovered, for 5 minutes.

Check that the beans are done; they should be tender but not falling apart. Remove the savory.

Add salt and pepper to taste and sprinkle with chopped parsley.

FOR 4 SERVINGS

Preparation: 1 hour
Cooking time: 10 minutes

5 1/2 pounds small fava beans
3/4 cup heavy cream
A sprig of fresh savory
Salt and freshly ground black pepper
1 tablespoon chopped parsley

See photograph on page 163.

Flans of Curried Peas
Flan de Petits Pois au Curry

✳

These exquisite little flans are wonderful with asparagus sauce made with butter (see page 22); they would be excellent as part of an all-vegetable meal.

FOR 4 SERVINGS

Preparation: 30 minutes
Cooking time: 45 minutes

10 ounces young peas in
their pods
2 eggs
½ cup heavy cream
A pinch of curry powder
1 teaspoon sugar
Salt

Shell the peas.

Preheat the oven to 300 degrees.

Bring a quart of water to the boil and add about 2 tablespoons salt. Add the peas, then immediately remove them, plunge them into cold water, and drain them. Purée them in a food processor, blender, or food mill, using the fine disk.

Bring a kettle of water to the boil.

In a bowl, whisk together the puréed peas, eggs, cream, curry powder, sugar, and salt to taste. Check for seasoning; you may want to add a little more curry powder.

Butter four 3-inch soufflé molds or custard cups and fill them with the mixture. Place the molds in a baking dish and add enough boiling water to come half way up the sides of the molds. Bake for about 30 minutes or until set.

Let the flans rest a few minutes, then unmold them onto warmed plates.

Peas with Fresh Mint
Petits Pois à la Menthe

✳

Such a simple recipe; I learned it in England years ago. It is a perfect combination of the fresh taste of mint and the sweetness of peas. Serve with young lamb chops.

FOR 4 SERVINGS

Preparation: 15 minutes
Cooking time: 5 to 10
minutes, depending on
the size of the peas

2¾ pounds fresh young
peas
1 teaspoon sugar
3 tablespoons butter
1 tablespoon chopped
fresh mint leaves
Salt

Shell the peas.

Bring 4 quarts of water to the boil and add a handful of salt. Add the peas and boil until done; if they are small and very fresh, they will need only a couple of minutes.

Drain the peas and put them in a casserole with the sugar, butter, and mint; stir over medium heat until the butter binds the dish together.

Check for seasoning and serve.

OPPOSITE PAGE:
Peas with Fresh Mint

My Purée of Peas

Purée de Petits Pois à ma Façon

✳

FOR 4 SERVINGS

Preparation: 20 minutes
Cooking time: 10 minutes

2¾ pounds medium peas,
　fresh or frozen
3 tablespoons butter
1 teaspoon sugar
Up to 10 tablespoons
　milk (optional)
Salt

Shell the peas if fresh, and save the pods (remove the thin internal membrane).

If using fresh peas, bring two 2- or 3-quart pots of water to the boil; add a handful of coarse salt, then the peas. Cook the peas and their pods separately, about 10 minutes. If using frozen peas, boil them until done, just a minute or so.

Drain the peas and their pods, and put them through the fine disk of a food mill, or purée them in a food

processor or blender. Cut the butter into small pieces, and add it to the purée along with the sugar. Beat with a wooden spoon.

If the purée seems thick, gradually add some hot milk. Season to taste with salt.

Serve quickly, lest the color fade. But if you have to keep the purée warm, pour a thin layer of hot milk onto the surface and hold it in a hot-water bath. When ready to serve, stir the milk into the purée.

Snowpeas with Red Bell Peppers

Pois Gourmands aux Poivrons Rouges

✳

A lovely palette of colors—and sweet flavors. You will like this springtime dish for its freshness and mildness.

FOR 4 SERVINGS

Preparation: 30 minutes
Cooking time: 10 minutes

1 red bell pepper
14 ounces snowpeas
2 medium oranges
6 tablespoons butter, cut
　into pieces
Salt and freshly ground
　black pepper

OPPOSITE PAGE:
*Snowpeas with
Red Bell Peppers*

Choose a firm, fleshy bell pepper. Peel it with a vegetable peeler, remove the seeds and internal ribs, and cut it into thin strips ¾ inch long. Set aside.

String the snow peas by breaking off the stems and pulling them away. Wash in cold water and drain in a colander.

Bring to the boil 5 or 6 quarts water, and add a handful of coarse salt. Add the snowpeas and boil them for 3 or 4 minutes, then plunge them into cold water. Drain in a colander.

Warm a serving platter in a slow oven.

With a vegetable peeler, strip the

zest from one of the oranges and place it into a saucepan large enough to hold the snow peas. Squeeze both oranges and add their juice to the zest. Bring to the boil and reduce until 2 tablespoons of juice remain. Remove the orange zest and add the butter; whisk until emulsified and creamy. Add the bell peppers and the snowpeas.

Season to taste with salt and pepper, and mix until warmed through; do not cover the casserole.

Serve immediately on the warmed serving platter.

Beans—Green and Others

GREEN OR YELLOW, long or short, thick or thin, flat or round—all beans should be delicate, crisp, stringless, and unblemished. In a word, they should be perfect. They have a tendency to rot, especially when soil adheres to them, so do not keep them long before cooking them. But if your harvest is bountiful, you can preserve them by canning, salting, or drying (see the section on preserving, page 251). Come winter, you'll welcome their summery flavor.

There is no end to the varieties of beans. You don't need to know them all; just remember the criteria listed above. Still, you should be aware of the general categories. First are the Italian beans, those big, flat, tender beans we cut with scissors into the traditional Provençal basil soup—*pistou*—or serve whole with *aïoli*. Then there are wax beans, yellow and meltingly tender; they are just delicious poached and served with butter and parsley. Finally, we have the standard green beans that are so good in salads. Many American markets now sell the very thin green beans that are popular in France, but these are often not at their freshest. Buy them if they are very fresh, or grow your own, but otherwise buy the freshest young green beans you can find, whatever their size.

I recommend fixing their green color by boiling them in salted water, but you have to follow the proper procedure. First, trim the ends and, if necessary, string them. Next, wash them carefully in cold water, drain them, and dry them in a towel.

Bring a great deal of water to the boil: for two pounds of green beans you will need six quarts of water and $2/3$ cup of coarse salt. When the water is boiling furiously, add half the beans and cook until tender. Cooking time will vary with the quantity, type, and freshness of the beans: thin, freshly picked beans may take only four minutes, while medium beans bought at the market could take 10 or 15 minutes. When they are done, remove the beans with a skimmer or tongs and put them into a bowl of ice water to stop their cooking; drain them immediately. When the water returns to the boil add the remaining beans and repeat the process.

Some people suggest adding baking soda to keep the color bright, but I do not advise this; it can affect your digestion and will make the beans too soft, spoiling their texture. (It also destroys many vitamins.)

When the beans are thoroughly drained, prepare them any way you like—with butter or hazelnut cream, for example. But do not let them stand too long, for they will quickly grow dry and shriveled.

With beans, wine should be delicate and easy to drink: a Bergerac from southwest France or a Saint-Émilion, for instance, will set off these fine, tender vegetables.

Warm Green Bean Salad

This salad is simple, yet delicious. Use very fresh green beans. Cook them in boiling salted water, drain them, and put them, still hot, into a salad bowl containing: a good vinaigrette made from wine vinegar and extra-virgin olive oil; two small green bell peppers, seeded and sliced into thin rounds; some finely chopped Italian parsley; one white onion, thinly sliced; a handful of black Niçoise olives; and salt and pepper. Mix well and serve immediately.

Purée of Green Beans and White Beans with Celery Leaves

Purée de Haricots Pape et de Cocos aux Feuilles de Céleri

✳

Tender, matte-green Italian flat beans become very soft when cooked and absorb the flavors of their sauce: that is why we use them in the basil-scented soupe au pistou.

White beans or cranberry beans—cocos in French—come from another branch of the family. If you raise them yourself and are using them fresh, wait until the beans are fully grown within their delicate green pods before shelling them. They will cook quickly and become wonderfully tender. My advice is not to let them cool after boiling, but to season them while still warm.

This summer purée is wonderful with roast veal or poached chicken. Leftovers can be stretched out with hot milk and cream to make an excellent soup; garnish it with a few celery leaves.

If you are using dried beans, soak them overnight in cold water, then cook them in unsalted water for about 2 hours or until very tender. Add a pinch of salt and the celery leaves in the last 20 minutes.

If you are using fresh beans, shell, wash, and drain them, then put them into a saucepan with the celery. Cover with cold water, add a handful of coarse salt, and cook over medium heat until very tender, 25 to 30 minutes.

Bring 4 quarts of salted water to the boil.

Trim and string the green beans. Put them into the boiling water and cook at a full boil for 15 to 20 minutes, or until very tender.

Drain both pots of beans, but do not discard the cooking liquid from the white beans. Do not let the beans cool.

Put all the beans and the celery through the fine disk of a food mill or purée them in a food processor or blender. While still hot, add the butter, stirring with a wooden spoon. If the purée seems too thick, gradually add a little of the cooking liquid from the white beans. Check for seasoning and add salt and pepper to taste; serve immediately.

If the purée has cooled, reheat it gently over hot water before serving.

FOR 4 SERVINGS

Preparation: 30 minutes
Cooking time: 1 hour

²/₃ cup fresh or dried beans (such as great northern or cranberry)
Leaves from 4 celery stalks
Scant 1 pound Italian flat beans
2 tablespoons butter, cut into pieces
Salt and freshly ground black pepper

OPPOSITE PAGE:
Green Beans Braised with Onions

Green Beans Braised with Onions
Fricassée de Haricots Verts aux Oignons

＊

FOR 4 SERVINGS

Preparation: 15 minutes
Cooking time: 25 minutes

1 3/4 pounds green beans
2 small onions
4 tablespoons butter
A sprig of fresh rosemary
Salt and freshly ground
  black pepper
2 tablespoons coarsely
  chopped parsley

Trim the ends of the beans with your fingers, and string them if necessary. Wash in cold water and drain in a colander.

Peel the onions and cut them into thin slices. Put them into a casserole or heavy saucepan with the butter and cook over medium-low heat, stirring with a wooden spoon, until the onions begin to turn golden. Add the beans, salt to taste, the rosemary, and 1/4 cup of water.

Cover the pan and cook over medium heat for about 15 minutes, or until the beans are very tender. Remove the lid and cook until the cooking liquid is gone.

Season the beans with pepper, check for salt, sprinkle with parsley, and serve.

Wax Beans with Chive Cream
Haricots Beurre à la Crème de Ciboulette

＊

FOR 4 SERVINGS

Preparation: 25 minutes
Cooking time: 25 minutes

1 3/4 pounds wax beans
  (or green beans)
2 medium shallots
2 egg yolks
3/4 cup heavy cream
2 tablespoons butter
Salt and freshly ground
  black pepper
A pinch of freshly grated
  nutmeg
2 tablespoons chopped
  parsley
2 tablespoons chopped
  chives
1/4 cup chervil leaves

Trim the ends of the beans with your fingers, and string them if necessary. Wash in cold water and drain in a colander. Bring 4 quarts of water to the boil and add a handful of salt.

Add the beans and cook for no more than 10 to 15 minutes; they should remain slightly crunchy. Drain in a colander but do not cool under cold water.

While the beans are cooking, peel and chop the shallots. In a small bowl, beat the egg yolks together with 1/4 cup of cream and set aside.

In a saucepan, cook the shallots in the butter until translucent but not browned. Add the remaining 1/2 cup cream, season with salt and a pinch of nutmeg, then add the beans. Simmer for 2 minutes.

Remove from the heat, then use a wooden spoon to stir in the egg yolk mixture, parsley, and chives.

Check for salt and add plenty of pepper. Stir gently so as not to break the beans.

Serve on a hot platter, garnished with chervil leaves.

Green Beans with Hazelnut Cream

Haricots Verts en Crème de Noisettes

✳

With proper attention to the quality of the ingredients, this will prove to be an amazingly elegant dish. Choose freshly picked, very thin green beans, non-ultra-pasteurized cream, and pure hazelnut oil pressed from toasted nuts.

FOR 4 SERVINGS

Preparation: 30 minutes
Cooking time: 15 minutes

1 pound thin green beans
½ cup hazelnuts
3 tablespoons heavy cream
2 tablespoons hazelnut oil
Salt and freshly ground
  black pepper
¼ cup chervil leaves

Trim the ends of the beans with your fingers, and string them if necessary. Wash in cold water and drain in a colander.

Soak the hazelnuts in warm water for 15 minutes; remove their skins, dry them, and cut them into slices. Run the sliced hazelnuts under the broiler for a moment to toast them lightly, or toast them in a microwave oven. Set aside.

Bring 4 quarts of water to the boil and add a handful of coarse salt. Add the beans and cook at a full boil for 10 to 15 minutes, uncovered.

When the beans are tender, drain and cool immediately in a bowl of ice water, but do not let them sit in the water lest they begin to lose flavor. Drain the beans and dry in a towel.

In a large bowl mix the cream and hazelnut oil and season with salt and pepper to taste. Add the beans and mix well. Mound the beans onto 4 plates and sprinkle with chervil leaves and toasted hazelnuts. Serve quite cool, but not too cold.

Lettuce and Radicchio

GREEN LETTUCE, red radicchio: leafy ruffles washed with pink and drenched with sunlight. These little plants are really good only when fresh from the garden, the base washed clean and the leaves barely rinsed in a drizzle of cold water and drained head-down in a colander.

People usually eat them as a salad, but don't forget how delicious they are when very gently braised.

Radicchio also makes fine fritters (see the section on fried vegetables in "The Right Way to Cook," page 247).

I like these leafy vegetables for their mild bitterness and their tenderness, but I refuse to cook them unless they come straight from the garden and show no signs of wilting.

Soft rosé wines, such as Cabernets from Anjou and Saumur, can tame the bitterness of these leaves.

OPPOSITE PAGE:
*Braised Radicchio
with Anchovies and
Black Olives
(recipe on page 140)*

Braised Lettuce with Fresh Savory
Laitues Braisées à la Sarriette

✳

FOR 4 SERVINGS

Preparation: 15 minutes
Cooking time: 45 to
    50 minutes

4 small heads of loose-
    head lettuce
½ cup plus 2 tablespoons
    chicken stock
A bunch of fresh savory
1 teaspoon sugar
Salt and freshly ground
    black pepper

Remove any wilted or blemished leaves from the lettuces and trim the stem ends, but leave the heads intact. Wash in several changes of cold water, then shake gently to drain.

Bring 4 or 5 quarts of water to the boil and add a handful of salt. Add the lettuces. When the water returns to the boil, remove them with a skimmer and cool them in a bowl of cold water. When cool, remove them and carefully squeeze out as much water as possible.

Cut each lettuce in half lengthwise and, with your hands, flatten each half on a cutting board. Fold the leaves down toward the root end, and pat the leaves together to form a rounded triangular shape.

Arrange the lettuce halves tightly in a casserole very generously greased with butter. Add the chicken stock, savory, and sugar. If the chicken stock has been salted, add no salt at this stage; if not, salt lightly.

Cook, covered, over medium heat for about 30 minutes. Then remove the lid and let the juices reduce to a syrupy consistency. Season with pepper, and check for salt.

Remove the savory and serve.

Braised Radicchio with Anchovies and Black Olives
Trévises Braisées aux Anchois et aux Olives de Nice

✳

FOR 4 SERVINGS

Preparation: 10 minutes
Cooking time: 30 minutes

8 small heads radicchio,
    preferably the long
    variety
2 savory sprigs
Salt and freshly ground
    black pepper
6 tablespoons olive oil
8 anchovy fillets (packed
    in oil)
1/3 cup black Niçoise
    olives, pitted

See photograph on page 139.

Sober in color but exuberant in aroma, this dish can be eaten hot or cold—but not too cold—with grilled country bread rubbed with garlic and sprinkled with good olive oil.

Wash the radicchio thoroughly and cut in half lengthwise.

Arrange the radicchio halves tightly in a casserole and add the savory, a little salt, and the olive oil. Add water to cover and cook, covered, over low heat for about 30 minutes. Alternatively, you can bring it to the boil, then put it into a preheated 300 degree oven for 30 minutes.

When done, remove the lid, arrange the anchovy fillets on top of the radicchio, sprinkle with pitted olives, and reduce the juices completely. Season with plenty of pepper.

Leeks

WHOEVER FIRST CALLED leeks "poor man's asparagus" was being a trifle hasty; they have little in common with asparagus, apart perhaps from their combination of green and white and the delicacy of their texture and flavor. The taste of leeks is closer to that of their near relative, the onion.

Leeks are the quintessential winter vegetable. They remain alone in the garden after everything else has been harvested, and their purple-blue shafts have a certain beauty. But when the ground freezes hard, they are impossible to dig up; they'll break off at ground level unless you remember to moisten the surrounding soil with warm water.

The thickness of leeks varies depending on the variety; thickness can be astonishing in such aptly named varieties as Elephant or Winter Giant.

Small leeks can be gently braised in butter and served with a cream sauce, or drizzled with good hazelnut oil and sprinkled with crushed roasted hazelnuts. Larger ones are better boiled or steamed and served with vinaigrette or béchamel.

But however you are going to cook them, always trim the root end and strip off one or two of the outermost layers. And wash them well in warm water to eliminate insects and soil.

An elegant white wine such as Pouilly-Fuissé or a light red such as Beaujolais will go well with the delicate but clear flavor and meltingly tender texture of leeks.

A Good Winter Soup

A simple soup, but one of the best for warming your winter evenings: trim the root end of some leeks and wash them carefully. Cut the white part into thin circles, and sweat them in a saucepan with a little butter over very low heat so they do not brown. Meanwhile, peel a few potatoes and dice them. When the leeks are very tender, add cold water and the potatoes. Add salt and cook for about twenty minutes over medium heat. Then raise the heat to high and boil hard for five minutes. With a whisk, break up the potatoes, but let some detectable pieces remain. Serve nice and hot with *crème fraîche* or sour cream on the side. When truffles are in season, you can certainly grate some generously into each plate. What a delicious way to start your dinner!

Gratin of Leeks with Beaufort Cheese
Blancs de Poireaux en Gratin de Beaufort

✳

FOR 4 SERVINGS

Preparation: 30 minutes
Cooking time: 45 minutes

5 large leeks (2¹/₂ pounds
  total)
1 tablespoon flour
1¹/₂ teaspoons sweet
  Hungarian paprika
2 tablespoons butter
1¹/₂ tablespoons *crème
  fraîche*, or 3 tablespoons
  heavy cream plus
  2 ounces mascarpone
3¹/₂ ounces Beaufort or
  Swiss Gruyère cheese,
  grated
A pinch of freshly grated
  nutmeg
Salt

Trim away the root ends and the greens of the leeks, then make 2 perpendicular cuts from the leaf end toward the root, cutting to within 3 inches of the root end. Wash the leeks carefully in warm water and tie them into a bundle with string.

Bring 2 cups of water to the boil and add about 2 tablespoons of salt. Add the bundle of leeks and cook for about 30 minutes. Remove them and drain well, pressing with a wooden spoon to squeeze out as much water as possible. Undo the bundle.

Mix the flour and the paprika, and dredge the leeks in this mixture.

Melt the butter in a skillet; when it begins to turn golden, add the floured leeks and brown them lightly on all sides.

Preheat the broiler.

Heat the cream (with the mascarpone if you are using it) and add the grated cheese and a pinch of nutmeg. Mix well until the cheese is melted, and season to taste with salt.

Arrange the leeks in a gratin dish or baking dish, spread the cheese mixture over them, and run under the broiler (not too close to the heat) until golden.

Spiced Braised Leeks
Poireaux Braisés aux Epices

✳

FOR 4 SERVINGS

Preparation: 15 minutes
Cooking time: 30 minutes

8 medium leeks (about
  3 pounds total)
2 garlic cloves
1 teaspoon caraway seeds
1 teaspoon coriander
  seeds
1 teaspoon black
  peppercorns
2 cups chicken stock
1 bay leaf
A sprig of fresh thyme
5 tablespoons olive oil
Juice of 1 lemon
Salt

OPPOSITE PAGE:
Spiced Braised Leeks

Trim away the root ends and the greens of the leeks, then wash them carefully in warm water. Peel and lightly crush the garlic.

In a dry skillet, briefly toast the caraway and coriander seeds, then add the peppercorns and grind to a powder in a mortar or a spice mill. Sift the powder through a fine strainer.

Bring the chicken stock to the boil; add the spice mixture, bay leaf, garlic, and thyme. Remove the pan from the heat, cover it, and let the mixture infuse for 10 minutes.

Arrange the leeks in a casserole and pour the spiced stock over them. Add the olive oil, lemon juice, and salt to taste (if your stock is already salted, salt lightly). Cook over low heat for about 30 minutes, covered.

When the leeks are tender, remove them from the casserole and arrange on a warm serving dish; keep them warm.

Strain and reduce the cooking liquid to a syrupy consistency and pour it over the leeks. Serve immediately.

PAGES
144–145:
*Bunches of
domestic
and wild
asparagus.
Pick them as
soon as their
stalks appear
if you want
them to
be tender.*

Vegetables of the Earth

Garlic

Back as far as the Gauls, we French were savoring the Bulb of Youth. Rabelais's Pantagruel stuffed himself on it. And for many people, garlic *means* French cooking. True enough, it appears in many of our traditional recipes, especially in Provence, where the regional accent often carries a hint of garlic from an *aïoli* or the *rouille* accompanying a bouillabaisse. But every corner of France uses plenty of garlic. In the Auvergne it joins forces with potatoes and cheese—young tomme de Laguiole—in that delicious and restorative dish *aligot*. In Burgundy it is combined with parsley to make the garlic butter in which we drown our snails. In Aquitaine it enlivens cassoulet. In Alsace and Lorraine it zips up sausages and freshly made cheeses. It all depends on your capacity for its rousing flavor.

In that connection, note that the bigger the head the tamer the garlic—especially true of elephant garlic—and that young, freshly dug garlic is gentler than garlic that has been dried for long keeping (it will keep for up to fourteen months). My favorite garlic is the small, very aromatic red-skinned variety that makes such elegant braids.

Choose good, hard garlic; the cloves will be full and will not have begun to sprout. If you grow your own, harvest some of the shoots in spring or early summer; eat them raw, chopped into a salad, with *fromage blanc*, or sprinkled on potatoes with cream.

When you need only a small quantity, by all means use a garlic press or grate the garlic on the tines of a fork held flat against a plate. But for larger amounts, you can certainly use a food processor.

Apart from its uses as a vegetable, garlic can also bind sauces; you can, for instance, mash some into a gravy. This technique dates back to the Middle Ages; in Provence we call it an *aiado*, and in other parts of France it is called an *aillée* or an *aillade*. Depending on the region, the garlic will be mashed either by itself or along with almonds, walnuts, parsley, or sorrel; the mixture is served with fish or roasted meat.

It will take a concentrated Saint-Joseph or Côte-Rôtie wine from the Rhône Valley to stand up to garlic's imposing presence.

Cooking Garlic

When cooked, garlic has a milder flavor and a meltingly tender texture. For those who find the flavor of garlic too powerful and bitter, tame it by putting it in cold salted water, bringing it to the boil, and boiling for three minutes; repeat this operation three to five times.

Boil older garlic four or five times; newly dug garlic requires only three repetitions. To make up a given volume of old garlic, use nearly double the weight in new garlic, for new garlic is much heavier than older, drier garlic.

As a rule, peel the garlic before blanching. To accompany a leg of lamb I generally leave the skins on and add the blanched garlic cloves to the roasting pan half way through the cooking; this prevents them from drying out or burning in the oven.

Fried Garlic

Gousses d'Ail Frites

✳

Peel the cloves of garlic and put them into a saucepan with 2 quarts of water and 3 tablespoons milk. Bring to the boil and cook for 3 minutes. Drain, discarding the cooking liquid. Repeat twice more; the last time add 1 teaspoon of coarse salt; make sure the garlic is very tender before draining.

Make bread crumbs by processing the bread in a food processor or rubbing it through a sieve.

Spread the flour on one plate and the bread crumbs on another. Break the eggs into a shallow bowl and add the remaining 3 tablespoons milk and the olive oil. Season with salt and pepper, and beat well with a fork.

Dredge the cooked garlic in the flour; place the cloves in a sieve and shake off the excess. Put them into the egg mixture; thoroughly coat with the egg, then use a fork to transfer them to the dish of bread crumbs. Roll them in the crumbs until completely coated. Spread them out on a drying rack or screen to dry for about 1 hour; do not refrigerate.

Heat the oil to 360 degrees and drop the garlic cloves in a few at a time. Let them brown evenly. Drain on paper towels, sprinkle with salt to taste, and serve.

FOR 4 SERVINGS

Preparation: 30 minutes
Resting time: 1 hour
Cooking time: 30 minutes

¾ pound garlic (7 or 8 heads), separated into cloves
12 tablespoons milk
6 to 8 slices white bread, crusts trimmed
¼ cup all-purpose flour
2 eggs
1 tablespoon olive oil
Salt
3 quarts corn or peanut oil, for deep-frying

See photograph on page 149.

Gentle Sautéed Garlic with Anise

Poêlée d'Ail Doux à l'Anis

✳

Don't be skeptical about the combination of garlic and anise. In this delicate recipe I have tamed the garlic; it is utterly gentle, in both texture and flavor. And besides, it will give you an excuse to come to Provence and tramp around the scrubland searching for wild fennel!

Peel the garlic; you should have about 6 cups peeled cloves. Place them in a saucepan with 3 quarts of water and bring to the boil. Boil for 3 minutes, and drain the garlic in a colander or strainer. Repeat this operation 4 times, using fresh water each time. For the final blanching, add some coarse salt to the water. Drain the garlic thoroughly.

Stem and finely chop the tarragon.

Over medium heat, melt the butter in a skillet; when it begins to turn golden, add the garlic and sauté until golden brown. Sprinkle with salt and add the *pastis*, tarragon, and some freshly ground pepper. Remove the garlic with a slotted spoon and keep warm on a serving dish; reduce the cooking juices until they form a sauce. Pour this sauce over the garlic and sprinkle with the fennel.

FOR 4 SERVINGS

Preparation: 1 hour
Cooking time: 45 minutes

1¾ pounds garlic, separated into cloves
A few fresh tarragon sprigs
4 tablespoons butter
Salt and freshly ground black pepper
2 tablespoons *pastis* (anise-flavored liqueur), such as Pernod or Ricard
A few wild fennel sprigs (or substitute 2 tablespoons fennel leaves and a pinch of fennel seeds)

See photograph on page 149.

For 4 servings

Preparation: 40 minutes
Cooking time: 30 minutes

3/4 pound garlic (7 or
  8 heads), separated into
  cloves
1 cup milk
3 tablespoons butter
Salt and freshly ground
  black pepper

Gentle Skillet-Browned Garlic

Gousses d'Ail Doux Rissolées

✱

When it has been duly subdued, garlic is very delicate, even discreet. Use this recipe as a vegetable dish or as a garnish for roasted or grilled meat, such as leg of lamb.

Peel the garlic cloves and put them into a saucepan with 2 quarts of water and 3 tablespoons milk. Bring to the boil, and let boil for 3 minutes. Drain, discarding the cooking liquid. Repeat 4 times more; the last time add some coarse salt and make sure the garlic is very tender before draining.

Melt the butter in a heavy skillet; when it turns light brown add the garlic and brown on all sides. Be careful not to break the tender cloves.

Drain, add salt and pepper to taste, and serve hot.

For 4 servings

Preparation: 30 minutes
Cooking time: 15 minutes

11 ounces garlic
  (5–6 heads), separated
  into cloves
1 quart chicken stock
A generous sprig of fresh
  savory
1/4 cup heavy cream
4 egg yolks
Salt and freshly ground
  black pepper
4 tablespoons butter
20 1/4-inch slices French
  bread (*baguette*)

My Garlic Soup

Soupe d'Ail à Ma Façon

✱

Here is my version of aigo boulido, *the Provençal garlic soup they used to give the dying to jolt them back to life. But even if you are hale and hardy, this soup will put a spring in your step.*

Peel the garlic and blanch the cloves in 4 changes of water (see previous recipes for details). Rinse in cold water and drain well. Bring the chicken stock to the boil, add the garlic and savory, and simmer over low heat for about 15 minutes, covered.

Preheat the broiler.

In a small bowl, blend the cream and egg yolks; season with freshly ground pepper. Melt the butter. Arrange the bread slices on a cookie sheet, brush them with the melted butter, and put under the broiler until brown. Arrange these croûtons on a serving plate.

Remove the savory from the soup. Purée the soup in a blender or food processor, pour some of it into the egg yolk mixture to temper it, then return all the soup to the pan. Stirring constantly, heat the soup until it just begins to simmer, being careful not to scramble the eggs. Immediately remove from the heat, add salt to taste, and strain into a warmed soup tureen. Serve the croûtons on the side.

OPPOSITE PAGE:
*Bottom right, Gentle Sautéed
Garlic with Anise; top right,
Gentle Skillet-Browned
Garlic; left, Fried Garlic.*

Asparagus

I ADORE asparagus—white, green, violet, or wild. Nothing in the garden moves me more than seeing its pearly, delicate shoots rising from the ground. Among our French varieties, I tend to prefer the violet asparagus grown in Provence, around Avignon, that each May come to the wonderful market of Isle-sur-la-Sorgue in great abundance. These are the most aromatic of asparagus; but I also like the white flesh of the big Alsatian asparagus that are the centerpiece of Rabelaisian banquets every year in the village of Hoerdt; and the thin, pink Loire Valley asparagus that grow near Orléans, and, farther afield, also near Sologne and Angoulème; and the Argenteuil asparagus grown in the sandy soil of Ile-de-France, which used to grace the tables of kings.

White asparagus are not particularly good with vinaigrette; they are better eaten with hollandaise sauce or with olive oil or melted butter.

Then, for Christmas, I am lucky to have wonderful thick, green asparagus, tender from top to toe and tasting of springtime; right through to mid-winter, my friend Raymond Blanc grows them at Lauris, in the Vaucluse, with the greatest of care.

Peeling asparagus takes a certain delicacy and know-how. It is best to do it just before cooking—certainly no longer than two hours in advance; any more and the asparagus can turn yellow and develop a stringy outer skin.

It is important to have a good, sharp vegetable peeler to avoid bruising or breaking your asparagus; I use one with a swivel blade. You must hold the asparagus at the proper angle to prevent breaking it. This should be about thirty degrees from the horizontal.

Begin with the blade of the peeler just below the head, where the color begins to get lighter, then, without exerting too much pressure, run the peeler to about $1/2$ inch from the base all around, then cut off the base.

Wild Asparagus

The wild asparagus we call *balais* in Provence grows in springtime in the scrubland (generally after fires), or in vineyards. It is dark green and very thin—no thicker than the tine of a fork. You eat only the tips, which must not be dried out when you pick them. Cook them for a minute or two in boiling water, cool them in cold water, drain them, and use them as one element in a lobster or squab salad.

Wild asparagus is very bitter, so you need only a small amount (fifteen to twenty spears) per person. Coat them with a tablespoon of dressing made of one tablespoon wine vinegar, a dash of Dijon mustard, five tablespoons olive oil, and salt and pepper.

Wash the peeled asparagus in cold water, drain, trim to a uniform length, and tie into bundles. Roll the asparagus in a damp towel and keep it cool until you are ready to cook it.

The most common cooking method for asparagus is to poach it in amply salted boiling water. Generally, this will take only a few minutes, but it all depends on size and freshness. Tiny wild asparagus, for instance, will cook in a minute.

I don't see any point in cooking asparagus standing up with the tips out of the water. If the asparagus is reasonably fresh the stalk will cook as quickly as the tip. On the other hand, you can certainly use an asparagus steamer—a high or long pan with a draining basket that will help you remove the cooked asparagus without damaging the tips.

Check for doneness by piercing the base with the point of a paring knife; it should meet no resistance.

Some cooks advocate steaming asparagus, but I see no advantage in this. But I do see the point of skewering uncooked asparagus tips and grilling them. They will grow nice and tender while remaining very slightly bitter.

Warm or hot asparagus is only enhanced by serving it handsomely arranged on an asparagus platter with a pierced insert to prevent it from sitting in its own liquid. Choose one in white porcelain or silver for green or violet asparagus, and a more elaborately decorated one for white asparagus; cover the asparagus with a slightly moistened white napkin.

To serve it cold, cool the asparagus in ice water immediately after cooking; to my mind, however, this diminishes the flavor.

But however you serve it, do not let your asparagus sit in water; this will damage both its texture and its flavor. Serve it with asparagus tongs; using a fork can damage the spears. In fact, these tongs are very useful for serving any cylindrical vegetable, such as carrots and hearts of palm.

The delicately acid flavor of Tavel or Palette rosés, served cool, is welcome with the violet asparagus of Provence. The delicate white asparagus from the Loire or Alsace calls for a more elegant white wine, such as a Meursault or a Sancerre.

Asparagus with Egg Sauce and Vegetable Confetti
Arlequinade d'Asperges à l'Oeuf

✳

OPPOSITE PAGE:
Asparagus with Egg Sauce and Vegetable Confetti

Peel the asparagus with a vegetable peeler and wash it in cold water. Divide it into 4 bundles and tie each with string; trim the asparagus to a uniform length.

Bring 5 to 6 quarts of water to the boil and add a handful of salt. Add the asparagus and cook 10 to 15 minutes or until tender.

Meanwhile soft-boil the eggs. Bring 1½ quarts of water to the boil, add the eggs, and cook for 5 minutes.

Warm 4 plates.

Soften, but do not melt, the butter in a metal bowl or a saucepan over warm water.

Shell the eggs under running cold water; take care—they will be very fragile. Mash the eggs in a bowl with a whisk. Season with salt and pepper, and add the softened butter. Keep the mixture warm in a tepid double boiler or in a cool oven.

Peel the red pepper with a vegetable peeler. Cut it in half lengthwise and remove the seeds, stem, and internal ribs. Cut the flesh into small dice. Wash and drain the chives, then chop them.

When the asparagus is done, remove it, and dry on a towel. Cut the strings and fan out one bundle of asparagus on each plate. Coat the asparagus tips with the egg sauce and sprinkle each serving with diced pepper and chives. Serve immediately.

FOR 4 SERVINGS

Preparation: 40 minutes
Cooking time: 20 minutes

3¼ pounds medium
  asparagus
6 eggs
4 tablespoons butter
Salt and freshly ground
  black pepper
1 red bell pepper
A bunch of chives

Asparagus-Tip Fritters
Beignets Croustillants de Pointes d'Asperges

✳

Whisk together the flour and beer to make a batter about the consistency of crêpe batter.

Peel, wash, and drain the asparagus. Cut the tips to about 4 inches in length; save the stalks for a soup (see page 156).

Heat the oil to 360 degrees. Thoroughly coat the asparagus tips with batter and carefully slip them into the hot oil.

Fry for 3 or 4 minutes, then turn the fritters. When golden brown, drain on paper towels.

Sprinkle with salt and serve immediately.

FOR 2 SERVINGS

Preparation: 30 minutes
Cooking time: 5 minutes

3 tablespoons flour
¼ cup cold beer
16 medium asparagus
  spears
1 quart corn or peanut oil,
  for frying
Salt

153

Asparagus with Parsley-Butter Sauce
Asperges à la Flamande

✳

Peel the asparagus with a vegetable peeler and wash it in cold water. Dry it with a cloth or with paper towels.

Cut each spear into 3 equal lengths; set aside the tips.

Melt 2 tablespoons butter in a saucepan and add the asparagus stalks. Season with salt, add 5 tablespoons warm water, cover the pan, and cook over high heat for 5 minutes.

Add the asparagus tips, cover the pan once again, and cook for an additional 10 minutes. Remove the lid and, still over high heat, reduce the cooking liquid to 3 to 4 tablespoons. Add the remaining 4 tablespoons butter, cut into small pieces, and the parsley. Add freshly ground pepper to taste and serve very hot.

FOR 4 SERVINGS

Preparation: 35 minutes
Cooking time: 25 minutes

3¼ pounds medium asparagus
6 tablespoons butter
Salt and freshly ground black pepper
3 tablespoons chopped parsley

Skewered Grilled Asparagus
Brochettes de Pointes d'Asperges Grillées

✳

I ate asparagus grilled on skewers for the first time in Japan; I learned that grilling spotlights its mild bitterness and heightens its flavor. The olive oil keeps the asparagus from drying out, and the fresh savory is like a burst of sunshine.

Peel, wash, and drain the asparagus; cut the tips to about 4 inches in length; save the stalks for a soup (see page 156) or a purée. Spread the asparagus tips on a plate and sprinkle with salt (this will tenderize them and make them less brittle).

Preheat the grill or the broiler to a moderate temperature.

Skewer the asparagus tips in groups of 5, using 2 skewers 1 inch apart to make it easier to handle them. Drizzle the asparagus with

olive oil, then broil or grill for 2 or 3 minutes; turn and cook for another 2 or 3 minutes.

Meanwhile, gently warm the remaining olive oil with some of the savory in a skillet or baking dish. When the asparagus is done, dip both sides in this scented oil.

Arrange the skewers on a serving platter, season with freshly ground pepper, sprinkle with more of the herb-scented oil, and garnish with a few sprigs of fresh savory.

FOR 4 SERVINGS

Preparation: 30 minutes
Cooking time: 6 minutes

40 thick asparagus spears
Salt and freshly ground black pepper
½ cup olive oil
Several fresh savory sprigs

OPPOSITE PAGE:
Skewered Grilled Asparagus

OPPOSITE PAGE:
Asparagus Quiche

Cream of Asparagus Soup
Velouté d'Asperges

✳

A delicate soup that you can make with the stalks left over from recipes that use only asparagus tips.

FOR 4 SERVINGS

Preparation: 20 minutes
Cooking time: 35 minutes

1 pound asparagus stalks
2 medium leeks, white part only
2 tablespoons butter
1 quart chicken stock
Salt
1½ tablespoons rice flour or cornstarch
2 tablespoons heavy cream
Fresh chervil sprigs

Peel, wash, and drain the asparagus, and cut each stalk into 3 or 4 pieces. Slice, wash, and drain the leeks.

Melt the butter in a saucepan; add the leeks, cover the pan, and cook over low heat for 8 minutes; be sure they do not brown. When the leeks are tender, add the asparagus and cover the pan again. Cook until the vegetables have rendered all their liquid and this has reduced completely, about 15 minutes.

Add the chicken stock and a little salt, bring to the boil, and simmer for 15 minutes.

Put the rice flour or cornstarch in a small bowl, add a little cold water, and mix well. Add to the soup, stirring constantly; let it boil briefly until thickened, then purée in a food processor or blender, or put the soup through the fine disk of a food mill. Strain through a fine sieve to remove any remaining fibers.

Return the soup to the saucepan and bring it back to the boil. Add the cream and immediately remove the pan from the heat.

Check for seasoning, garnish with chervil sprigs, and serve hot—either in a tureen or in individual bowls.

Asparagus Quiche
Quiche d'Asperges

✳

FOR 4 SERVINGS

Preparation: 20 minutes
Resting time for the pastry: 1 hour, then 30 minutes
Cooking time: 40 minutes

For the Pastry (pâte brisée)
½ cup cold butter
1⅔ cups all-purpose flour
1 egg
Salt

16 medium asparagus spears
2 eggs
1 cup heavy cream
Salt and freshly ground black pepper
1 tablespoon chopped chives

Make the pastry. Cut the cold butter into small pieces, blend it into the flour with your fingertips or a pastry blender, then add the egg and salt. Form the dough into a ball, flatten it slightly, wrap it in a towel, and refrigerate for 1 hour.

Roll the dough into a circle and line an 8-inch tart pan; trim away any excess pastry. Prick the bottom with the tines of a fork, and refrigerate for another 30 minutes.

Peel the asparagus, wash it, and cut it into ⅜-inch lengths. Bring 1 quart of salted water to the boil, then blanch the asparagus for about 2 minutes. Plunge immediately into cold water and drain well.

Preheat the oven to 350 degrees.

Mix the eggs and cream; season with salt and pepper, and add the chives.

Arrange the asparagus on the pastry; pour in the cream mixture and bake for 35 to 40 minutes or until set and lightly browned at edges.

Let the quiche rest for a few minutes before serving.

Scrambled Eggs with Asparagus and Truffles on a Crisp Shell

Brouillade d'Asperges aux Truffes en Couronne Croustillante

✳

FOR 4 SERVINGS

Preparation: 1 hour
Resting time: 6 hours
Cooking time: 20 to
   25 minutes

10 eggs
1 medium truffle
   (1 ounce), fresh or
   good-quality canned
Salt and freshly ground
   black pepper
24 medium asparagus
   spears (Provençal-type
   violet asparagus if you
   can get it)
7 tablespoons butter
2 sheets phyllo dough
1 tablespoon fresh chervil

Break the eggs into a bowl. Grate the truffle into the eggs and season with salt and pepper. Beat thoroughly with a fork, then cover the bowl with plastic wrap and leave at room temperature for about 6 hours to let the eggs absorb the truffle flavor.

Preheat the oven to 400 degrees and bring 2 quarts of salted water to the boil.

Peel and wash the asparagus. Cut off the tips to a length of 1½ inches. Cut the remaining stalks into 1½-inch lengths, then cut lengthwise into julienne strips the thickness of a wooden kitchen match.

Melt 3 tablespoons of butter, and brush it all onto the phyllo dough; the phyllo sheets must be supple, not brittle. Crumple the phyllo sheets loosely into an 8-inch ring mold.

Add the asparagus tips to the boiling water; cook for 5 to 10 minutes, or until *al dente*. Drain and keep warm.

Melt 4 teaspoons butter in a small skillet and add the julienned asparagus. Add salt and cook over high heat, stirring constantly, until the asparagus has rendered all its liquid and this has completely reduced.

Over medium-low heat, melt another 4 teaspoons butter in a saucepan; add the eggs and truffles. Stir constantly with a wire whisk and cook until creamy. Remove from the heat, and stir in the remaining 4 teaspoons butter, cut into small pieces. Check for seasoning and add salt and pepper. Cover the pan and keep warm by placing it in a hot (but not boiling!) water bath.

Put the ring mold into the hot oven for about 2 minutes, or until the phyllo dough is crisp, golden, and brittle but not deeply browned.

Unmold this golden crown onto a warmed serving dish. Put the julienned asparagus into the center, then mound the scrambled eggs on top of the asparagus. Garnish with the asparagus tips and the chervil.

Beets

OFTEN MUDDY and coarse-looking, the beet's rustic exterior conceals a sweet-tasting treasure. The shape is sometimes flat or, rarely, elongated; the color is occasionally yellow. But generally beets are round and, when cooked, a lovely shade of grenadine. They can take one or two hours to cook in boiling salted water, but this makes them fragile and their skins easily split; also, the flavor deteriorates as they boil.

I prefer to cook them in the oven or in the embers of an open fire. Granted, this takes patience—and a certain indifference to the gas or electric bill if you use your oven. Just wash them and put them on a baking sheet (adding no oil or fat) in a 300-degree oven. Then forget them for an hour or two, depending on their size. As they roast, their juices will concentrate and they will end up as balls of sugar—almost like a piece of fruit. They become the ideal partners for honey, sugar, almonds, and fruits such as red currants and oranges.

Beets are not eaten raw, but you can grate them and squeeze out their juice, then add it to vegetable soup or chicken broth, as the Russians do to make one version of borscht. Apart from its color, beet juice adds a very pleasant sweetness.

The fruity sweetness of beets cries out for light red wines such as Beaujolais-Village, or Bourgueil or Chinon from the Loire Valley.

Flavorful Salads

In France, beet salad is one of the classic winter salads (the other is endive). Try this variation: Mix equal parts of mâche, grated celeriac, and sliced beets. Dressed with a simple vinaigrette, this is a happy and delicious combination.

Let me also recommend another salad, made with Marie-Brizard Liqueur, to accompany roast duck or pork. It is colorful and easy to make: take some cooked (preferably roasted) beets, peel them, and cut them into large dice. Sprinkle with wine vinegar and salt, then let them marinate for two hours at room temperature. Drain them in a colander or strainer when you are ready to make the salad.

Whip a tablespoon of heavy cream with half a teaspoon of Marie-Brizard Liqueur. When it has begun to thicken, add the beets and a dash of Tabasco sauce. Serve this lovely pink salad immediately on a bed of pale-green lettuce, and sprinkle with a few fresh dill leaves.

OPPOSITE PAGE:
Beets with Red Currants

Beets with Red Currants
Betteraves aux Baies de Groseilles

✳

FOR 4 SERVINGS

Preparation: 10 minutes
Cooking time: 10 minutes
(plus cooking time for
the beets)

1¼ pounds cooked beets
(see page 159)
1 tablespoon light brown
or granulated sugar
¾ cup fresh red currants
Juice of 1 orange
2 tablespoons butter
A dash of *pastis* (anise-
flavored liqueur), such
as Pernod or Ricard
Salt and freshly ground
black pepper
4 small fresh dill sprigs

Peel the beets and cut them into julienne pieces about ⅛ inch thick and 1 inch long.

Put the sugar and 1 teaspoon of water into a small saucepan or skillet and heat it over medium heat until it begins to caramelize. Add the orange juice and the butter and cook until you have a thick syrup.

Keep 4 little bunches of currants for garnish and stem the remainder. Put the beets into the orange syrup and stir to coat evenly. Continue to cook over low to medium heat, stirring constantly, and add the currants. Cook for a scant minute, then add the *pastis* and season to taste with salt and pepper.

Divide the beets among 4 small plates and garnish each with a bunch of currants and a sprig of dill.

Beets with Orange and Almonds
Betteraves Rouges à l'Orange et aux Amandes

✳

FOR 4 SERVINGS

Preparation: 15 minutes
Cooking time: 30 minutes
(plus cooking time for
the beets)

1 generous pound cooked
beets (see page 159)
3 medium oranges, plus
½ orange
4 tablespoons butter
Salt and freshly ground
black pepper
A generous ⅓ cup
slivered almonds,
toasted
2 tablespoons chervil

Peel the beets and cut into ⅜-inch cubes. Grate the zest of half of one of the whole oranges. Squeeze the 3 whole oranges. Cut the additional orange half into slices or wedges for decoration, and set aside.

Put the orange juice, grated zest, and butter into a shallow saucepan or a skillet, along with some salt and the beets. Cook over medium heat for 15 minutes, stirring occasionally to move the beets around in the sauce. Then raise the heat and completely reduce the cooking liquid; the beets should be coated with an orange glaze. Check for salt, and add plenty of pepper.

Turn the beets into a warm serving dish and top with the toasted slivered almonds. Surround with the reserved orange slices and garnish with chervil. Serve immediately.

Carrots

THE GARDENER'S first pleasure of the carrot season comes in early spring, when it is time to thin the beds: reaching for the fringe of foliage and picking the sweet, tender baby carrots that take just a couple of minutes to cook in a covered pan with a little liquid. As the leaves spread and thicken, you can probe the roots with your fingernail, gauging their growth.

Carrots have everything going for them: attractive, aromatic leaves; vibrant color; sweet flavor. Raw, they are crunchy and succulent; cooked, they go with just about any ingredient—any aromatic herb or vegetable such as parsley, chervil, chives, or onions; and they are perfectly content to be paired with salt, sugar, honey—even vanilla and cinnamon.

Some are short and round; others are long with pointed or blunt ends; their color varies in vividness (some are almost white). They are all at their best when freshly picked, though they will keep well through the winter in a tub of sand protected from light and frost.

When buying carrots, opt for bunches with their leaves; if you are not going to cook them immediately, store them in a cool place without washing or trimming. Such very fresh carrots need not be completely peeled; just scrape them with the back of a knife and cut off the leaf end. If you have trouble getting decent carrots in wintertime, buy plenty in the summer or fall, and either store them in sand in your cellar or can them (see page 251).

You can cook young, tender carrots in a covered casserole with a minimum of water; they will retain all their flavor. But large carrots are best cooked in boiling salted water, either whole or cut into chunks or slices; you can then use them in delicious purées, soups, flans—even cakes, scented with vanilla or cinnamon and served with whipped cream.

Choose a wine that will not compromise their enormous sweetness, such as a rosé from the Côtes-de-Provence, a white from Anjou, or even a young red Burgundy from the Côte de Beaune.

Carrot Flans

Carrots are perfect for making delicious, beautiful-looking little flans to serve as a first course. You can make them in advance and briefly reheat them in a hot-water bath or in the microwave.

Just purée some cooked carrots and add some eggs, milk, and cream. Season with your choice of spices or herbs, and bake in a hot oven, in a hot-water bath, for half an hour.

Top to bottom: Flans of Curried Peas (recipe on page 128); Cauliflower Flans (recipe on page 110); Spinach-Coconut Flans (recipe on page 121); Carrot Flans with Cinnamon (recipe on page 165).

Carrots with Chive Cream Sauce
Crémée de Carottes à la Ciboulette

✳

Peel the carrots and cut them into julienne (³/₁₆ by 1 inch). Wash in cold water, drain, and dry on paper towels.

Put the carrots into a saucepan with the butter, sugar, a pinch of salt, nutmeg, and about 2 cups of water. Cover the pan and cook over medium heat for about 20 minutes.

Uncover and raise the heat; completely reduce the cooking liquid.

Chop the chives.

Add the lemon juice to the carrots and bring to the boil; add the cream and boil for a minute or so.

Check for seasoning and turn out into a warmed serving dish; sprinkle with the chopped chives.

OPPOSITE PAGE:
Carrots with Chive Cream Sauce

FOR 4 TO 6 SERVINGS

Preparation: 30 minutes
Cooking time: 25 minutes

8 to 10 medium carrots
  (1 ³/₄ pounds total)
2 tablespoons butter
1 teaspoon sugar
Salt
A pinch of freshly ground
  nutmeg
A small bunch of chives
1 tablespoon lemon juice
1 ¹/₂ tablespoons heavy
  cream

Carrot Flans with Cinnamon
Flans de Carottes à la Cannelle

✳

You can serve these flans for dessert accompanied by a good quality Muscat de Beaumes-de-Venise, that wonderful sweet wine from the Rhône Valley. Or sauce them with an onion cream as a delicious accent to their delicate flavor, and serve them as an appetizer.

Preheat the oven to 300 degrees.

Wash and peel the carrots; cut them into thin slices and put them into a saucepan with the butter, sugar, cinnamon, and orange zest. Add water to cover, put the lid on the pan, and cook over low heat for 5 minutes, then uncover, raise the heat, and cook until the liquid has completely reduced. The carrots should be very tender and lightly caramelized. Put them into a blender or food processor.

Put a kettle of water on to boil.

Season the cream with salt and pepper, and bring it to the boil. Add the cream to the carrots and purée thoroughly. Add the egg and the egg yolk and blend again.

Butter four 3-inch soufflé molds or custard cups and fill them with the carrot purée. Place them in a baking dish and add boiling water to come half way up the sides of the molds.

Bake for about 40 minutes or until set, and remove from the oven. Let the flans rest for 15 minutes before unmolding.

FOR 4 SERVINGS

Preparation: 20 minutes
Cooking time: 50 minutes
Resting time: 15 minutes

3 medium carrots
  (7 ounces total)
2 teaspoons butter
1 teaspoon sugar
A pinch of ground
  cinnamon
Grated zest of 1 orange
³/₄ cup heavy cream
Salt and freshly ground
  black pepper
1 egg
1 egg yolk

See photograph on page 165.

Fricassée of Carrots and Green Peppers
Fricassée de Carottes aux Poivrons Verts

✳

FOR 4 TO 6 SERVINGS

Preparation: 30 minutes
Cooking time: 20 minutes

8 to 10 medium carrots
   (1¾ pounds total)
1 large green bell pepper
Juice and zest of ½ orange
A pinch of ground
   cinnamon
1 generous teaspoon
   honey
4 tablespoons butter
Salt and freshly ground
   black pepper
Fresh coriander leaves,
   for garnish

Peel the carrots, wash them, and slice them into thin rounds. Peel the green pepper with a vegetable peeler. Cut it in half lengthwise and discard the seeds, stem, and internal ribs. Slice into thin strips.

Cut the orange zest into fine julienne and blanch it for 10 seconds in boiling water. Cool in cold water and drain.

Put the carrots in a saucepan along with the cinnamon, honey, butter, orange juice, salt and pepper, and ¾ cup of water.

Cover and cook over high heat for 10 to 15 minutes, depending on how fresh and tender your carrots are. Remove the lid and completely reduce the cooking liquid. Let the carrots brown very lightly.

Stir in the green pepper and the orange zest.

Turn out into a warmed serving dish and garnish with coriander leaves.

Carrot Cake with Apricots
Gâteau de Carottes aux Abricots

✳

FOR 4 SERVINGS

Preparation: 10 minutes
Cooking time: 45 minutes

2 small carrots
   (3½ ounces total)
Scant ½ cup dried
   apricots
⅔ cup all-purpose flour
½ cup sugar
1½ teaspoons baking
   powder
4 eggs
¼ cup corn or peanut oil
1 teaspoon vanilla sugar
A pinch of freshly grated
   nutmeg
Salt

OPPOSITE PAGE:
Carrot Cake with Apricots

Peel the carrots and wash them in cold water. Cut into chunks and put into a saucepan with cold water to cover. Bring to the boil and cook until tender. Purée in a food mill, blender, or food processor.

Cut the dried apricots into small cubes and soak in warm water for 20 minutes.

Preheat the oven to 350 degrees, and lightly grease an 8-inch cake pan with oil.

Put the flour into a bowl along with the sugar, baking powder, eggs, oil, vanilla, puréed carrots, nutmeg, and a pinch of salt. Mix well with a wire whisk until thoroughly blended.

Drain the apricots and stir them into the cake batter. Pour the batter into the cake pan and bake for about 35 minutes, or until a tester inserted in the center comes out clean.

Remove the cake from the oven and let it rest for about 5 minutes before unmolding onto a cooling rack. Serve warm with an apricot purée and whipped cream.

166

Salsify, Black Salsify, and Japanese Artichokes (Crosnes)

SALSIFY AND black salsify—also known respectively as oyster plant and viper's grass (or scorsanera)—are close relations; both of these root vegetables grow only in sandy soil. Salsify is white, while the rarer scorsanera has black skin. They have an elegant flavor and a meltingly tender texture, but are a nuisance to peel: your vegetable peeler is constantly bumping into their fibrous knots, and the saplike liquid they exude sticks to your fingers and turns black. As you peel them, immediately put them into a bowl of cold water acidulated with some white vinegar or lemon juice. To clean your hands, dry them well, then dip a wedge of lemon in salt and rub it over your hands before rinsing in cold water. Or rub your hands with white vinegar.

Do not leave these roots soaking in water for long; drain them and cut them into two-inch lengths, then blanch them in a flour-and-water *blanc* (see page 244) and finish them by gently braising in a casserole, perhaps with veal stock. You can also dip the pieces of blanched salsify or black salsify in batter and fry them to make delectable fritters.

Opt for a balanced but not excessively powerful Cabernet Sauvignon, such as Médoc, Graves, Saint-Émilion, or Côtes-de-Duras.

Crosnes are also known as Japanese or Chinese artichokes and, indeed, come from Asia, although the French have been growing them for years. They are little, pearly, deeply ridged rhizomes.

There is no point in even trying to peel them. Just wash them and lightly brush them under water. You can tell they are fresh by their light beige color; they should not have begun to turn brown. Also, they should be firm to the touch. When you have cleaned them, cook them in boiling salted water for about fifteen minutes. Their flavor is as delicate as that of salsify; it comes to the fore with rich or assertive sauces such as cream sauces on the one hand or parsley and garlic on the other. *Crosnes* are excellent with roasted white meats such as veal and pork, and make elegant, original fritters and delicious gratins.

These mild-tasting nuggets go well with balanced red wines from Tuscany, such as Tignanello (a blend of Cabernet Sauvignon and the traditional Tuscan Sangiovese), or from the Médoc.

Japanese artichokes (crosnes): raw, cooked in a blanc, *and with parsley and garlic (see recipe on page 172).*

Salsify Shoots for Salad

Salsify and black salsify keep well through the winter in a tub of sand. Trim away the leaves at the very top of the root and bury the salsify under about four inches of sand. After about a week, little white shoots will begin to appear; these have a slightly bitter flavor and are delicious in salads, dressed with a vinaigrette made with walnut or hazelnut oil.

Salsify with Orange Syrup

Salsifis au Sucre d'Orange

✳

Peel the salsify with a vegetable peeler, trim the ends, and put into a bowl of cold water acidulated with the vinegar.

Cut the salsify into 2-inch lengths; cut the thicker pieces in half lengthwise.

Prepare a *blanc*. Put the flour in a small strainer, hold it over a saucepan, and slowly pour 2 quarts of cold water through it, stirring to disperse the flour evenly. Add the salsify and coarse salt to taste; bring to the boil and cook for 5 minutes. Turn off the heat, cover the pan, and let stand for 20 minutes.

With a vegetable peeler, remove the zest from half an orange and cut it into fine julienne. Put the zest into boiling water; when it returns to the boil, drain and cool in cold water. Set aside.

Drain the salsify in a colander and rinse under warm running water. Dry in a towel.

Heat the butter in a skillet. When it begins to color, add the salsify and cook until golden. Sprinkle with the sugar; let this caramelize. Then add the orange juice and reduce it to a thick syrup.

Add salt and pepper to taste and serve hot, garnished with the orange zest and chervil leaves.

FOR 4 SERVINGS

Preparation: 30 minutes
Resting time: 20 minutes
Cooking time: 15 minutes

9 or 10 medium salsify
 (1¾ pounds)
¼ cup white vinegar
2 tablespoons flour
½ medium orange
3 tablespoons butter
1 teaspoon sugar
½ cup orange juice
Salt and freshly ground
 black pepper
Fresh chervil, to garnish

Salsify with Meat Glaze

Salsifis au Jus

✳

Peel the salsify with a vegetable peeler, trim the ends and put into a bowl of cold water acidulated with the vinegar. Cut the salsify into 2-inch lengths.

Prepare a *blanc*. Put the flour in a small strainer, hold it over a saucepan, and slowly pour 2 quarts of cold water through it, stirring to disperse the flour evenly. Add the salsify and salt to taste; bring to the boil and cook for 5 minutes. Turn off the heat, cover the pan, and let stand for 20 minutes.

Drain the salsify thoroughly and dry it in a towel.

Heat the butter in a skillet until it begins to color and sauté the salsify until golden.

Add the stock and reduce to a syrupy consistency.

Add salt and pepper to taste and serve on a hot dish, sprinkled with parsley.

FOR 4 SERVINGS

Preparation: 30 minutes
Resting time: 20 minutes
Cooking time: 25 minutes

9 or 10 medium salsify
 (1¾ pounds)
¼ cup white vinegar
2 tablespoons flour
2 tablespoons butter
½ cup rich chicken, pork,
 or veal stock or cooking
 juices
Salt and freshly ground
 black pepper
3 tablespoons chopped
 Italian parsley

OPPOSITE PAGE:
Salsify with Meat Glaze

Japanese-Artichoke Fritters

Beignets de Crosnes

✳

FOR 4 SERVINGS

Preparation: 20 minutes
Resting time: 15 minutes
Cooking time: 20 minutes

14 ounces Japanese
   artichokes (*crosnes*)
¹/₂ cup white vinegar
2 or 3 lemons
²/₃ cup all-purpose flour
9 tablespoons cold beer
3 quarts neutral vegetable
   oil, for frying (such as
   corn or peanut oil)
Salt

Clean the Japanese artichokes by brushing them under water, then soak them in a bowl of cold water acidulated with the vinegar; drain them and refrigerate for 15 minutes.

Cut each lemon into 8 wedges.

Mix the flour and beer in a bowl; it should be the consistency of thick crêpe batter. Add the chilled Japanese artichokes to the batter and mix well.

Heat the frying oil to 360 degrees.

With a tablespoon, place portions of battered Japanese artichokes into the hot oil. Make only about 8 fritters at a time to prevent the oil temperature from dropping. Turn the fritters occasionally with tongs and remove them when they are golden brown, about 5 minutes. Drain on paper towels.

Sprinkle with salt and serve with the lemon wedges.

Japanese Artichokes with Parsley and Garlic

Crosnes en Persillade

✳

FOR 4 SERVINGS

Preparation: 30 minutes
Resting time: 1 hour
Cooking time: 20 minutes

1 generous pound
   Japanese artichokes
   (*crosnes*)
¹/₂ cup white vinegar
2 tablespoons flour
A sprig of fresh savory
2 medium shallots
1 garlic clove
6 tablespoons butter
3 tablespoons chopped
   Italian parsley
Salt and freshly ground
   black pepper

Wash and brush the Japanese artichokes under water to remove all soil. Put them into a large bowl along with 4 quarts of water and the vinegar, and let them soak for 1 hour. Drain them and rinse well under running water.

Put the Japanese artichokes into a large saucepan. Place the flour in a small strainer, hold it over the pan, and pour cold water through it until all the flour is dispersed. Add water to make a total of 3 quarts. Add 2 tablespoons salt and the sprig of fresh savory.

Bring to the boil and cook for about 5 minutes. Let the Japanese artichokes cool in their cooking liquid before draining them thoroughly.

Meanwhile, chop the shallots and garlic.

When the Japanese artichokes are cool and dry, heat the butter in a skillet until it begins to color, add the Japanese artichokes, and sauté until just golden. Add the shallots and continue to sauté for another 3 or 4 minutes.

Remove from the heat, add the parsley and garlic, and season with salt and pepper. Toss well and serve immediately.

Variation: In the final step you can replace the parsley and garlic with ¹/₄ cup of heavy cream.

See photograph on page 169.

Turnips, Parsnips, and Rutabaga

Too MANY PEOPLE turn up their noses at turnips; I think they are wrong, because good turnips are delicate vegetables with a deliciously sweet flavor. The various kinds look very different: long and white; round and streaked with purple (these are called *raves* in some parts of France); or even yellow-orange or long and black.

The flavor varies, too. My preference is for white turnips, especially young and tender ones about the size of your finger, cooked with a pinch of sugar and generously buttered. The bigger purple-tinged turnips have a stronger flavor; with potatoes and cream, or just glazed with butter and sugar, they are fit for a king. They add a distinctive aroma to broths; I consider that no decent *pot-au-feu* can be without a few purple turnips—or, better still, the large yellow ones that I regret to say are so rare in today's French markets.

Whatever the variety, choose small, firm turnips with a smooth, thin skin. They can be cottony and wormy if too big. Come spring, make a point of getting some bunches of turnips with their leaves; this is when they are at their best.

Here in France, parsnips (which look very much like big white carrots) are hardly grown except in the west and in the Channel Islands—which is a pity, because their marked flavor is most welcome in *pot-au-feu* and in gratins. Their forwardness needs to be subdued with creamy, gentle sauces, and at the same time there is a delicious chemistry between parsnips and potatoes. Cook them like carrots.

Rutabaga, the shape of a flattened spinning top and green or yellow in color, still has bad wartime associations for many people in France. In small quantities, it adds a pleasant flavor to *pot-au-feu*, but it can easily stand alone. Nicely cooked, with a well-seasoned cream sauce, it will surprise you with its delicate flavor and texture.

As for wine, accompany all these vegetables with a red Chinon from the Loire Valley; it will add a soft flowery note and a mild astringency.

Turnip and Potato Soup

It saddens me that we seem to have forgotten good, rustic, warming, simple soups like this one. They exemplify French family cooking at its best.

Over very low heat, cook a sliced leek (white part only) in a little butter. Add a quarter-pound of turnips, peeled and sliced thin, and $1^1/_4$ cups of peeled, cubed potatoes. Stir with a wooden spoon and add cold water or chicken stock. Add salt and bring to the boil. Cook until the potatoes begin to fall apart. Purée in a blender or food processor. Bring some milk to the boil with a good chunk of butter and add this to the soup. Return to the boil; turn off the heat as soon as it boils, season with a pinch of freshly grated nutmeg, and serve.

Little Turnips with Red Currants

Petits Navets aux Groseilles

✳

OPPOSITE PAGE:
*Little Turnips with
Red Currants*

In this recipe, the sweetness of the turnips mates nicely with the acidity of the red currants. Your guests may be nonplussed when you serve them these pink vegetables but, believe me, they will love them. Serve this dish with roast duck; it's a delicious and unusual update of the traditional combination of duck and turnips.

Set aside 4 nice little sprigs of red currants for decoration. Stem the remainder and put them into a small saucepan with 4 tablespoons of water. Bring to the boil, then immediately turn off the heat. Pour the red currants and water through a strainer over a bowl; press on the currants with a wooden spoon to extract as much juice as possible. Discard the currant residue and set the juice aside.

Peel the turnips with a vegetable peeler. If some are much larger than others, try to trim them all to more or less equal size. Put them in a saucepan with lightly salted water, bring to the boil, and cook for a few moments; drain the turnips.

In a casserole or heavy saucepan, combine the currant juice, chicken stock, half the butter, turnips, and sugar. Add salt (carefully if your stock is already salted), cover the casserole, and cook over medium heat for 5 minutes; uncover and raise the heat to high. Completely reduce the liquid, stirring to glaze the turnips. Finally, add the remaining butter and some freshly ground pepper.

Arrange the buttery glazed turnips on 4 warmed plates or a warmed serving dish. Decorate with the reserved sprigs of currants and, and if you were able to find any, a few currant leaves.

FOR 4 SERVINGS

Preparation: 30 minutes
Cooking time: 15 minutes

1 cup fresh red currants
8 very small turnips
   (14 ounces total)
½ cup chicken stock
2 tablespoons butter
1 tablespoon sugar
Salt and freshly ground
   black pepper
A few red currant leaves
   for decoration
   (optional)

My Mother's Creamy Gratin of Turnips and Potatoes

Crémée de Navets et de Pommes de Terre de ma Mère

✳

An elegant, delicious, very rich dish that I am sure will win over even benighted souls who view turnips as poor-people's food. It was one of my favorite dishes back in the days when my mother used to make it for me.

FOR 6 SERVINGS

Preparation: 15 minutes
Cooking time: 45 to 50
minutes

4 firm waxy potatoes,
such as red-skinned
(1 pound total)
4 medium white turnips
(1 pound total)
1¼ cups heavy cream
Salt and freshly ground
black pepper
A pinch of freshly grated
nutmeg
2 to 3 ounces Swiss
Gruyère cheese, grated
3 tablespoons butter, cut
in pieces

Wash, but do not peel, the potatoes and put them into a pan of cold salted water; bring to the boil and cook for 20 minutes. You can also steam them.

Peel the turnips and cook in the same manner, but for 15 minutes; they should be tender but still somewhat firm.

Preheat the oven to 350 degrees.

Cool the potatoes and turnips in cold water until you are able to handle them. Peel the potatoes and cut both the potatoes and the turnips into ⅛-inch slices.

Pour the cream into a deep skillet or wide casserole; season with salt, pepper, and nutmeg, and bring slowly to the boil. Add the potatoes and turnips and mix carefully to avoid breaking the slices.

Turn the mixture into a buttered gratin dish or baking dish. Sprinkle with grated cheese and dot with butter. Bake for 20 to 30 minutes. If the top is not browned by this time, raise the oven heat to 475 degrees, or run under the broiler for a moment.

FOR 4 SERVINGS

Preparation: 15 minutes
Cooking time: 20 minutes

6 tablespoons whole
butter, or 4 tablespoons
clarified butter
1 tablespoon cornstarch
1 tablespoon
confectioners' sugar
1/2 teaspoon ground
cardamom
3 medium turnips of
uniform shape
(9 ounces total)
Salt

OPPOSITE PAGE:
*Turnip Galettes with
Cardamom*

Turnip Galettes with Cardamom
Galettes de Navets à la Cardamome

✳

If using whole butter, clarify it. Melt it in a small saucepan over low heat. Let the white solids settle and skim off the clear butterfat.

Put 1 tablespoon of this clarified butter into each of four 4-inch crêpe pans; if these are unavailable, you can make this recipe in a single 10-inch skillet, preferably nonstick.

Mix the cornstarch, confectioners' sugar, and cardamom in a small bowl; add about 2 tablespoons cold water and blend with a small whisk.

Peel the turnips, cut off the tops and bottoms, and cut into very thin

(about ¹⁄₁₆-inch) slices of approximately equal diameter.

Dip each slice in the cornstarch mixture before adding it to the buttered crêpe pans or skillet; overlap the slices by about ⅜ inch in a petal arrangement to form four 4-inch pancakes.

Put the crêpe pans or skillet over medium heat. When the first side is golden brown, in about 10 minutes, turn the crisps with a pancake turner or wide metal spatula and brown the second side for 10 minutes.

Salt just before serving.

Gratin of Parsnips and Potatoes
Gratin aux Panais et Pommes de Terre

✳

FOR 4 SERVINGS

Preparation: 10 minutes
Cooking time: 50 minutes

7 medium parsnips
  (14 ounces total)
3 medium potatoes
  (14 ounces total)
1 cup heavy cream
1/4 cup milk
A pinch of freshly grated
  nutmeg
Salt and freshly ground
  black pepper
2 ounces Swiss Gruyère
  cheese, grated
1 teaspoon butter

Peel the parsnips and cut them into 1/8-inch slices. Cook them in 4 quarts of salted water for about 20 minutes, or until very tender.

Wash, but do not peel, the potatoes and put them in a pan with cold salted water to cover. Bring to the boil and cook for about 20 minutes, or until tender.

Cool the potatoes in cold water until you can handle them. Peel them and cut them into slices the same thickness as the parsnip slices.

Preheat the oven to 400 degrees.

Pour the cream and milk into a saucepan and season it with nutmeg, salt, and pepper. Bring to the boil and add the parsnips and potatoes. Simmer for about 10 minutes, watching to make sure it does not boil over.

Turn the mixture into a buttered gratin dish or baking dish, making sure the vegetables are evenly distributed. Sprinkle with grated cheese and bake for 20 minutes, or until the top is golden.

Rutabaga in Parsley Cream Sauce
Rutabagas en Crémée de Persillade

✳

FOR 4 SERVINGS

Preparation: 25 minutes
Cooking time: 30 to 35
  minutes

2 1/4-pound rutabaga
1 medium potato
1/2 garlic clove
1/4 cup heavy cream (and a
  little more if needed)
Salt and freshly ground
  black pepper
A pinch of freshly grated
  nutmeg
1/3 cup chopped parsley
3 tablespoons chopped
  chives

Even people who lived in France during and after the war, and who have less than fond memories of rutabaga, will probably like this dish. Serve a red wine—perhaps a Chanturgues from near Clermont-Ferrand.

Peel the rutabaga and cut into 1/2-inch cubes. Wash thoroughly in cold water Peel the potato and cut into 1/4-inch cubes; wash and dry thoroughly.

Put the rutabaga into a pan of cold salted water; bring it to the boil and cook for 20 minutes. Drain in a colander.

Bring 1 quart of salted water to the boil. Place the potato in the boiling water and cook for about 7 minutes; drain and set aside.

Peel the garlic and mince it very fine.

Pour the cream into a skillet or a wide saucepan; add salt and bring to the boil. Immediately add the potato (while still warm) and cook over low heat until it begins to fall apart. Be ready to add a tablespoon or two of additional cream if the mixture becomes too dry. Now add the rutabaga (also still warm), nutmeg, garlic, parsley, and chives, and stir to blend.

Make sure the rutabaga is heated through, and season with salt and pepper before serving.

Onions, Chive Plants, and Shallots

MARINADES, SALADS, soups, roasts, *pot-au-feu*, fricassées, fish stews, court-bouillons, sauces—in a word, French cooking. What would it be without onions? In every situation, they add their own sweetly spicy note, their unobtrusive, appealing viscosity—a sense of "cooking" without which a dish will seem incomplete. But why not let the onion, which makes an invaluable contribution to all the finest dishes, star in recipes of its own?

Springtime marks the appearance of little, opalescent white onions, which are so good nibbled raw or sliced into salads. When cooked, glazed with a little sugar, they grow tender quickly, and make a fine accompaniment to a roast, especially pork or veal. When the green parts are tender, they too can be eaten, sliced raw into salads or fresh cheeses, or cooked and puréed, to savor, for instance, with veal chops or veal kidneys.

The large yellow onion we use through the winter brings its forceful flavor to stocks, court-bouillons, and soups. And when you have removed their beautiful skins (which can be used to color clear soups and tint the shells of hard-boiled eggs), you can cut them into slices that are so good deep-fried, either plain or in batter.

In France, red onions (round and elongated varieties) appear in the market in summertime plaited into braids. They have a gentle, slightly sweet flavor and are often eaten raw, sliced into salads, and dressed with olive oil and good wine vinegar, or simply sprinkled with coarse salt. There is a Hawaiian variety of onion that people say can be eaten out of hand like an apple, but I must confess I haven't tasted it.

Any variety you buy must be hard to the touch; it must not have begun to sprout, and it must be free of mold. If you cannot eat all your onions immediately, store them in a dry, airy place away from the light.

Don't tell me. When you chop onions you just can't hold back the tears, even when you create a breeze in the kitchen. An effective solution is to cut your onions under running water, but this washes away part of the juice—and hence the flavor. So resign yourself to suffering occasionally

A Special Onion-Rice Purée

Preheat the oven to 275 degrees.

Line the bottom and sides of a shallow casserole (with a tight-fitting lid) with thin slices of unsmoked bacon or fresh salt pork (or try blanched pancetta or bacon). Cut at least 2 1/4 pounds of white or yellow onions into very thin slices, season with salt, and add to the pan. Cover with a layer of strips of smoked bacon. Put the lid on the pan and bake for at least two hours.

Meanwhile, bring a quart of salted water to the boil and add some rice (about 1/4 of the weight of the onions, a generous cup or so). Boil for seven or eight minutes, then drain in a strainer or colander.

When the onions are meltingly tender, remove the top layer of bacon and stir the rice into the onions. Replace the bacon, cover again, and return to the oven for another forty minutes, or until the rice and onions are very tender. Then discard the bacon and salt pork and purée the onions and rice in a food mill, blender, or food processor. Add four tablespoons of butter and beat with a wooden spoon. Serve nice and hot as an accompaniment to roast meat.

in a good culinary cause.

Chive plants look like baby scallions, but their green tops are even thinner than those of the chives we use as an herb. They are closely related to white onions; they fall somewhere between these on the one hand and shallots and chives on the other. (You can sometimes find similar plants in Asian markets.) In France chive plants come to market only for a short period from mid-spring to early summer. Most people don't even notice them and, unfortunately, they are becoming rarer. Just trim them slightly and cook them with a little veal roast—in a covered pan with butter over low heat. They will melt into a sweet puddle,

perfuming the meat through and through. What a treat!

There are two main kinds of shallots: little gray ones and the plumper pink ones. They recall the onion, at least as far as their sugar content goes, and have an intense flavor in which I personally detect animal notes; perhaps that explains why they go so well with red meat. The gray shallot has a very concentrated flavor and is not eaten on its own, but is used in sauces.

All these bulbs, whose flavors grow so gentle with cooking, can be just as good with a white Hermitage or a Pouilly-Fuissé as with young red wines such as Coteaux d'Aix, Juliénas, or Côtes-de-Provence.

Little Glazed Onions with Currants (recipe on page 182).

Roasted White Onions

Oignons Blancs Rôtis

✳

FOR 4 SERVINGS

Preparation: 15 minutes
Cooking time: 1 hour

12 medium white onions
  (1–1½ pounds total)
¾ cup coarse sea salt
4 tablespoons butter
  (optional)
Juices from roast meat or
  meat stock, reduced and
  enriched with 2
  tablespoons butter
  (optional)

White onions roasted with coarse salt are a treat either by themselves or with roast veal. You can also wrap them in aluminum foil and cook them in the embers of your fireplace.

Preheat the oven to 300 degrees.
   Clean but do not peel the onions. Spread the coarse salt on a roasting pan and arrange the onions on the salt, root end down. Roast for 40 minutes, and check for tenderness by piercing the onions with the point of a small knife; it should go in easily. If they are not done, continue to roast, checking them occasionally.
   When the onions are cooked, remove the root end and the 2 outer layers of peel. Serve with coarse salt, or coated in melted butter, or with a little meat gravy or reduced stock enriched with butter.

OPPOSITE
PAGE:
*One of the
many varieties
of shallots.*

Glazed Pearl Onions
with Dried Currants

Petits Oignons Glacés aux Raisins de Corinthe

✳

FOR 4 SERVINGS

Preparation: 25 minutes
Cooking time: 30 minutes

1¼ pounds white pearl
  onions
3 tablespoons dried
  currants or raisins
4 tablespoons butter
1 tablespoon sugar
½ cup chicken stock
1 bay leaf
Salt and freshly ground
  black pepper

This dish is even better with pearl onions fresh from the garden. It is a delicious first course, but I also recommend it with roast pork or veal, braised ham, or grilled leg of suckling pig.

Peel only the papery outer skin from the onions. Soak the currants in warm water for 10 minutes, then drain them.
   In a heavy saucepan, combine the butter, onions, sugar, chicken stock, and bay leaf.
   Cook over medium heat for 15 to 20 minutes, depending on the size of the onions. Check for tenderness by piercing an onion with the point of a paring knife. When the onions are done, add the currants. Completely reduce the cooking liquid over high heat; let the onions caramelize and glaze. Season to taste with salt and pepper, and remove the bay leaf before serving.

See photograph on page 181.

Onions Braised in Sherry

Oignons Braisés au Sherry

✳

FOR 4 SERVINGS

Preparation: 15 minutes
Cooking time: 2¼ hours

8 medium onions, white
   or yellow
2 tablespoons butter
1 tablespoon sugar
½ cup dry Sherry, such
   as fino
1 teaspoon tomato paste
½ cup chicken stock
2 bay leaves
2 tablespoons soy sauce
1 teaspoon potato starch
   or cornstarch
Salt and freshly ground
   black pepper

Peel the onions, wash them, and dry with paper towels. Preheat oven to 275 degrees.

Melt the butter in a heavy casserole and add the onions, sugar, and Sherry. Bring to the boil and reduce the liquid by half. Stir the tomato paste into the chicken stock and add to the casserole. Season with salt, taking care if your stock is salted.

Add the bay leaves and bring to the boil. Cover the casserole and put it into the oven. Bake for about 2 hours, checking the onions from time to time; you should be able to pierce them with the point of a knife.

(The dish can also be cooked on top of the stove over very low heat.)

When the onions are done, remove them with a slotted spoon and put them on a serving platter. Over medium heat, reduce the cooking liquid to about 3 tablespoons. Mix the soy sauce with 2 tablespoons water in a small bowl and whisk in the potato starch. Stir the soy mixture into the simmering onion liquid. If the sauce is too thick, thin it with a little water.

Season with salt and pepper to taste, remove bay leaves, and pour sauce over the onions. Serve immediately.

Purée of White Onions

Purée d'Oignons Blancs

✳

FOR 4 SERVINGS

Preparation: 15 minutes
Cooking time: 50 minutes

2¼ pounds white onions
6 tablespoons butter
¼ cup rice, preferably
   medium grain
1 bay leaf
1 chicken bouillon cube
   or 1 tablespoon highly
   concentrated chicken
   glaze
Salt and freshly ground
   black pepper

Preheat the oven to 250 degrees.

Peel the onions and cut them into very thin slices. Put them into a casserole with half the butter, the bay leaf, 2 tablespoons of water, and a pinch of salt. Cover the casserole and bake it for 40 to 45 minutes, or cook it on top of the stove over extremely low heat.

The onions must remain uncolored; from time to time, check them and stir, adding a little hot water if the cooking juices begin to disappear.

While the onions are cooking, simmer the rice in salted water for about 20 minutes, until the grains are swollen.

When the onions are very tender, add the chicken glaze or crumble in the bouillon cube and stir well.

Put 4 soup plates into the oven to warm. Drain the rice and add to the onions. Cover the casserole and cook over the lowest possible heat for 5 minutes, or until any remaining liquid is absorbed. Remove the bay leaf and purée the onions and rice in a food processor or blender, or through the fine disk of a food mill.

Stir in the remaining butter; check for salt, add pepper to taste, and serve in the warmed soup plates.

Braised Chive Plants

Cives de Saint-Jean dans leur Jus

✳

Unfortunately, these wonderful vegetables rarely come to market. They are ready to harvest around the Feast of St. John the Baptist (June 24), hence the French name cives de Saint-Jean.

My mother used to brown a round roast of veal in a casserole, then cover it with chive plants and cook it with the lid on. Was it good!

If you cannot find chive plants, use very small scallions, but trim away much of the green.

Trim the roots of the chive plants, remove the outer skin from the white parts, and wash.

Melt the butter in a casserole and add the chive plants. Salt to taste, cover, and cook over medium-low heat for about 20 minutes. Uncover the casserole and reduce the juices to a syrupy consistency.

Serve in the casserole.

Note: You can also cut up the chive plants and sauté them in butter for barely more than a minute. Mix them into some beaten eggs and scramble them for a real feast. But be sure to use nearly as much chive as egg.

FOR 4 SERVINGS

Preparation: 15 minutes
Cooking time: 30 minutes

2¼ pounds chive plants
  or baby scallions
3 tablespoons butter
Salt

Roasted Whole Red Shallots

Échalotes Rouges Rôties en Gousses

✳

A rustic dish to serve with a friendly country dinner, especially with steaks grilled over a wood fire and garnished with poached marrow and coarse sea salt.

Preheat the oven to 275 degrees.

Wash the unpeeled shallots in warm water. Trim the tops and root ends, then place them in a roasting pan. Roast for 35 to 40 minutes.

Serve the shallots unpeeled; or you can pop them out of their skins by squeezing between thumb and index finger, then toss them in melted salted butter.

FOR 4 SERVINGS

Preparation: 10 minutes
Cooking time: about
  45 minutes

1 generous pound
  medium red shallots
2 tablespoons salted
  butter, melted (optional)

Shallots in Red Wine

Échalotes au Vin Rouge

✳

OPPOSITE PAGE:
Shallots in Red Wine

Don't be scared of the shallot's powerful flavor. As shallots cook, they become as soft as velvet. Still, use an intense wine such as a Côtes-du-Rhône for the sauce, and serve this dish with roast tenderloin of beef or with grilled steak.

FOR 4 SERVINGS

Preparation: 15 minutes
Cooking time: 20 to
   30 minutes

14 ounces medium
   shallots, all the same
   size
6 tablespoons butter
¾ cup chicken stock
1 teaspoon sugar
Salt and freshly ground
   black pepper
A sprig of thyme
1 cup red wine

Peel the shallots and trim the tops and root ends.

Heat half the butter in a heavy saucepan or casserole and add the shallots. Cook until lightly golden on all sides, then add the chicken stock, sugar, a pinch of salt, and the sprig of thyme.

Over high heat, reduce the cooking liquid completely, then add the wine and boil down until only 1 or 2 tablespoons of sauce remain. The shallots should be very tender.

Remove the pan from the heat and add the remaining 3 tablespoons of butter; stir to melt the butter into the sauce and to coat the shallots evenly.

Check for salt and season with pepper before serving.

Red Shallot Omelette

Omelette aux Échalotes Rouges

✳

This rustic omelette will be delicious if you take care to use red shallots, which are sweet and tender when cooked. Gray shallots will be too bitter. The omelette is nothing but a mid-morning snack, but with a glass of Sancerre it will certainly hold you until lunchtime.

FOR 4 SERVINGS

Preparation: 10 minutes
Cooking time: 8 minutes

4 medium red shallots
   (about 3 1/2 ounces
   total)
8 eggs
1 tablespoon chopped
   Italian parsley
Salt and freshly ground
   black pepper
2 tablespoons butter

Peel the shallots and cut into thin slices.

Beat the eggs with the parsley, and add salt and pepper to taste.

Melt the butter over low heat in a large, preferably non-stick omelette pan and add the shallots. Cook them for a minute or two, taking care not to brown them.

Add the egg mixture and stir well until the eggs begin to set; if necessary, lower the heat to prevent the bottom of the omelette from burning. When the omelette is cooked, but still slightly runny, fold it over in the pan and turn it out onto a plate.

Potatoes

EVERYONE WHO GROWS potatoes is a treasure-hunter at heart. At the end of summer, it is a real joy to thrust your spade into the soil to extract the pearls that accumulate in a tangle of roots beneath each plant. You let them dry in the sun for a few days, then place them in wire crates in a cool, dry, dark place to keep them from sprouting and to protect them from frosts. Potatoes could be the subject of a book in themselves (and indeed have been); there are so many diverse varieties and ways of preparing them.

You need to choose your potatoes according to the dish you want to prepare. For a soup or ragout, or for mashed potatoes, choose starchy potatoes that will crumble easily when cooked, and avoid new potatoes of any variety. For roasting, sautéing, and frying, use more firm-fleshed varieties. For potato salads, choose new potatoes with fine-textured flesh. Baked potatoes call for a very tasty, slightly mealy flesh.

These distinctions are important. If you mash a waxy roasting potato you will wind up with a yellowish, gummy, and liquid purée, whereas good mashed potatoes should be mealy and white—you should be able to stand up a spoon in them. On the other hand, if you use mealy potatoes for skillet-roasting or in potato salad, they will tend to fall apart in cooking.

In France, real potato enthusiasts rank the *Ratte* above all other varieties; these small fingerling potatoes are now grown in many areas of the United States and you may be able to find them in specialty stores and at farmers' markets. Their name comes from the way a little bit of root often remains attached, like a rodent's tail. *Rattes* are delicious and are best eaten plain, just steamed, salted, and coated in fresh butter. When they are very tiny you can serve them as "potato buckshot": just sauté them for a few minutes without peeling them.

There is almost no end to recipes involving potatoes, and I will not attempt to touch on them all. But let me give you a few hints that should be helpful.

When you are going to boil potatoes (peeled or unpeeled), always start them in cold water; they tend to toughen when dropped into boiling water. Don't forget the salt: a good handful of coarse salt for each two pounds of potatoes and two quarts of water. You can also flavor the water—if the potatoes are destined to be mashed, for instance— with a little piece of bay leaf, one or two sprigs of thyme, a clove of garlic, or a small onion. The potatoes will take about twenty

Smashed Potatoes with Niçoise Olives

This easy recipe is marvelous with roast pork, poultry, beef, or, best of all, lamb.

Boil or steam a pound of potatoes. Peel them immediately (but avoid burning yourself by working under running cold water). Warm half a cup of good, fruity olive oil in a small saucepan. Coarsely mash the hot potatoes with a fork, then incorporate the olive oil. You want to come upon pieces of potato as you eat. Finally, add about a third of a cup of pitted black Niçoise olives. Be careful when you add salt: because of the olives, you must not oversalt the dish. Mound into a serving dish and sprinkle with coarsely chopped parsley.

minutes to cook, from the time the water comes to the boil. But always check for doneness by piercing with the point of a knife; it should slip in with no resistance—and it is always better to overcook a potato than to undercook it.

When you steam potatoes, you can also scent the water—with bay leaves, for example.

When skillet-roasting potatoes in lard, bacon fat, or oil, use a heavy cast-iron, or enameled cast-iron, pan and be sure to get the fat hot enough to prevent the potatoes from sticking. And before you place them into the very hot fat, the potatoes must be completely dry. In fact, if they are not too dirty, just wipe them in a towel rather than washing them. If you ignore this advice, you risk spattering yourself with burning hot fat, and not quickly searing the potatoes, which can make them stick.

Always start these stove-top roasted potatoes over high heat, uncovered; occasionally slip a spatula under the potatoes to keep them from sticking, then when they are nice and brown all over, cover the pan and lower the heat. The potatoes are done when they are tender through. Add salt and pepper only just before serving, because salt has a tendency to destroy the crispness of roasted or fried foods.

The texture and even the flavor of skillet-roasted potatoes changes depending on how you cut them before cooking. Some people swear by large cubes; others by long slices (they quarter the potatoes lengthwise, then cut each quarter into thin slices the long way), and still others by rounds of various thicknesses. I have no intention of sparking a quarrel, so I shall keep my opinion to myself. Just try all three shapes and choose your favorite.

There is much to say also about "French" fries, as Americans call them, even though they are also the national dish of Belgium. Children love them no matter how well or badly they are cooked, but the fact is that they can be disastrous if prepared carelessly.

First, choose a firm variety of potato (in the United States, Russets are ideal); and please, please keep away from presliced or frozen potatoes, which are tasteless and generally drenched in preservatives. Peeling each potato and carefully wiping the French fries dry can take a certain amount of patience, but as far as cutting them up goes, you can buy an inexpensive French-fry cutter or an attachment for your food processor.

Whether you use an electric or stove-top deep-fryer, get yourself a frying basket with a handle, which will make it easy to drain the potatoes after each frying. Use a neutral-tasting vegetable oil that can stand the high temperatures needed for crisp French fries, such as peanut, sunflower, corn, or canola oils, or the solid coconut-oil shortening sold in France under the name of *Végétaline*. Make sure the oil is very clean and that it has not been used to fry anything but potatoes—least of all fish, which will give the oil a very strong flavor. Frying oil must be completely clear; it must not have darkened and must on no account be used more than four times.

Heat the oil to 360 degrees (see "The Right Way to Cook," page 247), and lower the basket of potatoes. Cook for about five minutes, raise the basket, and let it drain. When the potatoes have drained thoroughly, return them to the oil and repeat the procedure twice or three times more, or until the potatoes are golden but not dark brown. Drain and serve immediately. French fries will not wait! Salt only at the last moment.

Potatoes can also be sautéed in hot oil, using either raw or parboiled potatoes. The first will be firmer, the second more tender. This too is a question of personal taste, but it also depends on the type and size of the potatoes. The bigger and firmer the potato, the more likely it is that you will want to parboil it.

Various oven cooking methods also yield fine results. You can arrange slices of peeled potatoes in a baking dish with some cream and seasonings, or just wrap whole potatoes in aluminum foil and place them in the hot embers of the fireplace. For an informal meal, give each diner a foil-wrapped package; everyone will enjoy opening it, then slitting the skin of the potato and slathering it with butter, cream, or well-seasoned *fromage blanc*.

Another delicious way of cooking potatoes is to grate the peeled potatoes, either raw or parboiled, then form them into large pancakes. Depending on the region and the recipe, you can add eggs to bind the pota-toes, plus seasonings such as onions, herbs, and salt and pepper. The pancakes are then cooked in a skillet in hot oil and turned half way through the cooking (sliding them on to a plate to help turn them). These disks of golden shreds are called *criquettes* in central France and the Dauphiné, *râpées* in Lorraine, and *roesti* in Switzerland. They make an unusual but always welcome first course, and can also be served with grilled or roasted red meat.

Potatoes go as well with red wines as with white, depending on preparation and seasonings. For a purée with basil (see page 191), I recommend a floral-scented white Cassis. Potatoes roasted with bay leaves (page 192) call for a red country wine such as a Saint-Pourçain, a Gaillac, or a Saint-Chinian. But what about French fries or roasted potatoes? I merely put the question on the table—there is no single answer, so I recommend choosing a wine to match the meat with which you are serving them.

Potato Purée with Basil

Mousseline au Basilic

✳

This beautiful pistachio-green purée has a wonderful sun-drenched flavor; it will not survive waiting or reheating, so prepare it at the last minute.

Peel the potatoes and cut them into ³/₄-inch slices. Rinse in cold water and put into a saucepan with cold salted water to cover. Bring to the boil; skim away any scum that rises in the early stages of cooking.

Meanwhile, wash and drain the basil leaves and purée them in the blender with 2 tablespoons of olive oil and a pinch of salt.

Peel the garlic and lightly crush it. Put the garlic cloves and the remaining ¹/₂ cup of olive oil into a small saucepan and heat it over very low heat.

When the potatoes are done (in less than 30 minutes), drain them and put them through the fine disk of a food mill or a potato ricer. Remove the garlic from the warm oil. Mix the potatoes vigorously with a wooden spoon, gradually adding the garlic-scented oil. Continue mixing until the purée is very smooth.

Stir in the basil purée. If the mixture is too dry, add a little hot milk.

FOR 4 SERVINGS

Preparation: 15 minutes
Cooking time: 30 minutes

5 or 6 large potatoes
  (2¹/₄ pounds total)
About 30 fresh basil
  leaves
¹/₂ cup plus 2 tablespoons
  olive oil
Salt
2 garlic cloves
³/₄ cup scalded milk
  (optional)

Milk-Infused Mashed Potatoes

Pommes Purée Fondue au Lait

✳

Peel the potatoes and cut them into ³/₄-inch slices. Rinse in cold water and put in a saucepan with cold salted water to cover. Bring to the boil; skim any scum that rises in the early stages of cooking. Cook for about 20 minutes.

Toward the end of the 20 minutes, heat the milk over low heat, and keep it warm.

When the potatoes are nearly cooked, but still firm, drain them in a colander. Add the potatoes to the milk and cook over low heat until the potatoes are very tender and have absorbed all the milk.

Cut the butter into chunks.

Put the potatoes through the fine disk of a food mill set over the pan in which they cooked. Dot the potatoes with butter, and blend well with a wooden spoon, stirring vigorously until you have a very smooth purée. If the mixture seems dry, add a little boiling milk. If it needs salt, dissolve some in hot milk before adding it.

It is best to serve these potatoes immediately, but if necessary you can keep them warm, covered, in a hot-water bath.

FOR 4 SERVINGS

Preparation: 20 minutes
Cooking time: 40 minutes

5 or 6 large potatoes
  (2¹/₄ pounds total)
1 quart whole milk, plus
  additional if needed
6 tablespoons butter
Salt

My Mother's Potato Turnover

Pâté aux Pommes de Terre de ma Mère

✳

For 4 servings

Preparation: 20 minutes
Resting time for the
 pastry: 1 hour
Cooking time: 50 minutes

For the Pastry (pâte brisée)
½ cup lard or butter
1⅔ cups all-purpose flour
1 egg
1 tablespoon water
Salt

3 medium boiling potatoes
 (1 generous pound)
Salt and freshly ground
 black pepper
1 egg
2 tablespoons heavy
 cream
1 tablespoon chopped
 chives

In the central French regions of Berry and the Bourbonnais, they love turnovers as much as they love potatoes, and the two are felicitously combined in this recipe—which, for me, symbolizes a mother's tender loving care.

Make the pastry by cutting the lard into the flour, then adding the egg, water, and a pinch of salt. Gather into a ball and set aside to rest in a cool place, covered with a towel, for at least 1 hour.

Put the potatoes into a saucepan filled with cold salted water. Bring to the boil and cook for 10 or 15 minutes. When the potatoes are just cool enough to handle, peel them and cut them into ⅜-inch slices.

Preheat the oven to 400 degrees.

Roll out the dough into a circle just less than ¼ inch thick. Put it onto a baking sheet and arrange the potatoes, overlapping, over half the circle, leaving a ¾-inch border.

Sprinkle with a little salt and pepper, moisten the border with a little water, and fold the dough over to make a turnover.

Brush the surface of the turnover with beaten egg, and bake for about 30 minutes.

Remove from the oven, and cut a small circular hole in the center of the pastry. Pour in the cream.

Sprinkle with salt, pepper, and chopped chives, and eat while still very hot.

Note: You can make this a more elegant dish by using all-butter puff pastry and grating a truffle into the cream.

Bay-Scented Roasted Potatoes

Pommes Rôties au Laurier

✳

For 4 servings

Preparation: 15 minutes
Cooking time: 40 to
 50 minutes

8 medium potatoes,
 such as red-skinned
12 large fresh bay leaves
Salt
¾ cup chicken stock
½ cup olive oil

OPPOSITE PAGE:
Bay-Scented Roasted Potatoes

Preheat the oven to 400 degrees.

Peel, wash, and dry the potatoes. Cut slits into each potato every ⅜ inch; cut nearly all the way through, but be careful to keep the potatoes in one piece. Cut the bay leaves into ½-inch strips.

Oil a baking dish just large enough to hold the potatoes; put the potatoes into the pan and slip a piece of bay

leaf into each slit. Sprinkle with salt (very little if your chicken stock is already salted). Bring the chicken stock to the boil and pour it over the potatoes; drizzle with the olive oil.

Bake, uncovered, for about 40 minutes. The potatoes should be very tender and nicely browned; no cooking liquid should remain.

Serve in the baking dish.

Radishes

HERE'S ANOTHER VEGETABLE to crunch when just picked. The freshness of a radish quickly fades, and it grows dry. Apart from its peppery notes, the flavor is not terribly interesting. Radishes are generally eaten raw and unpeeled, perhaps dipped in salt. Too often, the leaves are thrown away, yet they make an elegant mousse (see page 195) and a delicious soup.

Also, the leaves are the best indicator of how fresh the radishes are; you should certainly avoid bunches whose foliage is crumpled or yellow—or, even worse, missing altogether. Opt for small radishes; they have a tendency to get too hot-tasting when very large. Don't bother at all with radishes that are not hard to the touch and that could have a pulpy texture.

There are several varieties—some round, some flattened, some red, some pink, sometimes white at the bottom. Try as many of the various kinds as you can find; they taste somewhat different. Among French varieties, my favorite is the red *Cerise*; I find it the freshest tasting and the crunchiest.

In eastern France, the big and long black-skinned radishes are very popular. When peeled these have a pearly white, very spicy flesh. They are grated like carrots and eaten in salads.

With radishes, have nothing more complicated than a cold glass of rosé from Provence to drink.

Radish Salad

Trim and peel a bunch of small radishes. If the leaves are in good condition, you can save them for soup. Wash the radishes in cold water, dry them in a towel, and cut them into thin slices. Sprinkle with coarse sea salt and olive oil. You can also arrange radish slices on top of salted fresh goat cheese. Serve the cheese as a first course, in little individual rustic bowls with grilled or toasted country bread drizzled with olive oil.

Pink Radishes with Radish-Leaf Purée

Radis Roses en Mousseline de Feuilles

✳

Radishes are pleasant to eat raw, just dipped in salt and served with bread and butter, or in a green salad, but they lose their slightly peppery flavor when cooked too much.

The leaves, however, have a delicate flavor. Cooked and puréed, they make a beautiful backdrop for the little red pearls themselves.

Cut off the radish leaves and set aside. Trim the root ends and soak the radishes in a bowl of cold water.

Thoroughly wash the leaves in cold water. Bring a pan of salted water to the boil and add the radish leaves. Cook for 2 or 3 minutes. Cool them under cold water, and drain well. With your hands, squeeze out as much water as possible. Purée the leaves in a blender or food processor.

In another pan of boiling salted water, cook the radishes for a minute or two; drain them.

Heat the butter in a skillet; when it begins to color, add the puréed radish leaves. Stir well with a wooden spoon, then add the radishes.

Add salt and pepper to taste, and serve on individual plates.

FOR 4 SERVINGS

100 to 120 tiny pink
  radishes (no bigger than
  1/2 inch in diameter),
  with their leaves
2 tablespoons butter
Salt and freshly ground
  black pepper

PAGES 196–197:
*Pattypan squash look better
than they taste; I like them
best in a gratin, with a
flavorful mushroom stuffing
(recipe on page 199), or
stuffed, as a before-dinner
snack (recipe on page 198).*

Vegetables from Afar

MY PASSION FOR vegetables knows no boundaries, and I indulge it wherever I travel. Nose, eyes, and palate alert, I ferret out new flavors and new aromas everywhere I go. My search always bears fruit: it is a windfall for food lovers that the whole world is bursting with edible treasures.

Asian cooks have a way of bringing out the best in their vegetables, with a highly developed economy of means, seriousness, and aesthetic sense. Eating bamboo shoots can be like biting into the living fibers of the plant, freshly picked by a true artist—just for us.

In the Caribbean, my impression is of the ebullience of nature on display in the marketplace, even in the heart of the cities. The closest thing I've ever seen to a cornucopia is these pyramids of multicolored tropical fruits, with their gorgeous shapes and their heady perfume dispersing in the sunlight. In the islands, the recipes, too, reflect a generosity that ignores our petty traditional distinctions. Fruits are eaten as vegetables and vegetables as fruit; bananas are fried into chips; the potatoes are sweet; and the flavors, from mild to hot, are combined in a simple way to please our taste buds.

In the past few years, I've also begun to discover the culinary wealth of North America, and I've already made some great finds. In the United States, you have those wonderful, sweet sugar-snap peas, a cross between the English pea and the snowpea. I don't have to tell an American reader that all you need to do is snap off the two ends, boil them for a few seconds, and finish them with salt, pepper, and butter.

You may think I am naïve, but I sometimes find the pioneer way of life reflected in North American cooking: nothing detracts from the true flavor of the produce. Cooking and seasoning are simple. Ears of corn are lightly grilled and drenched with fresh butter. And in Quebec and New England, they simmer tiny white beans in an iron pot with bacon and maple syrup.

I wish I could share more of these riches, but very few so-called exotic vegetables are available in France, except in specialized or ethnic groceries. It doesn't matter; in this chapter I just want to crack open the door and widen the horizons of your appetite—horizons that can be infinite.

A Pretty Hors d'Oeuvre

For a decorative cocktail party snack, take enough baby pattypan squash to cover the outside of a medium pumpkin. Boil them in salted water for seven or eight minutes, then cool in cold water and drain. Cut off and reserve the tops; hollow the squash and fill them with a salad of tiny shrimp dressed with mayonnaise, a tablespoon of grapefruit juice, a dash of cognac, and some chopped dill. Replace the tops and attach the stuffed squash to the outside of a pumpkin, using wooden skewers or long toothpicks. Affix some sprigs of parsley or dill between the squash for garnish.

Gratin of Pattypan Squash
Pâtissons au Gratin

✳

Pale green, prettily scalloped pattypan squash are much grown in the United States. Their mild, subtle flavor recalls that of zucchini and requires delicate treatment. Buy the smallest ones you can, because the skin grows tough when they get much bigger than an inch and a half across. If they are larger than that, poach them in boiling water, then scoop out the flesh and serve a colorful salad in the shells.

Trim the base of the mushrooms and rinse them; do not let them soak in water because they will become soggy. Drain them, and add them to a bowl containing the lemon juice; toss to coat the mushrooms evenly. Chop them very fine, either by hand or in a food processor or meat grinder.

Peel and chop the shallots; you should have about 2 tablespoons. Melt 1½ tablespoons of butter in a skillet and add the shallots; let them cook, but not brown, until soft, then add the mushrooms and cook over moderate to high heat for about 10 minutes. Add salt, and stir well with a wooden spoon.

Turn the mushrooms into a strainer over a bowl to collect all remaining liquid rendered by the mushrooms; reserve this liquid.

Bring 3 quarts salted water to the boil. Wash and drain the squash, then boil them for 7 to 8 minutes, or until tender. Cool them in cold water, drain them, and put them on a towel to dry.

Preheat the oven to 400 degrees.

Melt 2 tablespoons of butter in a saucepan over medium heat. Add the flour and mix well with a whisk. Before the flour begins to brown, add the cold milk and continue to whisk. Add the reserved mushroom liquid, salt to taste, and a pinch of nutmeg. Simmer over low heat for 2 or 3 minutes, then add the cream. Bring to the boil, add the mushrooms, and bring to the boil once again. Check for salt, add pepper to taste, and keep warm.

Peel and chop the garlic.

Melt the remaining 2 tablespoons of butter in a skillet; when it begins to color, add the squash and toss to coat well. Add salt, pepper, and the garlic.

Arrange the squash in a gratin dish or baking dish and cover with the mushroom sauce. Sprinkle with grated cheese and bake until the sauce is bubbling and topped with a nice golden crust. Serve immediately.

FOR 4 SERVINGS

Preparation: 30 minutes
Cooking time: 50 minutes

4 ounces white
    mushrooms
Juice of 1 lemon
2 shallots
5½ tablespoons butter
Salt and freshly ground
    black pepper
1 generous pound baby
    pattypan squash
1 tablespoon flour
¾ cup milk
Freshly grated nutmeg
2½ tablespoons heavy
    cream
1 garlic clove
2 ounces Swiss Gruyère
    cheese, grated

Spicy Plantain Chips
Chips de Plantains Piquantes

✳

You can serve these unusual chips as a before-dinner snack or with a curry or any other dish with a spicy sauce. You'll find plantains in Latin American and Caribbean markets and in many supermarkets. They have a rather floury flesh and are not sweet like bananas. Don't buy very ripe ones for this recipe. To make even chips quickly, I recommend slicing them with a stainless-steel mandoline or other slicing gadget.

FOR 4 SERVINGS

Preparation: 5 minutes
Cooking time: 10 minutes

3 plantains (not too ripe)
1¹/₂ quarts vegetable oil,
   for frying
Salt
Cayenne pepper

Peel the plantains and preheat the oil to 360 degrees.

Set the blade of the *mandoline* or other slicing gadget to just over ¹/₁₆ inch. Hold it over the fryer and slice the plantains directly into the hot oil; this will prevent them from sticking together. If you are slicing them manually or with a food processor, drop the chips into the oil one at a time.

Fry until golden, 5 to 10 minutes, then remove with a skimmer and drain on paper towels.

Mix some salt and a pinch of cayenne pepper; sprinkle the chips with this mixture just before serving (if salted too soon, the chips could lose their crispness).

These chips (unsalted) will keep for 2 or 3 days in a very dry place.

FOR 4 SERVINGS

Preparation: 5 minutes
Cooking time: 10 minutes

2¹/₄ pounds canned hearts
   of palm
2 tablespoons flour
1 teaspoon ground ginger
3 tablespoons butter
2 tablespoons soy sauce
4 tablespoons chopped
   fresh coriander

Hearts of Palm with Ginger
Coeurs de Palmier Dorés au Gingembre

✳

In the tropics, hearts of palm are gathered from young sabal palms no taller than about three feet. Fresh hearts of palm, seasoned with nothing more than salt, pepper, olive oil, and lemon juice, have the aroma of hazelnuts, but it is nearly impossible to buy them in France or the United States outside of Florida. So we use canned hearts of palm; they are not as flavorful, but they taste surprisingly close to the fresh product. If you can buy fresh hearts of palm at your local Asian or Caribbean market, do so by all means; just poach them in salted water before using them in these recipes.

Drain the hearts of palm, rinse them thoroughly, and dry them with paper towels.

Blend the flour and the ginger and dredge the hearts of palm in this mixture.

Heat the butter in a skillet until it begins to take color, add the hearts of palm, and cook until golden on all sides. Add the soy sauce, and turn the hearts of palm with tongs until evenly glazed with soy sauce.

Arrange on a serving platter and garnish with the coriander.

Gratin of Hearts of Palm with Almonds
Coeurs de Palmier en Gratin d'Amandes

✳

Peel and finely chop the shallot; heat 3 tablespoons butter in a heavy saucepan over low heat and cook the shallot for a few minutes, until tender but not browned. Whisk in the paprika, then the flour. Blend well and cook this roux over very low heat for 2 or 3 minutes.

If you are using the bell pepper, remove the stem, seeds, and internal ribs, then cut it into small dice. Melt 2 tablespoons of butter in a small skillet, add the bell pepper and cook over low heat until very tender.

Whisk the milk and half of the cream into the flour-paprika roux, stirring vigorously to prevent lumps. Add salt to taste and simmer for 2 minutes; you will have a creamy sauce. Add the optional bell pepper and set the sauce aside.

Preheat the broiler.

Drain the hearts of palm, rinse them thoroughly, and dry them with paper towels.

Heat the remaining 3 tablespoons of butter in a skillet; when it begins to color, add the hearts of palm and cook until lightly golden on all sides. Arrange them in a gratin dish or baking dish and cover them with the paprika-cream sauce.

Whip the remaining 6 tablespoons of cream until it begins to thicken, and whisk in the egg yolks. Top the hearts of palm with the egg yolk mixture.

Sprinkle with slivered almonds and broil until golden.

FOR 4 SERVINGS

Preparation: 30 minutes
Cooking time: 20 minutes

1 shallot
6 tablespoons butter, plus 2 tablespoons if using bell pepper
1 teaspoon sweet Hungarian paprika
1/3 cup all-purpose flour
1 red bell pepper (optional)
2 1/2 cups milk
12 tablespoons heavy cream
Salt
2 1/4 pounds canned hearts of palm
2 egg yolks
2 1/2 tablespoons slivered blanched almonds

Chayote and Sweet Potatoes Stewed with Coconut and Curry

Compotée de Chayotes et de Patates Douces au Curry-Coco

✳

Chayote is a tropical member of the squash family originally from Central and South America. It remains less common in France than in the United States, though it is sold in fancy groceries, and nowadays even in the marketplaces of Nice and Cannes. Among other cuisines, it is much used in Caribbean Creole cooking; and in the Canary Islands they include it in a wonderful version of pot-au-feu. Chayote is perfectly nice simply boiled and served with butter and parsley, but I like it best as part of a mixture; I sometimes even add it to ratatouille.

FOR 4 SERVINGS

Preparation: 40 minutes
Cooking time: 45 minutes

1 medium onion
2 tablespoons butter
³/₄ cup heavy cream
5 tablespoons
  unsweetened dried
  coconut
2 firm tomatoes
2 chayote (10 ounces total)
3 large sweet potatoes
  (1¼ pounds total)
2 garlic cloves
1 teaspoon cardamom
  seeds
2 whole cloves
2 tablespoons mild curry
  powder
1¼ cups chicken stock
  (optional)
Salt

Peel the onion and chop finely; sauté in a heavy saucepan or casserole over low heat with the butter. When lightly golden, set aside in the saucepan.

Bring the cream to the boil, then add the coconut. Turn off the heat and let the mixture steep for 10 minutes, then put through a fine sieve, pressing with a wooden spoon to extract as much coconut flavor as possible.

Cut the tomatoes in half crosswise, squeeze out the juice and seeds, then cut into large cubes.

Peel the chayote and remove the seeds, then cut lengthwise into slices. Cook in boiling salted water for 3 or 4 minutes, then drain, but do not cool.

Peel the sweet potatoes and cut into slices the same size as the chayote; cook in boiling salted water for 3 or 4 minutes, then drain, but do not cool.

Peel and lightly crush the garlic and add it to the pan with the cooked onion, along with the tomatoes, cardamom, cloves, and curry powder. Stir well, then add the coconut-flavored cream.

Put the pan over medium heat, then add the chayote and sweet potatoes with water (or, better, chicken stock) to cover. Add salt, cover the pan, and simmer over very low heat for about 20 minutes. Check the pan every so often to make sure the vegetables are not sticking. Serve in a heated vegetable dish.

It's spicy and good—heady with warming aromas.

Jamaican Roasted Pumpkin or Winter Squash

Courge Rouge Rôtie à la Jamaïcaine

✳

Jamaicans generally eat this dish with roast pork. Try to get a pumpkin picked at least a month before; it will be less watery and therefore tastier and easier to brown.

Preheat the oven to 550 degrees. Put the fat into a roasting pan and heat it in the oven until smoking hot (monitor the process to make sure the fat does not catch fire).

Meanwhile, cut the squash or pumpkin into large chunks, around 2½ or 3 inches on each side, and put them carefully into the hot fat. Return the pan to the oven.

Blend the sugar, cinnamon, and a pinch of salt. When the squash begins to brown, remove the pan from the oven and sprinkle the squash with the sugar mixture. Stir well with a wooden spoon to coat all surfaces, then return to the oven until the squash is a rich caramel color. Total cooking time should be around 40 minutes.

Drain the squash in a metal strainer or colander to remove excess fat.

Add freshly ground pepper and enjoy a real treat.

FOR 4 SERVINGS

Preparation: 15 minutes
Cooking time: 40 minutes

5 ounces beef suet (kidney fat), or generous ¾ cup corn oil, or 5 ounces coconut-oil shortening (*Végétaline*)
3¼ pounds red-fleshed pumpkin or winter squash
2 tablespoons light brown or granulated sugar
1 teaspoon ground cinnamon
Salt and freshly ground black pepper

Okra with Sweet-Potato Curry

Okras au Curry de Patate Douce

✳

Okra is grown in hot climates worldwide. It is used in many cuisines, including those of Africa, India, and the United States, and is particularly popular in the Caribbean. It has a rather neutral flavor and a mucilaginous texture, and is often used in mixed-vegetable stews. Occasionally it is just poached, tossed in butter, and served with curries or other spicy dishes. I like to combine okra with starchy vegetables such as sweet potatoes. I try to use the smallest okra I can find, because the seeds in the larger pods can be annoying to chew on.

FOR 4 SERVINGS

Preparation: 30 minutes
Cooking time: 45 minutes

1 garlic clove
1 medium onion
2 medium tomatoes
1 small sweet potato
2 tablespoons butter
1 teaspoon curry powder
1 cup chicken stock
Salt and freshly ground
   black pepper
14 ounces small okra
¼ cup chopped fresh
   coriander

Peel and chop the garlic. Peel and chop the onion.

Peel the tomatoes. Remove their stems and place them in boiling water for 15 seconds (or a little longer if they are not ripe). Cool them in a bowl of cold water; the skins should slip off easily. Cut them in half crosswise and squeeze out the seeds and liquid. Cut the tomatoes into ½-inch cubes.

Peel the sweet potato and cut into ½-inch cubes.

Melt the butter in a heavy casserole. Add the onion and cook over low heat until it begins to turn golden.

Add the garlic and tomatoes, and sprinkle with curry powder. Stir well

and add the chicken stock and sweet potato. Add salt to taste. Cover and cook over medium-low heat for 15 minutes.

Meanwhile, bring 3 quarts of salted water to the boil. Trim the ends of the okra, wash it, and add it to the boiling water. Cook at a full boil for 5 minutes, then drain.

Add the okra to the casserole and stir gently to avoid crushing the vegetables. Simmer over low heat for another 10 minutes, uncovered.

By now the cooking liquid should be reduced and somewhat thickened. Check for salt and season with pepper. Turn out into a warmed serving dish and garnish with coriander leaves.

Roasted Plantains
with Coconut Cream
Plantains Rôtis à la Crème de Coco

✳

OPPOSITE PAGE:
*Roasted Plantains with
Coconut Cream*

FOR 4 SERVINGS

Preparation: 30 minutes
Cooking time: 15 minutes

1¼ cups heavy cream
½ unsweetened dried
  coconut
A 2-inch cinnamon stick
1 tablespoon sugar
Salt
A pinch of cayenne
  pepper
4 ripe plantains
3 tablespoons flour
2 tablespoons butter

In a heavy saucepan bring to the boil a mixture of the cream, coconut, cinnamon, half the sugar, a pinch of salt, and cayenne pepper. When it comes to the boil, turn off the heat, cover the pan, and let the cream steep for 30 minutes.

Meanwhile, peel the plantains and cut them into 2-inch lengths. Mix the flour with the remaining ½ tablespoon of sugar and dredge the plantains in this mixture.

Heat the butter in a skillet. When it begins to turn golden, add the plantains and brown them lightly on all sides. Continue to cook for another 8 to 10 minutes.

Strain the coconut-infused cream through a fine strainer, pressing with a wooden spoon to extract as much liquid as possible. Check for seasoning. Pour the coconut cream onto a heated serving platter. Drain the plantains on paper towels and arrange them on top of the cream.

Baby Corn with Snowpeas
Petits Epis de Maïs aux Pois Gourmands

✳

FOR 4 SERVINGS

Preparation: 25 minutes
Cooking time: 15 minutes

14 ounces baby corn,
  preferably fresh, but
  canned or frozen
  if necessary
½ cup milk
10 ounces snowpeas
1 garlic clove
2 tablespoons butter
A sprig of fresh thyme
1 teaspoon sugar
Salt and freshly ground
  black pepper

If you were able to get fresh baby corn, remove the husks, and cook in 1 quart of water and the milk for 2 or 3 minutes. Drain and reserve.

For frozen or canned baby corn, drain and rinse well before using; no pre-cooking will be required.

Trim the ends from the snowpeas and string them. Peel and crush the garlic.

Melt the butter in a large skillet, then add the snowpeas, garlic, thyme sprig, and sugar. Add salt to taste and sauté over high heat for 2 or 3 minutes. Then add the baby corn and continue sautéing over high heat for another 2 minutes.

Remove the thyme and the garlic. Check for seasoning, add freshly ground pepper to taste, and serve.

Quinces in
Black Currant–Scented Cream
Coings à la Crème et aux Feuilles de Cassis

✳

I can imagine your surprise at reading this fruit recipe in a book of vegetable dishes. But there is no better "vegetable" than quinces to accompany venison or other game. Hare and partridge come to mind as well, but just think of the sight of a plump hen pheasant, moistened with a creamy sauce and surrounded by these rosy-colored nuggets of quince. They are delicious!

Rub the quinces vigorously with a towel to remove all traces of fuzz. Peel and quarter the quinces, then cut out the core and seeds. Do not discard the peel, core, or seeds; instead, place them on a piece of cheesecloth, gather the corners, and tie it into a bundle with a piece of cotton string. Put the bundle into a stainless-steel, enameled, or other nonreactive pot containing 2 quarts of lightly salted water, and heat over medium-low heat.

Cut each piece of quince lengthwise into 4 slices and add these to the pot. Cover and cook over low heat for 30 to 40 minutes, depending on the ripeness of the quinces. When the quinces are tender, remove the cheesecloth bundle and put it into a strainer over a heavy saucepan large enough to hold the quinces. Press hard with a wooden spoon to squeeze out as much juice as possible.

Bring this juice to the boil and reduce it to about 4 tablespoons. Wash and dry the black currant leaves if you are using them, then add the leaves or the black currants to the juice and continue cooking until reduced to a syrupy consistency.

Drain the quinces in a strainer or colander, discarding the water in which they were cooked.

Add the cream and the sugar to the quince–black currant syrup; season with salt and pepper to taste.

Return to the boil, remove the black currant leaves, and place the cooked quinces into the sauce. Bring back to the boil to reheat the quinces and serve.

FOR 4 SERVINGS

Preparation: 20 minutes
Cooking time: 1 hour

5 or 6 ripe plump quinces
  (2¼ pounds total)
20 black currant leaves or
  1 or 2 tablespoons black
  currants (fresh, frozen,
  or from a jar)
¼ cup heavy cream
1 teaspoon sugar
Salt and freshly ground
  black pepper

PAGES 212–213:
*A painter's palette of colors:
Old-Fashioned Nice-Style
Stuffed Vegetables (recipe on
page 216).*

Vegetable Medleys

Let's combine the beautiful vegetables that colorfully mark the seasons year-round. Of course, vegetables have different requirements for cooking and seasoning, so combining several in a single dish is not so simple. For a successful marriage you have to know the idiosyncrasies of all parties. But don't let this prevent you from having a try: the combinations will almost always be tasty, so long as you can find a note that will create harmony among all the vegetables in the dish. It could be butter, lovely fresh cream, oils vividly perfumed with fruits, or simply eggs—in omelettes, scrambled, or fried.

Break an egg into a hollow in a dish of ratatouille, put it into the oven for a while, and you'll have a real treat. And I can also recommend omelettes with vegetable purées (called *crespeou* in Provence), or standard rolled omelettes filled with mixed stewed vegetables or with tangy vegetables marinated in vinegar (see page 234).

On long summer evenings I often organize omelette parties for my friends, where they can choose among a variety of aromatic omelettes, both hot and cold. Spend as much time as you want with guests by preparing the omelettes a little in advance. Here are some ideas for fillings:

* Spinach wilted in olive oil with a little grated Parmesan cheese and some shredded fresh basil, or with a few chopped anchovies
* Peeled, chopped tomatoes with a hint of minced garlic and a little fresh thyme
* Swiss chard leaves and chopped sweet onions sautéed in olive oil
* Chopped garlic and walnuts
* Sliced zucchini sautéed in oil, with chopped parsley
* Slices of unpeeled eggplant browned in oil, with chopped garlic
* Equal parts of chopped parsley, chervil, and chives, with a little tarragon
* Sliced white onions, sautéed until golden
* Tiny wild asparagus just blanched for a minute in boiling salted water.

By the way, think what a lovely idea it would be to replace the traditional dinner-table flowers with a centerpiece of perfectly fresh vegetables—misted with water to make them look even fresher. For a somewhat baroque dinner party around a long table with silver candlesticks, you might even construct pyramids of fruit, vegetables, and herbs—endives, apples, lemons, and fennel, for instance. Such a sparkling, bright decoration would give a charming hint of the vegetable delights to come.

PAGE 215:
A variation on Eggplant Gratin Vieux Peygros (recipe on page 51), enriched with eggs.

Omelette Layer Cake

Here is how to make a delicious, colorful "layer cake" of omelettes. While the oven is heating to 375 degrees, prepare the eggs and fillings for a variety of omelettes (see the suggestions on this page).

Put the ingredients for each omelette in an oiled tart pan or cake pan and bake in a hot oven for ten minutes. Unmold the omelettes and stack them, brushing beaten egg between the layers to hold them together. Bake the cake for one or two minutes (no more!) and let it cool a while.

When it is lukewarm or at room temperature, cut it into wedges and serve it with a salad of mixed young greens (*mesclun*).

Old-Fashioned Nice-Style Stuffed Vegetables

Petits Farcis à la Façon du Vieux Nice

✳

A few (fewer and fewer!) restaurants hidden in the back streets of Nice's old town still serve this quintessentially Provençal dish. It is easy to prepare, but takes a long time, so you'll need patience. But I assure you that the results are worth the effort. Incidentally, nothing is stopping you from preparing more of one vegetable and less—or none—of another; create your own assortment.

Farcis are best eaten at the foot of an ocher façade, beneath a big green parasol, in sight of a fig tree and a fountain. They are a taste of nearby Italy.

FOR 4 SERVINGS

Preparation: 2 hours
Cooking time: 20 minutes

Tomatoes
1 tablespoon rice
4 small tomatoes
1 tablespoon sausage meat
4 fresh basil leaves, chopped
Salt and freshly ground black pepper
1 tablespoon butter

Zucchini
1 large firm zucchini
1 tablespoon olive oil
1 tablespoon heavy cream
1 egg yolk
1 tablespoon finely diced red bell pepper
1 tablespoon grated Parmesan cheese
1 tablespoon dry unseasoned bread crumbs
Salt and freshly ground black pepper

Artichokes
4 small artichokes
Juice of 1 lemon
1½ tablespoons finely diced carrot
2 tablespoons chopped onion
1 tablespoon butter
Salt
4 black Niçoise olives, pitted
¼ cup olive oil
2 tablespoons white wine

Mushrooms
6 small mushrooms, very finely chopped
1 teaspoon chopped chives
1 tablespoon reduced veal stock
½ garlic clove, minced
Salt and freshly ground black pepper
4 large mushroom caps

Tomatoes
Cook the rice in boiling salted water for 15 minutes, and drain. Do not cool the rice.

Meanwhile, cut off the top of each tomato and set the top aside. Hollow out the tomatoes with a spoon. Thoroughly mix the sausage meat, rice, chopped basil, and salt and pepper to taste. Stuff the tomatoes with this mixture, and replace the tomato tops. Put the tomatoes in an ovenproof dish with the butter.

Zucchini
Cut the zucchini into four 3-inch lengths. With a small teaspoon or melon baller, hollow out the sections, leaving about ½ inch shell. Blanch the zucchini in boiling salted water for 2 minutes, and set aside.

Chop the flesh you have removed and sauté it in olive oil until all liquid has evaporated. Put it into a bowl, and add the cream, egg yolk, diced red bell pepper, Parmesan cheese, and bread crumbs. Add salt and pepper to taste, and mix thoroughly.

Stuff the zucchini with this mix-

ture, and arrange them in a lightly oiled ovenproof dish.

Artichokes
Trim the leaves from the artichoke hearts and remove the hairy choke with a spoon. As you trim each heart, keep it from discoloring by placing it in a bowl of water acidulated with the juice of ½ lemon. Cook the artichoke hearts for 25 minutes in salted water with the juice of ½ lemon.

Meanwhile, cook the carrot and onion in a small, heavy saucepan with the butter. Cook over very low heat, covered, until very tender. Add a little salt.

When the artichoke hearts are done, drain them and top each one with a spoonful of the onion-carrot mixture, then with an anchovy fillet coiled into a circle on top of the stuffing, or half a Niçoise olive. Place the artichokes in a small ovenproof saucepan or baking dish with the olive oil and the white wine.

Mushrooms
Mix the chopped mushrooms, chives, concentrated veal stock,

garlic, and salt and pepper to taste; this stuffing should be dry, because the mushrooms will exude quite a bit of juice as they cook.

Stuff the mushroom caps with this mixture, and place them on an oiled baking sheet.

Onions

Peel the onions and blanch them in boiling salted water for about 15 seconds. Drain them and cool them in cold water. Cut the top off each onion, far enough down to enable you to hollow the onions out; leave the 2 outermost layers of flesh intact. Very finely chop the tops and the flesh you have removed, and cook with the olive oil over low heat until the onion is a tender purée and all the juices have evaporated. Put the purée in a bowl and add the egg yolk, cheese, basil, and salt and pepper to taste.

Stuff the onions with this mixture and arrange them in an ovenproof dish with the butter and chicken stock. Top each onion with some of the fried cubes of bread.

Zucchini Blossoms

Cut the eggplant, zucchini, and bell pepper into small cubes and, over medium heat, cook them with the olive oil for about 25 minutes to make a little ratatouille. Add the thyme and salt and pepper to taste.

Fill the zucchini blossoms with this ratatouille and close them around the stuffing with your fingers. Put them into an ovenproof dish with the butter.

Cooking the Farcis

Put all the various baking dishes into a preheated 325 degree oven and cook for 20 minutes.

Pour the juices from all the dishes into a small saucepan, bring to the boil, and add the butter and the chopped basil. Stir well and check for seasoning.

Arrange the stuffed vegetables on a serving platter. Drizzle the sauce over them and garnish with sprigs of fresh chives, basil, or parsley.

Onions
4 medium white onions
1 tablespoon olive oil
1 egg yolk
1 teaspoon grated Swiss
  Gruyère cheese
4 fresh basil leaves,
  chopped
Salt and freshly ground
  black pepper
1 tablespoon butter
2 tablespoons chicken
  stock
2 tablespoons tiny cubes
  of sandwich bread, fried
  in butter

Zucchini Blossoms
1 small eggplant
1 small zucchini
1 small green bell pepper
2 tablespoons olive oil
1 teaspoon fresh thyme
  leaves
Salt and freshly ground
  black pepper
4 zucchini blossoms
1 tablespoon butter

For the Sauce
2 tablespoons butter
2 fresh basil leaves,
  chopped
Salt and freshly ground
  black pepper
Chives, basil, or parsley,
  for garnish

See photograph on pages 212–213.

Orange-Scented Bourride of Vegetables
Bourride de Légumes à l'Orange

✳

The word bourride *generally refers to a kind of bouillabaisse made with white-fleshed fish. But it can also mean the foundation of that soup: an aromatic broth, or court-bouillon,* thickened with aïoli *and potatoes. Here, I fill it out with an assortment of other vegetables.*

For 4 servings

Preparation: 45 minutes
Cooking time: 40 minutes

4 medium carrots
4 medium turnips
4 small artichokes
4 small leeks, white part
  only
1 celery heart
¼ pound green beans
¼ pound fresh spinach
2 medium potatoes
1 medium onion
1 orange (not sprayed with
  chemicals, if possible)

Aïoli
2 egg yolks
½ potato, cooked
2 garlic cloves
1 cup olive oil
Salt and freshly ground
  black pepper

Bouquet garni
1 dried fennel stalk, or
  ½ teaspoon fennel
  seeds tied in a bundle
  of cheesecloth
A sprig of fresh thyme
3 parsley stems
1 bay leaf

5 tablespoons olive oil
6½ cups chicken stock
Salt and freshly ground
  black pepper
2 medium tomatoes (not
  too ripe)
4 egg yolks
2 tablespoons chopped
  parsley

⅜-inch slices of day-old
French bread (*baguette*),
dry but not toasted

Prepare the vegetables. Peel the carrots and turnips; trim the leaves from the artichoke hearts and remove the hairy choke with a spoon. Trim the leeks, wash them very carefully, and tie them in a bundle with string; cut the celery heart in quarters lengthwise and wash it. Trim the ends of the beans, string them, and wash them. Stem the spinach and wash it carefully. Peel the potatoes and cut them into ⅜-inch slices. Peel and chop the onion.

With a vegetable peeler, remove 2 strips of orange zest, avoiding the white pith.

Make an *aïoli* sauce using the listed ingredients, following the recipe on page 26. Assemble the *bouquet garni*.

In a wide, shallow pan or casserole, heat the olive oil over medium heat and cook the onion. When it begins to turn golden, add the chicken stock, *bouquet garni*, and orange zest. Bring to the boil and add coarse salt to taste (salt lightly if your stock is already salted).

Add the carrots, turnips, artichokes, leeks, celery and potatoes and cook over low heat for 25 or 30 minutes, covered.

Meanwhile, cook the green beans in boiling salted water for 10 minutes, then cool them in cold water.

Preheat the oven to 150 degrees and put in 4 soup plates to warm. Cut the tomatoes into thick slices.

Check the vegetables with the point of a small knife. They should be tender but still slightly firm. At that point, add the tomatoes, then, a minute later, the spinach.

When the spinach is cooked (a minute or two), turn off the heat. Use a skimmer or slotted spoon to remove the vegetables to the heated soup plates. Put the green beans back into the stock to warm, then drain them and add to the other vegetables. Put the plates back into the oven.

Put half the *aïoli* into a large bowl and whisk in the egg yolks. Add 2 cups of the hot vegetable broth, whisking continuously. Pour this mixture back into the soup pan and reheat over low heat, continuing to whisk continuously to prevent the eggs from scrambling.

When the soup starts to thicken to a creamy consistency—but definitely before it returns to the boil—remove the pan from the heat and strain the soup through a fine sieve.

Ladle some of this soup over each plateful of vegetables and garnish with chopped parsley.

Serve very hot, with the slices of bread and the remaining aïoli on the side, so diners can spread the bread with *aïoli* and dip it in their soup.

Three-Vegetable Quiche with Thyme
Quiche aux Trois Légumes et au Thym

✳

Serve this quiche as the first course of an elegant dinner. It takes some time—and a little skill—to make, but the result should meet all your expectations.

FOR 4 SERVINGS

Preparation: 1 hour
Resting time: 90 minutes
Cooking time: 65 minutes

For the Pastry (pâte brisée)
7 tablespoons butter
1⅓ cups all-purpose flour
1 egg yolk
Salt

14 ounces white
　mushrooms
3 tablespoons butter
Salt and freshly ground
　black pepper
2 small eggplants
　(11 ounces total)
6 tablespoons olive oil
A pinch of thyme leaves
5 or 6 medium tomatoes
　(18 ounces total)
½ small garlic clove,
　chopped
9 ounces spinach
A pinch of freshly grated
　nutmeg
1 cup heavy cream
2 eggs

Prepare the pastry. Soften the butter at room temperature or over tepid water. Make a well in the flour and put in the egg yolk, salt, and butter. With your fingertips, combine the ingredients; keep handling to a minimum. Form the dough into a ball, wrap it in a towel or plastic wrap, and refrigerate it for at least 1 hour.

Trim the base of the mushroom stems. Rinse the mushrooms quickly and dry them with paper towels. Cut them into thin slices.

Preheat the oven to 400 degrees.

Heat 1 tablespoon of butter in a skillet; add the mushrooms and salt to taste. Cook over high heat until the mushroom liquid has boiled away completely. Set aside in a cool place.

Peel the eggplant and cut it into slices 3/16 inch thick. Oil a baking sheet and arrange the eggplant slices in a single layer. Sprinkle them with salt, olive oil, and thyme. Bake for about 10 minutes, or until the eggplant slices have softened but not browned. Set aside in a cool place. Turn the oven down to 375 degrees.

Peel the tomatoes. Remove their stems and place them in boiling water for 15 seconds. Cool them in a bowl of cold water; the skins should slip off easily. Cut them in half crosswise and squeeze out the seeds and liquid. Cut into large dice.

Heat 1 tablespoon of butter in a skillet; when it turns golden, add the tomatoes. Raise the heat to high, season with salt and pepper to taste, and completely boil away the liquid from the tomatoes. Add the garlic, stir well, and pour the tomatoes into a fine strainer to drain any remaining juices.

Stem the spinach and carefully wash it in 2 or 3 changes of water; drain it and dry it with a towel.

Heat another tablespoon of butter in a skillet; when it begins to turn golden, add the spinach leaves. Season with salt, pepper, and nutmeg. Cook over high heat until all the spinach juices have boiled away, less than 1 minute. Set aside in a cool place.

Roll out the pastry and line a 9- or 10-inch tart pan with high sides. Prick the bottom with a fork, and refrigerate for 30 minutes.

With a whisk, mix the cream and eggs; add salt and pepper to taste.

Remove the pastry-lined tart pan from the refrigerator. Put in the mushrooms, then the eggplant. Pour in one-third of the cream-egg mixture, and bake for about 20 minutes.

Mix the tomatoes and spinach with the remaining cream-egg mixture. Pour this into the quiche and bake for another 20 minutes.

Remove the quiche from the oven and let it rest for 10 minutes before unmolding it—carefully, to avoid breaking the crust. Serve hot, warm, or cold.

Vegetable Stir-Fry with Sesame Oil

Sauté Minute de Légumes à l'Huile de Sésame

✳

This Chinese-influenced dish will let you see vegetables in another light: fresh, crisp, vividly colorful. The whole cooking process must take less than 10 minutes, otherwise the vegetables will become too soft. Note that the recipe is for two servings: if you try to make it in larger quantities the texture will suffer. If you need to feed more than two people, divide the ingredients among several pans.

Peel, wash, and drain the carrot, onion, and celery, and dry them thoroughly in paper towels; cut into very thin slices. Shred the cabbage and chop the garlic, keeping them separate from the others.

Heat the corn oil in a wide casserole, skillet, or wok over very high heat. When the oil begins to smoke, add the carrot, onion, celery, and ginger. Sprinkle with a little salt and stir well.

After 5 minutes, add the cabbage (be sure it is thoroughly dry) and the garlic. Stir well and continue to cook, uncovered, over high heat. Three or 4 minutes later, add the sesame oil, soy sauce, and butter.

Season with salt and pepper to taste and garnish with coriander leaves.

FOR 2 SERVINGS

Preparation: 20 minutes
Cooking time: 9 minutes

1 medium carrot
1/2 medium onion
1 celery stalk
1/2 small cabbage (about 9 ounces)
2 garlic cloves
3 tablespoons corn oil
A 1-inch chunk of fresh ginger
Salt and freshly ground black pepper
1 teaspoon roasted sesame oil
1 tablespoon soy sauce
2 tablespoons butter
A handful of fresh coriander

Baked Summer Vegetables with Two Cheeses

Tian de Légumes d'Eté aux Deux Fromages

✳

When you cut into this rustic dish, it will exude the aromas of the Provençal countryside. For a complete summer meal, make it and serve it in a dish that resembles a southern French tian—a glazed earthenware baking dish. It is flavorful enough to stand on its own, but it would also be delicious with a few sautéed veal scallopini.

FOR 4 SERVINGS

Preparation: 45 minutes
Cooking time: 90 minutes

2 large onions (10 ounces total)
5 tablespoons olive oil
1 large firm eggplant (1 pound)
3 medium zucchini (1 pound total)
3 medium tomatoes (1 pound total)
½ pound mozzarella cheese
2 garlic cloves
1 teaspoon oregano leaves
Salt and freshly ground black pepper
3 tablespoons grated Parmesan cheese

Preheat the oven to 400 degrees.

Peel the onions, cut them into thin slices, and cook them in a saucepan with 3 tablespoons of olive oil, over moderately low heat, until they begin to turn lightly golden.

Peel the eggplant and cut into ¼-inch-thick slices. Grease a baking sheet with a little olive oil, sprinkle it with salt, and arrange the eggplant slices in a single layer. Bake for 5 or 10 minutes, or until the eggplant slices have softened but not browned.

Reduce the oven temperature to 325 degrees.

With a vegetable peeler, remove strips of peel from the zucchini, leaving alternate stripes of peeled and unpeeled flesh. Cut into rounds ³/₁₆ inch thick.

Wash and dry the tomatoes, remove their stems, and cut them into slices ³/₁₆ inch thick.

Cut the mozzarella in half, then into slices of the same thickness as the vegetables.

Peel and finely chop the garlic and mix it into the cooked onions; add the oregano leaves. Spread this onion mixture into a 12-inch square baking dish.

Arrange the eggplant, zucchini, tomatoes, and mozzarella on top of the onions: 1 slice of eggplant, then 1 of zucchini, 1 of tomato, 1 of mozzarella, and so forth. Stand the slices on their edges rather than laying them flat.

Sprinkle with salt and pepper and with the remaining olive oil.

Bake for about 1 hour. The vegetable juices should have evaporated and the vegetables should have begun to caramelize.

Press down the vegetables with a fork, sprinkle with grated Parmesan, and bake for another 10 to 15 minutes.

Serve in the baking dish, either hot or cold; this dish reheats perfectly well.

Pie of Tiny Vegetables with Lettuce

Pie de Petits Légumes aux Feuilles de Laitue

✳

A melange of baby vegetables under a golden crust: as beautiful as it is delicious, because all the vegetables I've chosen for this dish will keep their bright color as the pie cooks. Put the pie together in advance and refrigerate it before baking, because the results will be all the better if the crust has had plenty of time to rest.

FOR 4 SERVINGS

Preparation: 30 minutes
Resting time: 1 hour
Cooking time: 1 hour

For the Pastry
7 tablespoons butter
Salt
1 1/3 cups all-purpose
   flour

For the Filling
4 ounces baby carrots
4 ounces baby turnips
4 ounces baby zucchini
4 ounces tiny new
   potatoes
2 tablespoons butter
4 ounces white pearl
   onions
1 teaspoon sugar
Salt and freshly ground
   black pepper
1 small head of lettuce
1/2 cup shelled peas
   (about 11 ounces in the
   pod)
1/2 cup shelled young
   fava beans (about 14
   ounces in the pod)
3 tablespoons heavy
   cream
2 tablespoons chopped
   parsley
1 egg

Make the pastry. Put the butter, 1/2 cup water, and a pinch of salt in a saucepan and heat until the butter is completely melted. Put the flour into the bowl of an electric mixer, add the hot butter mixture, and mix at low speed until well blended. (Alternatively, use a wooden spoon or rubber spatula in a large mixing bowl.)

Put the dough on a plate, cover it with plastic wrap, and refrigerate it for at least 1 hour.

Peel the baby vegetables. If some are much larger than the others, trim them so that all the pieces are more or less the same size.

Melt the butter in a heavy casserole, and add the pearl onions and carrots. Sprinkle with the sugar and some salt, cover the pan, and cook over low heat for 10 minutes. Add the turnips, zucchini, and potatoes. Put the lid back on the casserole and cook over very low heat for another 15 minutes, until all the vegetables are tender. The steam from the vegetables' own juices should be enough to cook them; if not, add a few spoonfuls of hot water.

Meanwhile, separate the leaves of the lettuce, wash them, and dry them well in a towel.

When the vegetables are cooked,

add the peas, fava beans, and cream. Bring to the boil, turn off the heat, season with salt and pepper to taste, and allow to cool.

When they are cold, put the vegetables into an oval earthenware or china dish about 2 1/2 inches deep. They should fill the dish by three-fourths and no more. Sprinkle with the chopped parsley and cover with the lettuce leaves.

Break the egg into a small bowl, add a tablespoon of cold water, and beat well with a fork or a small whisk.

Put the dough on a well-floured board and roll it thin (less than 1/8 inch thick). Cut out an oval large enough to cover the pie dish plus a 3/8-inch overhang.

Brush some beaten egg onto the border of the pie dish and lay the pastry oval on top of the dish, pressing well with your fingers to make it adhere to the edge. Brush the surface of the pastry with beaten egg.

Use the excess pastry to make some decorations in the shape of leaves and arrange them on the pie crust; the egg wash will hold them in place. Brush the decorations with beaten egg.

Put the pie in the refrigerator

for at least 15 minutes to firm the pastry.

Preheat the oven to 400 degrees.

Place the pie dish on a baking sheet and bake for 10 minutes, then reduce the oven temperature to 350 degrees and bake for another 20 minutes.

When done, transfer the pie dish to a platter lined with a folded napkin and serve hot.

A Fricassée from My Father's Garden
Fricassée du Jardin de mon Père

✳

My love for vegetables dates from when I was a tiny child and tasted this fricassée for the first time, its ingredients straight from my father's garden. For the best results you should ideally go out to your own vegetable garden and pick what you need, either at dawn or after the sun has set. But if you can get up early and visit a local farmers' market first thing in the morning, you should be able to get wonderfully fresh vegetables.

One thing: Eat this dish all by itself. It is perfectly capable of standing on its own.

If you are using salt pork or pancetta, blanch it in boiling water for 2 minutes.

Remove the outermost layer from the onions; cut off the roots and, if you are using spring onions, the green shoots. Wipe with a towel.

Rinse the lettuces under cold water and drain on a towel. Leave them whole.

Scrape the carrots with a small knife to remove their delicate skin; cut off the roots and leaves. Leave them whole, and simply wipe them with a towel to clean them.

Cut off the roots and leaves of the turnips and peel them with a vegetable peeler. Leave them whole, and simply wipe them with a towel to clean them.

Discard any peas that are too large. Do not wash them.

Rub the potatoes with your fingers under cold running water to clean them. (Do not leave them to soak in water.) Dry them in a towel.

Put a teaspoon of butter and the bacon strips into a heavy casserole. Sauté, stirring constantly, for 2 or 3 minutes, but do not let the bacon brown.

Add the onions, carrots, turnips, peas, and potatoes, along with $1/4$ cup cold water and the salt. Stir well. Place the lettuces on top of the vegetables, cover the casserole, and cook over medium-low heat for 20 to 30 minutes. To tell whether the fricassée is done, use the potatoes as a gauge: when the point of a small knife pierces them easily, everything will be fully cooked.

When the vegetables are done, add the remaining butter. Taste for salt and—most important—serve immediately. This dish will not wait.

FOR 4 SERVINGS

Preparation: 30 minutes
Cooking time: 30 minutes

5 ounces unsmoked bacon (or salt pork or pancetta), cut into matchstick pieces
12 small white pearl onions
4 small lettuces
About 20 baby carrots
About 20 baby turnips
2 cups very small peas (about $3 1/4$ pounds in the pod)
8 or 9 very small new potatoes (9 ounces)
5 tablespoons butter
1 teaspoon salt

Baby Carrots and Turnips with Garlic Cloves
Casserole de Carottes et de Navets aux Gousses d'Ail

✳

OPPOSITE PAGE:
Baby Carrots and Turnips with Garlic Cloves

The whole point of this very simple recipe is the quality of the vegetables, which must be extremely fresh and tender. It is probably best to wait for springtime, when you are most likely to find baby carrots and turnips at their peak.

FOR 4 SERVINGS

Preparation: 30 minutes
Cooking time: 45 minutes

Cloves from 2 large heads
  of garlic (3½ ounces)
9 ounces baby carrots
5 ounces baby turnips
3 tablespoons butter
1 teaspoon sugar
Salt and freshly ground
  black pepper
3 tablespoons coarsely
  chopped parsley

Peel the garlic and put into a saucepan with 1 quart of cold salted water. Bring to the boil and cook for 2 or 3 minutes. Drain the garlic. Repeat this procedure 4 times more. Set the garlic aside.

Peel the carrots and the turnips (if they are very young and tender, the carrots should need only to be scraped with a knife to remove their fine skin). Put them into a heavy saucepan with ¼ cup of water, a pinch of salt, 2 tablespoons of butter, and the sugar. Cover and cook over medium-low heat for 15 minutes. Remove the lid, raise the heat to high, and completely reduce the cooking juices.

Put the remaining tablespoon of butter in a skillet over medium heat; when it begins to turn golden, add the garlic and sauté it until lightly golden. Add the garlic to the carrots and turnips.

Season with salt and pepper, sprinkle with parsley, and serve in a warmed serving dish.

Roasted Caramelized Vegetables
Compotée de Légumes Confits

✳

FOR 4 TO 6 SERVINGS

Preparation: 30 minutes
Cooking time: 2 hours
  5 minutes

1 sweet potato
1 large potato
10 garlic cloves
6 large tomatoes
½ teaspoon marjoram
  leaves
½ teaspoon savory
  leaves
¼ cup chopped parsley
6 tablespoons grated
  Parmesan cheese
2 medium-small eggplants
Salt and freshly ground
  black pepper

(continued on page 228)

I simply have to share this recipe—it has given me great pleasure ever since my friend Antoinette first made it for me in the glorious village of Saint-Clair, near le Lavandou.

Preheat the oven to 400 degrees.

Peel the potato, sweet potato, and garlic. Remove the stems from the tomatoes and blanch tomatoes in boiling water for 15 seconds; remove the skins and set aside.

Put the marjoram, savory, parsley, garlic, and 4 tablespoons of the Parmesan cheese into a blender or food processor; blend until finely chopped.

Generously grease an 8- or 9-inch heatproof charlotte mold or casserole with olive oil; add the remaining 2 tablespoons of grated Parmesan and shake to coat the bottom and sides.

(continued from page 226)

10 tablespoons olive oil
2 red bell peppers
2 medium zucchini
2 large onions
1 sprig each of savory and
   marjoram, for garnish

Cut the eggplants lengthwise into
$^1/_8$- to $^1/_4$-inch slices, and line the
mold with these slices.

Cut the potato and sweet potato
into $^1/_8$-inch slices and layer them
into the mold on top of the eggplant.

Add salt and pepper, then one-third
of the garlic-herb mixture. Sprinkle
with 2 tablespoons of olive oil.

Peel and seed the bell peppers and
cut them into strips; add them to the
charlotte mold.

Cut the zucchini into $^1/_8$-inch
slices and layer them into the mold
on top of the peppers. Top with a
third of the garlic-herb mixture, add
salt and pepper, and sprinkle with
another 2 tablespoons of olive oil.

Cut the onions into thin slices
and add them to the mold.

Cut the tomatoes in half crosswise
and squeeze out the seeds and juice.
Chop them roughly and mix in the

remaining garlic-herb mixture and
some salt and pepper. Add the tomatoes to the charlotte mold and sprinkle with the remaining olive oil,
leaving just enough to grease a circle
of parchment paper or waxed paper
the diameter of the mold.

Lay the greased paper on top of
the charlotte mold, cover very tightly
with its lid or with aluminum foil,
and bake for 30 minutes.

Lower the oven temperature to
225 degrees and leave for $1^1/_2$ hours.

At the end of that time, remove
the mold from the oven and place it
on top of the range, over high heat,
for about 2 minutes to brown the
bottom thoroughly. Unmold onto a
serving platter.

Spoon away the excess oil and
decorate the top with a sprig each
of savory and marjoram, arranged
crosswise.

Vegetable Barigoule with Garden Herbs
Barigoule de Légumes aux Herbes du Jardin

✳

The Provençal word barigoule *originally referred to a type of wild mushroom (the*
Lactarius deliciosus, *or saffron milkcap, which looks something like a chan-*
terelle) and hence to a way of preparing it—the same way used for tiny artichokes.
This old southern French recipe deserves to be revived; it is a happy blend of the
untamed flavors of the thickets and scrubland with those of a Provençal garden.

FOR 4 SERVINGS

Preparation: 30 minutes
Cooking time: 50 minutes

1 medium carrot
12 white pearl onions
6 tablespoons olive oil
$3^1/_2$ ounces salt-pork rind
   (optional)
3 garlic cloves
A sprig of thyme
A sprig of savory
$^1/_2$ cup dry white wine
Salt and freshly ground
   black pepper

(continued on page 229)

Peel and slice the carrot; peel the
pearl onions. Put them into a heavy
saucepan with 2 tablespoons of olive
oil and cook over low heat until the
onions begin to turn golden.

If you are using it, blanch the salt-
pork rind in boiling water for 3 minutes; drain.

Peel and slice the garlic and add it

to the carrot and onions along with
the sprigs of thyme and savory, the
salt-pork rind, a generous tablespoon
of olive oil, the white wine, and a few
tablespoons of water. Add a little salt,
cover the saucepan, and cook over
low heat for 20 minutes.

Meanwhile, prepare the basil
liaison. Crush the garlic to a purée

and blend it with the basil, olive oil, and pepper.

Trim away the outermost two or three layers of leaves from the baby artichokes. Cut off ³/₄ inch of the tips, and trim the stems to ³/₄ inch; peel the remaining stems with a vegetable peeler. Cut the artichokes in half lengthwise and dip them for a moment in some cold water acidulated with the lemon juice.

Trim the asparagus, leaving only 2¹/₂ or 3 inches of the tips. Wash in cold water and drain.

Remove the outer layer from the little scallions; keep only the white parts. Rinse quickly in cold water and drain.

Trim the ends of the mushroom stems; if they are very dirty, rinse them quickly and drain immediately, but if they are reasonably clean just wipe them with a damp cloth.

When the pearl onion mixture has cooked for 20 minutes, remove the rind and herbs; add the scallions and artichokes. Replace the lid and cook over very low heat for 10 minutes. Add the asparagus tips and cook for another 10 minutes or so. Check all the vegetables with the point of a small knife: they should be tender all the way through.

While the vegetables are cooking, salt the mushrooms and sauté them over high heat in the remaining 3 tablespoons of olive oil until all their liquid has completely reduced. Drain the mushrooms and add them to the saucepan with the other vegetables when these are done.

With the lid off, reduce the cooking juices until they have become slightly syrupy in consistency.

With a slotted spoon, divide the vegetables among 4 heated plates.

Add the basil liaison to the reduced cooking juices. Check for salt and spoon over the vegetables.

Garnish each plate with fresh basil, chervil, parsley, and coriander.

This dish can be served hot or lukewarm, as you prefer.

For the Basil Liaison
1 garlic clove
3 tablespoons chopped fresh basil
3 tablespoons olive oil
Freshly ground black pepper

8 baby artichokes
Juice of ¹/₂ lemon
24 asparagus spears
8 very thin scallions
6 ounces chanterelles or *Lactarius* mushrooms
Fresh basil, chervil, parsley, and coriander, for garnish

Basil-Scented Tiny Vegetables

Pistou de Petits Légumes

✳

A delicate, comforting dish: like Provence in the spring. Never, never reheat it, or you'll ruin it; on the other hand, it is delicious lukewarm. Try to get freshly picked young vegetables, but failing that, buy the smallest and tenderest ones you can find.

Peel the carrots, onions, and potatoes. Wash the zucchini and cut off the ends. Stem the spinach, wash it thoroughly, drain it, and dry on a towel.

If the carrots, zucchini, and potatoes are not really baby varieties, cut them into julienne of uniform size. Cut the fennel into strips.

Pour 3 tablespoons of olive oil into a heavy casserole and add the onions and fennel. Cover the pan and cook over low heat for about

Preparation: 30 minutes
Cooking time: 30 minutes

5 ounces carrots
4 ounces white pearl onions
7 ounces small new potatoes
5 ounces small zucchini
5 ounces spinach

(continued on page 230)

(continued from page 229)

1 head fennel
6 tablespoons olive oil
Salt and freshly ground
    black pepper
2 thyme sprigs
¾ cup shelled peas
    (a little over 1 pound
    in the pod)
2 ripe tomatoes
2 garlic cloves
25 fresh basil leaves

10 minutes. Add the carrots, potatoes, salt to taste and a sprig of thyme, plus ¼ cup warm water.

Cook for another 15 minutes or so, covered, or until the carrots and potatoes can be pierced easily with the point of a knife. Now add the peas and spinach and continue to cook, covered, for another 5 minutes.

Meanwhile, peel the tomatoes: Remove their stems and place them in boiling water for 15 seconds. Cool them in a bowl of cold water; the skins should slip off easily. Cut them in half crosswise and squeeze out the seeds and liquid.

Peel the garlic. Wash the basil leaves carefully and dry them. Put the garlic and basil into a blender along with the remaining 3 tablespoons of olive oil, the tomatoes, and salt and pepper to taste. Blend to a thin purée; if it is not smooth enough, put it through a fine strainer.

Pour off and reserve the vegetable cooking juices. There should be about 4 tablespoons; if there is much more than that, reduce the juices as necessary. Thicken with the tomato-basil-garlic purée and pour onto a heated serving platter. Put the cooked vegetables on top of this sauce, garnish with the remaining sprig of thyme, and serve, hot or lukewarm.

FOR 4 SERVINGS

Preparation: 30 minutes
Cooking time: 20 minutes

4 firm-fleshed potatoes
4 baby artichokes, small
    and fresh enough to
    slice and eat raw
10 tablespoons olive oil
The very pale heart from
    1 head of celery
4 small scallions
⅓ cup small black
    Niçoise olives, pitted
Salt and freshly ground
    black pepper
2 tablespoons chopped
    Italian parsley

OPPOSITE PAGE:
*Potato, Artichoke, and
Olive Salad*

Potato, Artichoke, and Olive Salad

Salade de Pommes de Terre et d'Artichauts aux Olives de Nice

✳

The important elements in this unpretentious dish are the olive oil, which must be very full-flavored and fruity, and the potatoes, which must be firm-fleshed and not ruined by overcooking.

Wash the potatoes but do not peel them. Put them in well-salted cold water, bring to the boil, and cook for about 20 minutes or until tender.

Meanwhile, cut away the outer leaves of the artichokes until you reach the pale, tender interior leaves. Cut the artichokes into thin slices, put them into a bowl, and coat them with 5 tablespoons of olive oil to keep them from discoloring. Pour the remaining olive oil into a large salad bowl.

Wash the celery and scallions, and cut them into thin slices; add them to the artichokes.

When the potatoes are done, peel them while still hot (you can use an oven mitt to hold them) and slice them into the large salad bowl. Add the olives and artichoke mixture, season with salt and pepper to taste, and mix gently to avoid breaking the potatoes. Sprinkle with chopped parsley and serve immediately.

A Simpler Ratatouille
Ratatouille en Trois Coups de Cuiller à Pot

✳

People often avoid cooking ratatouille because it takes so long to prepare well. But this dish will actually save you time, because it is the basis of so many summer recipes, which is why I recommend making plenty. It is excellent with any roast meat, red or white. It is especially good with lamb. My version of the traditional recipe has been designed to make your life simpler. You'll see: nothing could be easier.

FOR 8 TO 10 SERVINGS

Preparation: 30 minutes
Cooking time: 1 hour
  10 minutes

3 white onions
5 green frying peppers
10 tablespoons olive oil
2¼ pounds medium
  eggplants
2¼ pounds medium
  zucchini
2¼ pounds medium
  plum tomatoes
5 garlic cloves

For the Bouquet Garni
1 celery stalk
1 parsley sprig
1 thyme sprig
1 bay leaf

Salt and freshly ground
  black pepper

Preheat the oven to 400 degrees.

Peel the onions; cut the onions and peppers into thin slices. Cook them over medium-low heat in a heavy casserole, covered, with 3 tablespoons olive oil for about 15 minutes. Take care that they do not brown.

Meanwhile, peel the eggplants and cut them into large cubes. Wash and slice the zucchini, but do not peel them.

Put the eggplants and zucchini into 2 separate baking dishes, sprinkle with salt and olive oil, and bake until tender, 15 to 20 minutes.

Remove the stems from the tomatoes, cut them in half, and squeeze out the seeds and juice. Cut them into chunks.

Peel and finely slice the garlic.

Lower the oven temperature to 300 degrees.

Add the zucchini, eggplants, tomatoes, garlic, and the *bouquet garni* to the casserole containing the cooked onions and peppers. Add pepper to taste, cover the casserole, and bake in the oven for about 30 minutes.

Variations: Ratatouille is versatile, and will always be appealing and fresh when you serve it in a new way. It will seem very different when served cold on toasted country bread than when served hot.

Seasonings will also change it. Here are some possibilities: parsley chopped together with garlic and, perhaps, some anchovies; mint chopped with garlic; coriander and garlic; basil and garlic; or little black Niçoise olives and, possibly, sliced hard-boiled eggs and tuna packed in olive oil.

You can also make it into a gratin: spread some ratatouille in a baking dish, sprinkle it with bread crumbs and grated Swiss Gruyère cheese, and bake it in a hot oven.

For a completely different gratin, use a small ladle to make some depressions in the ratatouille, break an egg into each depression, and bake until the eggs are set.

You can also serve ratatouille with scrambled eggs or as the filling for an omelette with herbs mixed into the eggs.

Baby-Vegetable Cakes
Galettes de Légumes Nouveaux

✳

Phyllo dough is used in endless ways in the Middle East. If you think the phyllo dough you've bought is too thin, you can use a double sheet.

Stem the spinach, wash it carefully, and dry it on paper towels.

Peel and lightly crush the garlic and put it into a skillet with 1 teaspoon of butter. Heat over high heat, and when the butter begins to turn golden, add the spinach and sauté, stirring constantly with a wooden spoon, until nearly all the water from the spinach has evaporated. Season with salt and pepper to taste. Remove the garlic clove and put the spinach into a strainer over a bowl to collect any remaining juices.

Peel the pearl onions and carrots. Put them into a small casserole with a teaspoon of butter, a pinch of salt, the sugar, and a sprig of thyme. Add water to cover and cook over medium heat until all the water has boiled away, about 10 minutes. Continue to cook the onions and carrots until golden, then put them on a plate. Remove the thyme.

Blanch the peas in boiling salted water for a few seconds; drain.

Cut away the outer leaves of the baby artichokes until you reach the pale, tender leaves of the heart. Cut the artichokes lengthwise into quarters and put them immediately into some cold water acidulated with half the lemon juice.

Preheat the oven to 525 degrees.

Put the olive oil into a casserole with the remaining lemon juice and add the artichokes. Season with salt and pepper and add a sprig of savory. Cover the casserole and cook over medium-low heat for about 10 minutes. Set the artichokes aside.

Melt the remaining butter in a small saucepan.

Place 4 small tart rings (5 to 6 inches in diameter) on a baking sheet. Brush the phyllo sheets generously with melted butter and lay them into the tart rings, letting the excess dough hang over the edges (you will be folding it over the filling). Save the remaining butter for the sauce.

Put a layer of spinach in each pastry, then arrange the carrots, onions, peas, and artichokes on top. Fold the excess dough over the filling, place in the oven, and bake for 8 minutes.

Meanwhile, bring to the boil the juice that drained from the spinach. Put it into a blender along with the remaining melted butter and the basil leaves; blend thoroughly to make a lovely, vivid green sauce.

When the cakes are done, put them on 4 heated plates. Garnish with sprigs of thyme and savory and a cherry tomato. Neatly pour some basil sauce around each vegetable cake.

FOR 4 SERVINGS

Preparation: 30 minutes
Cooking time: 1 hour

5 ounces spinach
1 garlic clove
4 tablespoons butter
Salt and freshly ground
  black pepper
20 pearl onions
20 baby carrots
A pinch of sugar
5 thyme sprigs
1 cup shelled peas
  (a little over 1 pound
  in the pod)
6 tiny artichokes
Juice of 1 lemon
2 tablespoons olive oil
5 savory sprigs
4 sheets phyllo dough, or
  8 if very thin
20 fresh basil leaves
4 cherry tomatoes

Tangy Mixed Vegetables in Vinegar
Méli-Mélo de Légumes Piquants au Vinaigre

✳

For 6 servings

Preparation: 20 minutes
Marination time: 3 to
    4 weeks

2 medium tender carrots
¼ chayote
2 small white onions
2 pale celery stalks
½ red bell pepper
½ green bell pepper
¼ medium cucumber
¼ head cauliflower
2 small green tomatoes
1 garlic clove
1 small hot chili pepper
1 bay leaf
½ teaspoon coarse sea salt
1 quart distilled white
    vinegar

See photograph on page 249.

This is less a dish than a wonderful condiment to serve with cold meat, pâtés, sausages, and fish. You should add new vegetables from time to time, even if you don't have everything in the recipe on hand, because the vegetables will lose their crunch after a long soak in the vinegar.

Peel the carrots, chayote, and onions. Cut the cucumber in half lengthwise and remove the seeds.

Cut the carrots, chayote, celery, bell peppers, and cucumbers into strips. Divide the cauliflower into florets.

Thoroughly wash and dry a 2-quart crock or glass jar. Add all the vegetables, plus the garlic, chili pepper, bay leaf, and sea salt. Fill with vinegar.

Tightly seal the crock or jar and leave it for 3 to 4 weeks in a cool, dark place.

Molded Vegetable Gratin
as Served in Mougins
Gratin de Légumes Mouginois

✳

For 6 to 8 servings

Preparation: 1 hour
Cooking time: 40 min-
    utes, then 1 hour
    10 minutes
Resting time: 5 to 6 hours

4 very ripe plum tomatoes
1 small fennel bulb
15 tablespoons olive oil
2 medium white onions
3½ ounces spinach
1½ red bell peppers
1 medium eggplant
1 small zucchini
3 garlic cloves
1 teaspoon thyme leaves
A sprig of savory
A sprig of rosemary
4 sage leaves
Salt and freshly ground
    black pepper

This dish takes a while to prepare—though it is not difficult—but you can put it together in advance. So please do try it. It is both beautiful and delicious and will bring you a ray of Mougins sunlight—especially if you sauce it with a good tomato coulis, perhaps scented with star anise.

Peel the tomatoes. Remove the stems and place them in boiling water for 15 seconds. Cool them in a bowl of cold water; the skins should slip off easily. Cut them in half crosswise and squeeze out the seeds and liquid. Chop them roughly, sprinkle with salt, and put in a strainer to drain.

Trim and slice the fennel. In a covered casserole, cook it for 40 min- utes with 2 tablespoons of olive oil, water to cover, and some salt. Then remove the lid and completely reduce all the cooking liquid. Set the fennel aside.

Peel and slice the onions; cook them in the same way as the fennel, with 2 tablespoons of olive oil and 2 tablespoons of water, but for only 20 minutes; remove the lid and completely reduce all the cooking liquid. Set the onions aside.

Stem the spinach and wash and drain it thoroughly. Heat 3 tablespoons of olive oil in a skillet over high heat. When it begins to smoke, add the spinach plus salt to taste. Sauté until all liquid has completely reduced. Drain in a strainer or colander.

Char the peppers under the broiler or over a gas flame. When they are blackened all over, wrap them in newspaper; they will continue to steam as they cool. Leave until completely cool and remove the skin with your fingers. Remove the stems, seeds, and internal membranes, and drain the flesh on paper towels.

Heat 3 tablespoons of olive oil in a skillet over medium-high heat. Add the tomatoes and cook until all their juices have reduced. Return them to the strainer in which they had been draining.

Preheat the oven to 425 degrees.

Peel the eggplant and cut lengthwise into slices a little less than $^1/_4$ inch thick. Spread some oil on a baking sheet, sprinkle it with salt, and arrange the eggplant slices on it in a single layer. Drizzle with olive oil and sprinkle lightly with salt. Bake for 10 minutes and transfer the eggplant to a plate (it could take

on a metallic flavor if left on the baking sheet).

Do the same for the zucchini, but do not peel them.

Reduce the oven temperature to 300 degrees.

Peel and finely chop the garlic, and mix it with the thyme.

Add half the garlic mixture to the tomatoes and half to the cooked fennel.

Oil a deep 7- or 8-inch springform pan (such as a cheesecake pan) with olive oil. Lay the sprigs of savory and rosemary and the sage leaves in the pan. Line the bottom and sides of the pan with alternating, overlapping pieces of pepper and zucchini.

Layer the pan with the fennel, half the eggplant, the spinach, and then the remaining peppers and zucchini. Continue with the onions, tomatoes, and finally the remaining eggplant. Season to taste with salt and pepper.

Cover the pan with aluminum foil and bake for 1 hour and 10 minutes.

Remove the pan from the oven, weight the vegetables with 2 or 3 plates, and leave to cool for 5 or 6 hours. Unmold onto a serving platter.

You can serve this dish at room temperature or reheat it in the microwave oven.

PAGES 236–237:
A springtime lunch under the olive trees, featuring the first vegetables of spring.

All-Vegetable Menus

In this book, I've done my best to present the broadest possible range of vegetable recipes from which you can draw ideas for menus completely composed of vegetable dishes. You can choose them according to the season, the circumstances, the quality of available produce, and the style and tastes of your dinner guests.

But don't forget that an all-vegetable menu must be as well balanced as a traditional one; it should include one or two light appetizers, a more substantial main course, and a dessert.

Menus are better for being organized around a theme. This gives them a coherence and unity that please both the mind and the palate. Choosing a theme also gives you the opportunity to harmonize the table setting with the menu.

Here are some menus that I like because they evoke my favorite regions of France. My friends have enjoyed them very much. But do not be shy about devising your own menus. All the recipes in this book are at your disposal.

A Menu for a Country House
✴

Potato, Artichoke, and Olive Salad (page 230)
Salade de Pommes de Terre et d'Artichauts aux Olives de Nice
Baked Summer Vegetables with Two Cheeses
(page 222)
Tian de Légumes d'Eté aux Deux Fromages
Spinach with Goat Cheese Toasts (page 118)
Epinards aux Croûtons de Rigotte

A white Châteauneuf-du-Pape (Domaine Clos des Papes), with its straw-yellow color and its forceful aroma combining honey and toasty notes, and its full and well-balanced flavors, will be wonderful with the potato-artichoke salad and the summer vegetables.

A Sun-Drenched Menu
✴

Zucchini and Pearl Onions with Cardamom (page 66)
Courgettes et Petits Oignons à la Cardamome
Eggplant Gratin Vieux Peygros (page 51)
Gratin d'Aubergines du Vieux Peygros
Carrot Cake with Apricots (page 166)
Gâteau de Carottes aux Abricots

With the zucchini and the eggplant, the ideal wine is a Clos Saint-Joseph, a nicely balanced red wine from near Nice. It has a strong garnet color and is vivid and deep in flavor. Its pleasantly straightforward aroma is redolent of berries. A sumptuous accompaniment to the Carrot Cake with Apricots is a Muscat de Beaumes-de-Venise from the Domaine de Durban. You will be dazzled by its golden color; its elegant, powerful aroma with mango, mint, and citrus notes; and its balance—freshness over a rich liqueur foundation.

A Menu from Old Nice
✴

Eggplant with Black-Olive Stuffing (page 43)
Aubergines Farcies aux Olives Noires
Caramelized Sautéed Tomatoes (page 79)
Tomates Estrancinnées
Old-Fashioned Nice-Style Stuffed Vegetables
(page 216)
Petits Farcis à la Façon du Vieux Nice
Swiss Chard Pie Niçoise (page 88)
Tourte de Blettes à la Niçoise

Drink a salmon-pink Bellet rosé with the eggplant and the tomatoes; it is a lively wine full of exotic aromas, and silky and fresh to the taste. The stuffed vegetables and the chard pie call for a warm-tasting, gently spicy wine, such as a red Coteaux des Baux (Domaine de Trévallon) with its fine dense color, and its engaging aroma—simultaneously elegant and powerful.

An Island Menu
✴

Hearts of Palm with Ginger (page 200)
Coeurs de Palmier Dorés au Gingembre
Chayote and Sweet Potatoes Stewed with
Coconut and Curry (page 202)
*Compotée de Chayotes et de Patates Douces
au Curry-Coco*
Roasted Plantains with Coconut Cream (page 208)
Plantains Rôtis à la Crème de Coco

The briskness of a classic Bandol—generous, with a long-lasting flavor—will enhance the hearts of palm and the chayote. With the plantains, try a *vin de paille* produced by Rollet: a flashy, rare, and precious wine.

A Menu from the Auvergne
✳

Winter Squash Soup (page 61)
Soupe à la Courge
Celery Hearts with Walnut Oil (page 99)
Coeurs de Céleri à l'Huile de Noix
Gratin of Parsnips and Potatoes (page 178)
Gratin aux Panais et Pommes de Terre
Beets with Orange and Almonds (page 160)
Betteraves Rouges à l'Orange et aux Amandes

Begin on a note of supple strength, by accompanying the soup and the celery with a floral- and honey-scented Saint-Joseph. A red Bellet will mate to perfection with the richness of the gratin and will also be a lovely drink with the beets.

A Provençal Menu
✳

Eggplant Bundles with Tomato Coulis (page 48)
Ballotins d'Aubergines au Coulis de Tomates
Orange-Scented Bourride of Vegetables (page 218)
Bourride de Légumes à l'Orange
Zucchini Pound Cake with Pine Nuts (page 65)
Cake de Courgettes aux Pignons

An elegant Bandol rosé (Moulin des Costes) will nicely counter the gentle sharpness of the eggplant, highlight the delicacy of the Swiss chard in which it is bundled, and serve as a fresh-tasting support for the *bourride* of vegetables. A beautiful end to this meal is to drink a powerful, aristocratic, balanced, spicy wine from the Domaine de Trévallon in the Coteaux d'Aix with the zucchini pound cake.

Childhood Memories
✳

Endives with Almond Cream (page 114)
Endives au Lait d'Amandes Douces
Spinach with Eggs (page 118)
Feuilles d'Epinards aux Oeufs
My Mother's Creamy Gratin of Turnips
and Potatoes (page 175)
Crémée de Navets et de Pommes de Terre de ma Mère
Quinces in Black Currant–Scented Cream (page 211)
Coings à la Crème et aux Feuilles de Cassis

With the endives and spinach, I recommend a young, golden, brilliant, crystal-clear Crozes-Hermitage. You will be charmed by its flowery aroma with hints of citrus, and its big, generous flavor. For the turnips and the quinces, what is needed is the richness of a Côte-Rôtie, with its complex, concentrated aroma of coffee, cocoa, berries, vanilla, and truffles.

A Visit to Lorraine
✳

Three-Vegetable Quiche with Thyme (page 220)
Quiche aux Trois Légumes et au Thyme
Smothered Red Cabbage (page 108)
Fondue de Chou Rouge
Bay-Scented Roasted Potatoes (page 192)
Pommes Rôties au Laurier
Winter Squash and Tapioca Flan (page 59)
Flan de Courge au Tapioca

An Alsatian Pinot Noir would be splendid with the quiche and the red cabbage: a cherry-red wine with a powerful and engaging aroma, and a nice balance that will charm your taste buds. With the squash flan, you will be captivated by a golden *vin de paille* produced by Domaine Chave, with its honey and candied-apricot notes and exotic aftertastes.

And Farther to the North . . .
✳

Brussels Sprouts with Chestnuts (page 110)
Choux de Bruxelles aux Châtaignes
Spiced Braised Leeks (page 142)
Poireaux Braisés aux Epices
Pie of Tiny Vegetables with Lettuce (page 224)
Pie de Petits Légumes aux Feuilles de Laitue
Beets with Red Currants (page 160)
Betteraves aux Baies de Groseilles

With the Brussels sprouts try a deep-purple Chinon, with its aromas of cherry and undergrowth and its supple, balanced, and generous flavor. (Serve it slightly chilled.) The rest of the menu is nice with a red Bandol (from the Domaine Ott), fairly well developed and supple; it will remind you of black currants, raspberries, and red currants and will leave your mouth tasting just delicious.

A Springtime Menu
✳

Baby Artichokes en Barigoule (page 40)
Petits Artichauts Violets en Barigoule
Buttered Young Fava Beans (page 127)
Févettes au Beurre Frais
Baby-Vegetable Cakes (page 233)
Galettes de Légumes Nouveaux
Fennel with Figs Scented with Bay Leaves (page 70)
Cocotte de Fenouil aux Figues et au Laurier

With the artichokes, let me suggest a white Côtes de Provence (from the Maîtres Vignerons de Saint-Tropez) with its green-highlight appearance and its lively, fruity flavor. The fava beans, the vegetable cakes, and the fennel also demand a Côtes de Provence, but a red one this time, with its blackberry, black currant, and licorice notes. Chill it just a bit to highlight its perfectly balanced, supple tannic flavor.

A Winter Menu

✳

Gratin of Leeks with Beaufort Cheese (page 142)
Blancs de Poireaux en Gratin de Beaufort
Cabbage with Mushroom Stuffing (page 105)
Chou Farci aux Champignons
Pumpkin Tart (page 63)
Tarte à la Citrouille

With the leeks, serve the subtle, lively, and balanced flavors of a white Bellet. This wine owes its charm to the variety of grapes from which it is made—the Rolle, which is grown only in the vicinity of Nice. The stuffed cabbage and the pumpkin tart call for a robust wine, such as a red Bandol from the Domaine Tempier. Open it a little while before the meal to allow the air to free up its blackberry, black currant, and licorice aromas.

A Lubéron Menu

✳

Monsieur Jourdan's Zucchini Galette
(page 65)
Galette de Monsieur Jourdan
Scrambled Eggs with Asparagus and Truffles
on a Crisp Shell (page 158)
*Brouillade d'Asperges aux Truffes
en Couronne Croustillante*
Eggplant Cake (page 52)
Gâteau d'Aubergines
Honey-Crusted Spinach Leaves (page 122)
Feuilles d'Epinards en Croûte de Miel

With the first two courses I recommend a fully mature white Hermitage (produced by J.-L. Chave); the Marsanne grape develops wonderfully as it ages in the bottle. A good choice for the eggplant and the spinach is a wine from the Coteaux des Baux—crystalline and brilliant to the eye, and spicy to the nose. This up-front wine combines elegant tannic and almost animal notes with the flavors of berries and candied fruit. If a wine can be said to melt in your mouth, then this one does.

A Cold Buffet Under the Arbor

✳

Tian of Eggplant, Bell Peppers, and Savory (page 54)
Tian d'Aubergines aux Poivrons Doux et à la Sariette
Pumpkin Purée with Olive Oil (page 60)
Purée de Potiron à l'Huile d'Olive
Tomato-Oregano Tarts (page 83)
Tartes aux Tomates et à l'Origan
Braised Radicchio with Anchovies and
Black Olives (page 140)
Trévises Braisées aux Anchois et aux Olives de Nice
Glazed Pearl Onions with Dried Currants (page 182)
Petits Oignons Glacés aux Raisins de Corinthe
A Simpler Ratatouille (page 232)
Ratatouille en Trois Coups de Cuiller à Pot

Serve all these dishes with a bottle of good, fruity olive oil (perhaps from the Les Baux Valley) and thick slabs of grilled country bread (rubbed with garlic for those who like it that way). A basket of fresh fruit will do for dessert. To drink, offer a rosé from Malherbe, a seaside wine with orange-blossom highlights in its color and fruity aromas.

Summer in Provence

✳

Skewered Grilled Asparagus (page 155)
Brochettes de Pointes d'Asperges Grillées
Cauliflower Flans (page 110)
Flans de Chou-Fleur
Basil-Scented Tiny Vegetables (page 229)
Pistou de Petits Légumes
Green Tomato Jam (page 78)
Confiture de Tomates Vertes

The asparagus and cauliflower will be at their most elegant with a white Hermitage produced by Jaboulet. This complex thoroughbred wine will enchant you with its aromas of irises, new-mown hay, unroasted coffee beans, and almonds. The *pistou* and the tomato jam would be good with a Côtes de Provence rosé from the Domaine de Saint-Baillon, fragrant with flowers, peaches, and honey. It is most elegant to drink—seductive and velvety.

OPPOSITE
PAGE:
*Green Tomato
Jam (recipe
on page 78)—
dessert for the
Summer in
Provence Menu
(see page 239).*

PAGES
242–243:
*Golden brown,
crisp summer-
time vegetable
fritters.*

The Right Way to Cook

Vegetables are a true product of the soil and of the labor of patient gardeners. My respect for vegetables obliges me to treat them with the dignity they deserve: painstaking harvesting, careful selection, meticulous trimming, and—above all—the best possible cooking, cooking that does them full justice. All too often, vegetables are the victims of clumsy cooks. For years it had been common to cook them and re-cook them until all their flavor and texture disappeared, until they had been reduced to what could aptly be called a "vegetative state." But in their naïve antagonism to the old practices, the proponents of *nouvelle cuisine* ended up with a result that was just as excruciating. To my mind, a vegetable just briefly exposed to a burst of steam is an abomination that cannot be justified even by the desire for a crunchy texture.

The truth lies elsewhere—with common sense and a love of food. When you cook vegetables, cook them properly. To do this, you need to understand and learn the various techniques, and there is nothing complicated about them.

Cooking in Water

Cooking in water is without question the most common method. Most vegetables can be cooked in this way, apart from some of what I call the sun-drenched vegetables—eggplants, zucchini, tomatoes, and bell peppers—which are much tastier baked, braised, fried, or grilled. But different vegetables require different methods.

Cooking Vegetables in Water

	Boiling Water	Cold Water	Blanc
Artichoke hearts			x
Artichokes	x		
Asparagus	x		
Beets		x	
Belgian endive			x
Broccoli	x		
Cabbage	x		
Cardoons			x
Carrots	x	x	
Cauliflower	x		
Celery root (celeriac)			x
Corn	x		
Fennel			x
Garlic		x	
Green beans	x		
Japanese artichokes (crosnes)			x
Jerusalem artichokes (sunchokes)		x	
Parsnips	x	x	
Peas	x		
Potatoes		x	
Rutabaga		x	
Spinach	x		
Swiss chard stalks			x
Swiss chard greens	x		
Turnips	x	x	
Winter squash	x		

Green vegetables—such as green beans, cabbage, cauliflower, broccoli, asparagus, and spinach—should be poached in boiling salted water. A good two pounds of vegetables require five quarts of water with one or two handfuls of coarse salt. The water should be at a rolling boil; to keep the vegetables green, you should never cover the pan and you should cook only a small quantity at a time. This will let the water return to the boil more quickly, ensuring a firm texture and bright color.

There is still no better way of telling when vegetables are done than to pierce them with the blade of a small knife—or to taste one. When they are done, remove them from the pan with tongs or a skimmer, and plunge them into a bowl of very cold water, possibly containing ice cubes, and then drain them as soon as they are cold.

It is difficult to be precise about cooking times for every vegetable. These vary depending on freshness (the fresher the vegetables are, the less time they take to cook), with size, and on the temperature at which the vegetables were stored. Nonetheless, the table on page 244 will give you some guidelines.

Starchy vegetables such as potatoes, dried beans, and lentils, and some root vegetables such as beets, Jerusalem artichokes (sunchokes), and rutabaga, will toughen if put straight into boiling water. Therefore they should be started in cold salted water and gradually brought to the boil. The rest of the process is the same as for poaching. Other root vegetables such as carrots, turnips, and parsnips can be started in either cold or boiling water.

Finally, some vegetables, when peeled or trimmed, tend to oxidize from contact with air or salted water: the flesh begins to turn black or brown. These vegetables include artichokes, cardoons, the stalks of broad-stemmed Swiss chard, Japanese artichokes (*crosnes*), fennel, salsify and black salsify, Belgian endive, and celery root (celeriac). To retain their appetizing pale color, after peeling them you should immediately place them in a bowl of cold water acidulated with the juice of half a lemon or a tablespoon or two of white vinegar.

Then you should cook the vegetables in a flour-and-water *blanc*. Hold a fine-mesh strainer over a deep pot and place four tablespoons of flour in the strainer. Pour a slow stream of cold water through the flour, stirring with a whisk to make the flour disperse and pass through the strainer. When the pot contains the amount of water you need (three to five quarts for two pounds of vegetables), add the juice of a lemon or a tablespoon of white vinegar, plus a handful of salt. Put the trimmed, washed, and drained vegetables into the pot and turn on the heat. You do not need to cover the pan, but watch it carefully to make sure the flour-and-water mixture does not boil over.

Steaming

All vegetables can be steamed—except for Japanese artichokes (*crosnes*), salsify, black salsify, Swiss chard stalks, cardoons, and artichoke hearts (which will discolor), and eggplant.

Steaming has the advantage of not waterlogging the vegetables and of preserving their texture and flavor. Very aromatic vegetables such as carrots, parsnips, and fennel can lose some of their flavor when boiled; the same is true for zucchini, whose delicate flavor holds up to steaming but loses all its appeal when the vegetable is cooked in water.

Nowadays you can choose among a wide variety of steamers; on the whole, they all yield the same results. Chinese bamboo steamers are easy to find, and they have the advantage that they can be used over any pan of a suitable size. Plus, by stacking several steamers you can cook meat, fish, rice, and vegetables all at the same time—although I don't recommend stacking them more than three high, because the steam grows weaker as it rises and cooking time increases on the uppermost tiers.

If you want to steam several vegetables at once—for an *aïoli*, say—put the longest-cooking vegetables in the bottom steamer, and fill the upper tiers with vegetables needing less cooking time. Here is a suggested arrangement: kohlrabi, celery, white cabbage, potatoes, fennel, and leeks (except very young ones) take the longest. On the second tier could be baby artichokes, carrots, parsnips, cauliflower, turnips, and savoy cabbage. The tenderest, quickest-cooking vegetables are asparagus, broccoli florets, fava beans, green beans, peas, snowpeas, zucchini, spinach, and tomatoes. These can be

Cooking Times in Water
(time after water comes to the boil)

(*For 2 pounds of vegetables*)

Artichoke hearts	20 to 25 minutes
Artichokes	40 to 50 minutes
Asparagus	15 to 20 minutes
Beets	1 hour
Belgian endive	5 to 10 minutes
Broccoli	10 to 15 minutes
Cabbage	10 to 15 minutes
Cardoons	40 to 45 minutes
Carrots (medium)	20 to 25 minutes
Celery root (celeriac)	15 to 20 minutes
Corn	5 to 10 minutes
Fennel	15 to 20 minutes
Garlic	5 to 10 minutes (4 repetitions— see page 146)
Green beans	10 to 15 minutes
Japanese artichokes (*crosnes*)	15 to 20 minutes
Jerusalem artichokes (sunchokes)	15 to 20 minutes
Peas	10 to 15 minutes
Parsnips	20 to 25 minutes
Rutabaga	15 to 20 minutes
Spinach	3 to 5 minutes
Swiss chard stalks	15 to 20 minutes
Swiss chard greens	5 to 10 minutes
Turnips	15 to 20 minutes
Winter squash	10 to 15 minutes

arranged in higher steamers, or can be added to the lower ones when the longer-cooking vegetables are done.

Steamers often do not fit the water pan properly, especially those not made for a particular pan, like bamboo steamers. But you can improvise a tight seal. Make a thin flour-and-water paste and soak a clean dish towel in it. Wrap the towel around the junction between pan and steamer; the heat will quickly set the paste, ensuring a good seal and, hence, the maximum flow of steam up into the food.

Do not bother salting the water; rather, sprinkle the food with coarse sea salt. The condensing steam will gradually melt the salt and thoroughly season the food. On the other hand, you can certainly scent the water with herbs or spices to go with the vegetables you are cooking—for example, bay leaves, thyme, celery, fennel, rosemary, sage, mint, cinnamon, and so forth.

Finally, when the vegetables are done (which you can check by piercing them with the point of a knife), serve them immediately, for they can wilt all too easily. Drizzle your steamed vegetables with olive oil, cream, or your choice of sauces (see "Sauces and *Coulis*," page 15).

And never chill steamed vegetables in cold water before serving them. If you want to use them in a salad, let them cool gradually to room temperature.

Oven Cooking

The advantage of the oven is that it lets you cook vegetables at very low temperatures (250 to 275 degrees) for a very long time. I recommend it for concentrating the sugars of vegetables such as beets and onions. You will also get excellent results from potatoes, eggplant sliced and arranged on an oiled baking sheet, and bell peppers. (See the chapters on those vegetables.)

The oven is also good for braising. Put one or more vegetables into a heavy casserole with very little liquid and cook, covered, at between 300 and 350 degrees; the heat will surround the food and will rob it of none of its juices or its flavor.

You can also bake gratins in earthenware or enameled-iron dishes. The filled dish should go into a preheated 350- to 375-degree oven.

Sautéed Vegetables

Some vegetables are delicious simply sautéed—seared in a skillet with hot (but not burnt) oil or butter. Try this with onions, cucumbers, and the ingredients of a ratatouille: eggplant, zucchini, bell peppers, and tomatoes. To sauté successfully, keep the pan and its contents moving to prevent sticking.

The Asian version of sautéing is stir-frying in a wok, a round-bottomed pan made of steel designed for use over an open flame (gas or solid fuel). Flat-bottomed versions are also available, as are rings to set under the wok for use on an electric range, but I feel an open flame gives the best results. Stir-frying the vegetables in hot oil keeps them somewhat crunchy and preserves their fresh flavors. Wok cooking is so quick that it should be done only at the last minute—once you have washed, drained, cleaned, and trimmed the vegetables. Here is how I cut vegetables for stir-frying:

A Nice, Brown Gratin

Gratins are usually topped with a cheese that melts nicely (such as Swiss Gruyère or Emmental; Italian fontina; or French Comté or cantal), with or without dry bread crumbs, and perhaps sprinkled with some dried herbs.

Here is a mixture that will give you terrific, gleaming, golden gratins: whip two tablespoons of cold heavy cream; when it forms soft peaks, whisk in an egg yolk. Season with salt and pepper and spread a thin, even layer of this mixture on top of your gratin (already cooked). Broil for a few moments, watching constantly, until it is perfectly browned. If you like, you can also stir a tablespoon of grated Parmesan or Swiss Gruyère cheese into the mixture.

ARTICHOKES: The hearts only, cut into slices $1/8$ inch thick, or into quarters

ASPARAGUS: The tips only, cut into julienne strips $1 1/2$ inches long

BEAN SPROUTS: Whole

BELGIAN ENDIVE: The hearts only, cut crosswise into $3/16$-inch slices

BELL PEPPERS: Strips $1 1/2$ inches long and $3/8$ inch wide

CABBAGE OR CHINESE CABBAGE: $3/8$-inch strips

CARROTS: $1/8$-inch slices or julienne strips

CAULIFLOWER OR BROCCOLI: In florets

CELERY: The heart only (with its leaves), cut into strips 2 inches long

EGGPLANT: Peeled and cut into $3/16$-inch slices or $3/4$-inch cubes

MUSHROOMS: Slices $1/8$-inch thick, or cut in quarters

ONIONS (WHITE): $3/16$-inch slices

PEAS: Shelled

SNOWPEAS: Whole (if young and tender)

Toss the prepared vegetables into a wok containing one tablespoon of a neutral vegetable oil, preheated over high heat. Cooking will take only five or six minutes.

Deep-Frying

The light-cooking brigade disparages deep-frying, but I am very fond of this traditional, very flavorful method so long as certain rules are followed—and given that some vegetables have little appeal when deep-fried (carrots, radishes, parsnips, kohlrabi, cabbage, and so forth).

First, select a neutral vegetable oil such as peanut, sunflower, or corn oil; other oils may not perform as well. If the oil has been used before, make sure it remains light-colored and clear. There must be no particles floating in the oil; if there are, strain them out carefully.

Put the oil into a range-top or electric deep-fryer and heat to 360 degrees. There is an easy way to tell whether a range-top fryer has come up to temperature, even without a thermometer. Moisten a wooden skewer or chopstick and submerge it in the oil; when bubbles rise vigorously

from the end of the chopstick, the oil has reached frying temperature. Much above 360 degrees, the oil will begin to smoke, will become less digestible, and could even catch fire. If it *should* catch fire, never pour water onto the flames; smother them by covering the pan.

Some vegetables can be fried as is. Just peel, wash, and dry them very carefully before cutting them up and putting them into the hot oil a few at a time, turning them to make sure they brown on all sides. If you drain the vegetables well on paper towels and keep them warm and dry, they can stay crisp for several hours, so long as you do not salt them until just before serving.

Celery root (celeriac), beets, potatoes, white of leek, celery leaves, Italian parsley, onion rings, plantains, and thinly sliced garlic can all be fried with no coating. But I prefer to protect the vegetables with a batter; this keeps them tender. Here is a light, crisp batter: mix a scant cup of all-purpose flour, $2 1/2$ tablespoons of cornstarch, and two teaspoons of baking powder with enough very cold water or beer to yield a creamy-thick batter. Add no salt or sugar; these soften the crust. Let me emphasize that the water or beer must be ice cold. Use the batter immediately, keeping it cold over a bowl of ice water.

Here is how to use this batter to make fritters. Remember, all frying is at 360 degrees:

BABY ARTICHOKES: Remove the leaves from the base, cut the artichokes in quarters lengthwise, dip in batter, and fry for 3 minutes.

ASPARAGUS: Peel the asparagus and dry thoroughly with a towel. Cut each spear into 2 equal lengths (about 3 inches long). Dip in batter and fry for 2 minutes.

BELGIAN ENDIVES: Use tiny endives, or remove the outer layers of leaves. Cut each endive heart in half lengthwise. Dip in batter and fry for 1 minute.

BELL PEPPERS: Cut the peppers in half lengthwise and remove the seeds and internal ribs. Cut into strips $3/8$ inch wide. Dip in batter and fry for 1 minute.

BROCCOLI AND CAULIFLOWER: Divide into florets. Use a fork to dip in batter, and fry for 2 minutes.

CELERY: Use only the leaves of the heart, with a little of the stalk attached. Dip in batter and fry for 45 seconds.

CORN: Cut the kernels from the cobs and mix them with one-fourth their volume in batter. Dip the fritters out by the teaspoonful directly into the hot oil. Fry for 1 minute. (Baby corn can be battered and fried whole.)

EGGPLANT: Peel the eggplant and cut into slices about 3/16 inch thick. Use a fork to dip in batter, and fry for 1 1/2 minutes.

GARLIC: Peel the cloves, then blanch them in 4 changes of water (see page 146). Drain, dredge in flour, dip in batter, and fry for 1 minute.

GREEN BEANS AND WAX BEANS: Use very thin beans (if very large, split lengthwise). Trim the ends and string the beans. Dip in batter and fry for 1 1/2 minutes.

ONIONS: Use medium onions. Peel them and slice them about 1/8 inch thick. Divide the slices into rings, dip them in batter, and fry for 1 1/2 minutes.

OKRA: Use small okra. Wash them and dry them thoroughly, dip in batter (holding them by the stem), and fry for 1 1/2 minutes.

PEAS: Shell the peas and mix them with one-fourth their volume in batter. Dip the fritters out by the teaspoonful directly into the hot oil. Fry for 1 minute.

RADICCHIO: Try to get the long rather than the spherical variety of radicchio, with its root still attached. Use the heart of each head and the root. Peel the root and cut the radicchio in quarters lengthwise. Dry well, dip in batter, and fry for 1 1/2 minutes.

SALSIFY AND BLACK SALSIFY: Use small salsify. Peel and keep in water acidulated with lemon juice. Drain, dry thoroughly, and cut into strips about 2 1/2 inches long. Dip in batter and fry for 2 to 3 minutes.

SNOWPEAS: String them, dip them individually in batter, and fry for 1 minute.

SPINACH: Wash the leaves (with a short length of stem attached) and dry them thoroughly. Dip in batter and fry for 20 seconds.

TOMATOES: Use green tomatoes or firm ones that are not fully ripe. You can keep the skin on or peel them. Cut them into quarters or eighths, depending on size, and discard all seeds, juice, and internal membranes. Dry the pieces of tomato flesh, dip them in batter, and fry for 45 seconds.

ZUCCHINI: Wash and thoroughly dry the zucchini, and cut into slices about 3/16 inch thick. Use a fork to dip in batter, and fry for 1 1/2 minutes.

ZUCCHINI BLOSSOMS: Remove the pistils and dip the blossoms in batter. Fry for 1 1/2 minutes.

OPPOSITE PAGE: To keep vegetables crunchy, there is nothing like pickling them in vinegar.

When the vegetable fritters are golden brown, remove them from the oil with a skimmer or slotted spoon, and drain them on a plate covered with paper towels. Salt just before serving.

Braising

Here, we slowly cook one or more vegetables with very little liquid; the heat should surround the vegetables. The best utensil is an enameled-iron or pottery casserole with a tight-fitting lid. You can braise over very low heat, or in a 300- to 350-degree oven. I use this technique for very fresh, tender vegetables—young vegetables fresh from the garden, for example—that can stand on their own and could lose flavor by quick cooking in lots of water.

Grilling

This technique is favored in Mediterranean countries like Italy and Spain, and is increasingly popular in the United States as well; it is still not often used in France. The results are delicious, for the vegetables retain their flavors without becoming oily.

The best grilling is done over the embers of a

fireplace or an outdoor barbecue or grill. But you can certainly use an electric grill (which will not fill the air with spent gas fumes), or even a heavy iron skillet or ridged range-top grill.

No matter what kind of grill you select, take care to clean it thoroughly after each use to remove all blackened cooking residues, which can be unhealthy. Do not use detergents on your grill.

Do not let open flames come in contact with the food; they will give it an unpleasant burnt flavor. Be patient with the fire; the coals should be covered with ash before you begin cooking.

Different vegetables need different grilling temperatures, so I recommend a grill that will let you adjust the distance of the food from the fire. To succeed in grilling, it is important that you learn how to judge the heat and grilling time required; these vary greatly depending on the vegetables, their size, their freshness, and their quantity. I urge you to experiment.

Sun-drenched vegetables such as tomatoes, bell peppers, and zucchini, as well as onions and artichokes, are delicious grilled then drizzled with a little olive oil. You might serve them plain to accompany meat or fish, or you could add a *coulis* of red bell peppers or tomatoes to an assortment of grilled vegetables.

Glazing

This is more a way of finishing vegetables and making them appetizingly glossy than a basic cooking technique. It is used with little fresh vegetables such as carrots, turnips, onions, asparagus tips, broccoli florets, beets, baby zucchini, baby fennel, garlic, peas, and snowpeas.

Peel and trim the vegetables and add cold, lightly salted water just to cover, along with a pinch of sugar and some butter (a little less than two tablespoons per pound of vegetables). Bring to the boil and simmer until the vegetables are tender. Then raise the heat to high and completely reduce the liquid with the pan uncovered. Don't let the vegetables brown.

Preserving Vegetables

My advice is always to chart as short a course as possible between garden and table. The longer vegetables wait, the more they deteriorate. Lettuce, for instance, is never as good as when it has just been picked, its leaves holding the freshness of the morning dew and the gentle warmth of the first rays of the sun. And when you taste a freshly picked radish, just wiped clean of soil, you feel that the earth itself has sprinkled it with pepper. A few days—even a few hours —later, that same radish will have much less to offer.

Many people adore frozen peas or green beans, and it is true that there has been remarkable progress in freezing technology in recent years. But I am suspicious about how serious these people are about food; if they had ever tasted freshly picked peas, even raw, they would see things differently. Let me remind you again that whenever you go to the market it is critical that you buy only very fresh vegetables and eat them as soon after purchase as possible.

Even though most vegetables are now available year-round, you can also opt for out-of-season vegetables preserved in one way or another. This is sometimes better than eating fresh but tasteless green beans, peas, and tomatoes. For preserving vegetables, choose the method that will do the least damage to the flavor.

STORING IN SAND: In temperate climates, root vegetables and tubers (carrots, parsnips, beets, turnips, celery root, kohlrabi, rutabaga, Jerusalem artichokes, salsify, black salsify, and long black or white radishes) keep well outdoors in a pit or in a barrel of sand in the cellar. Salsify kept this way will sprout delicious little leaves you can eat as a salad (see page 168).

DRYING: Vegetables such as green beans, leeks, bell peppers, chili peppers, and sliced eggplant can be dried. Use vegetables in good condition. Wash them, dry them thoroughly with a towel, and thread them onto a length of thin cotton or linen twine. Hang the strings of vegetables in an airy place, and leave until you need them. Before using, soak the dried vegetables in warm water— a few minutes for eggplant and peppers, and an hour for leeks and green beans.

Tomatoes dry nicely in the sun on wooden grids (see page 76). They can then be preserved in olive oil, but I do not recommend this because they often turn black or fall apart. Dried tomatoes store well in an airtight jar.

Before being gathered into bunches or woven into braids, garlic and onions must be dried either outdoors in the sun if time permits or indoors on grids. Then store them in wire crates or hang them up in a dry place.

SALTING: Cabbages—especially big white ones—can be preserved in coarse sea salt, either quartered or cut into strips, packed into stoneware or earthenware crocks. Fermentation brings out a nice acidic flavor, which you can modify by adding a bay leaf, a few juniper berries, or some caraway seeds. Back in the Bourbonnais, in central France, my parents also salted green beans that had grown a little too big. They put them in crocks with alternating layers of coarse sea salt. They would soak them in fresh water for twelve hours, then cook them in boiling water and serve them with cream and a parsley-and-garlic *persillade:* they were as tender a treat as you could ask for.

CANNING: Canning vegetables in sterilized pint glass jars yields excellent results, although you need a pressure cooker. You'll also need proper canning jars and a supply of new lids. I use this method for vegetables grown in plenty and that we have not had enough of during the season, such as green beans, peas, and tomatoes.

For green beans, I trim and string them, wash them, and blanch them for 5 minutes in boiling unsalted water. I cool them under running water, drain them, and pack them into the jars. I fill the jars with salted water (two tablespoons of salt per quart), close the jars, and process them at 10 pounds of pressure for 20 minutes.

Tomatoes, since they have a high enough acid content, can be canned and processed in a hot-water bath. Tomatoes can be canned whole, puréed, or as a *coulis* (see the recipe on page 29). Whole canned tomatoes can be a delicious winter accompaniment for roasted or grilled meats. Choose the nicest tomatoes: firm, smooth, and red, with no blemishes or dents; use the others for purées and *coulis.* Wash the tomatoes carefully in cold water, remove their stems, then briefly blanch them in boiling water so you can peel them. Fill the jars with peeled tomatoes, top with hot water or tomato juice, add a pinch of salt, then close jars and boil in a hot-water bath for 30 minutes.

To can puréed tomatoes, wash about 12 pounds of very ripe tomatoes; remove the stems and any bruised parts, then briefly blanch in boiling water and peel them. Cut the peeled tomatoes in half crosswise and squeeze out the juice and the seeds. Peel and chop two carrots, two small onions, and a clove of garlic; cook them in $1/2$ cup of olive oil until softened, then add a *bouquet garni* (a sprig of thyme, a sprig of savory, a bay leaf, some parsley, and, if you like, a few basil leaves). Add the tomatoes and cook over low heat for 45 minutes or until they become a thick purée. Season with salt, pepper, and a pinch sugar, and strain to remove all remaining seeds.

Fill canning jars, close jars, and process in a hot-water bath for 30 minutes.

Green beans, peas, and tomatoes are the vegetables I am most likely to put up in jars, but others can be very successful too. For instance, young little carrots tasting of the spring are most welcome in the middle of winter, when the farmers' markets can supply only woody old specimens. Use the youngest carrots you can. Do not peel them; just wash them under running water. Blanch them in boiling water for a couple of minutes, layer them into canning jars and fill the jars with salted water (one tablespoon of salt per quart). Process at 10 pounds for 25 minutes.

The asparagus season is brief but abundant. For canning, choose lovely fresh asparagus of more or less uniform length and thickness. Peel them with a vegetable peeler, trim the bases, wash them in cool water, then put them into a large bowl of very cold water.

Bring to the boil about 1½ quarts of water per pound of asparagus. Blanch the asparagus for five minutes, then chill in a bowl of ice water; leave them in the cold water for ten minutes. Place the asparagus in the canning jars tip down so you will not break the spears when removing them. Fill the jars with salted water (1½ tablespoons of salt per quart), seal, and process at 10 pounds for 25 minutes.

If any of the asparagus tips break off during preparation, you can put them up also and use them for soups, omelettes, or garnishes.

For all canning, be sure to check the seals after processing. Refill and reprocess any that have not sealed properly. Store canned vegetables in a dark, cool place.

PRESERVING IN VINEGAR: Some vegetables (such as cauliflower, onions, cornichons, cucumbers, bell peppers, baby corn, celery, and celery root) can be put up in jars and preserved in white vinegar or wine vinegar—in other words, pickled. Process the jars in a hot-water bath and store in a dark place. Eat the pickled vegetables quickly—do not keep them longer than two months, because they tend to get soggy.

FREEZING: Freezing seems to be overtaking canning in popularity. It can give you good results if you follow the basic rules and do not try to freeze every kind of vegetable. I don't recommend freezing watery vegetables such as tomatoes; they are a disaster. And I still prefer home-canned green beans to the frozen ones. On the other hand, freezing is very good for peas, shell beans, and spinach. My advice about freshness and quality are equally valid for freezing. If your only freezer is part of your refrigerator, process only small quantities; even then, since these units are not as cold as a deep freezer, there is always a risk that the temperature will not be cold enough. It is far better to use a stand-alone freezer.

Wash, trim, and meticulously dry your vegetables, then spread them on a plastic tray and put the tray into the freezer. Be sure the freezer is tightly shut, and leave the tray untouched for a few hours. When the vegetables are completely frozen, seal them in plastic freezer bags. This two-stage approach avoids getting large blocks of frozen vegetables. By flash-freezing first, the vegetables remain loose and separated, and you can take out only as much as you need at one time.

Conversions

Ingredients and Equipment Glossary

British English and American English are not always the same, particularly in the kitchen. The following ingredients and equipment used in this book are pretty much the same on both sides of the Atlantic, but have different names:

AMERICAN	BRITISH
beans (dried)— lima, navy, Great Northern	dried white (haricot)— beans
beets	beetroots
Belgian endive	chicory
bell pepper	sweet pepper (capsicum)
broiler/to broil	grill/to grill
celery stalk	celery stick
confectioners' sugar	icing sugar
cornstarch	cornflour
eggplant	aubergine
fava bean	broad bean
heavy cream (37.6% fat)	double cream (35–40% fat)
snow pea	mangetout
peanut oil	groundnut oil
pearl onion	pickling onion
scallion	spring onion
skillet	frying pan
squash	vegetable marrow
tuna	tunny
zucchini	courgette

Volume Equivalents

These are not exact equivalents for the American cups and spoons, but have been rounded up or down slightly to make measuring easier.

AMERICAN	METRIC	IMPERIAL
$^1/_4$ t	1.25 ml	
$^1/_2$ t	2.5 ml	
1 t	5 ml	
$^1/_2$ T (1$^1/_2$ t)	7.5 ml	
1 T (3 t)	15 ml	
$^1/_4$ cup (4 T)	60 ml	2 fl oz
$^1/_3$ cup (5 T)	75 ml	2$^1/_2$ fl oz
$^1/_2$ cup (8 T)	125 ml	4 fl oz
$^2/_3$ cup (10 T)	150 ml	5 fl oz ($^1/_4$ pint)
$^3/_4$ cup (12 T)	175 ml	6 fl oz
1 cup (16 T)	250 ml	8 fl oz
1$^1/_4$ cups	300 ml	10 fl oz
1$^1/_2$ cups	350 ml	12 fl oz
1 pint (2 cups)	500 ml	16 fl oz
1 quart (4 cups)	1 litre	1$^3/_4$ pints

Weight Equivalents

The metric weights given in this chart are not exact equivalents, but have been rounded up or down slightly to make measuring easier.

IMPERIAL	METRIC	IMPERIAL	METRIC
$^1/_4$ oz	7 g	12 oz	350 g
$^1/_2$ oz	15 g	13 oz	375 g
1 oz	30 g	14 oz	400 g
2 oz	60 g	15 oz	425 g
3 oz	90 g	16 oz (1 lb)	450 g
4 oz	115 g	1 lb 2 oz	500 g
5 oz	150 g	1$^1/_2$ lb	750 g
6 oz	175 g	2 lb	900 g
7 oz	200 g	2$^1/_4$ lb	1 kg
8 oz ($^1/_2$ lb)	225 g	3 lb	1.4 kg
9 oz	250 g	4 lb	1.8 kg
10 oz	300 g	4$^1/_2$ lb	2 kg
11 oz	325 g		

Oven Temperature Equivalents

OVEN	°F.	°C.	GAS MARK
very cool	250–275	120–140	$^1/_2$–1
cool	300	150	2
warm	325	160	3
moderate	350	180	4
moderately hot	375	190	5
	400	200	6
hot	425	220	7
very hot	450	230	8
	475	240	9

Butter

Some confusion may arise over the measuring of butter and other hard fats. In the United States, butter is generally sold in a one-pound package, which contains four equal "sticks." The wrapper on each stick is marked to show tablespoons, so the cook can cut the stick according to the quantity required. The equivalent weights are:

1 stick = 115 g /4 oz

1 T = 15 g / $^1/_2$ oz

Flour

American all-purpose flour is milled from a mixture of hard and soft wheats, whereas British plain flour is made mainly from soft wheat. To achieve a near equivalent to American all-purpose flour, use half British plain flour and half strong bread flour.

Sugar

In the recipes in this book, if sugar is called for it is assumed to be granulated, unless otherwise specified. American granulated sugar is finer than British granulated, closer to caster sugar.

Index of Vegetables

254

Acknowledgments

This book came about not just because I wanted to write a new cookbook. It is first and foremost a tribute to vegetables—those delicate, noble offspring of nature. I had the great pleasure of sharing my passion for vegetables with my chefs Michel Duhamel, Serge Chollet, Daniel Desavie, and Joël Manson; their assistance was invaluable. Charles-Henri Flammarion and Gisou Bavoillot are themselves enthusiastic followers of this fresh, honest type of cooking; they fell in quickly with the project and I am most grateful to them for allowing me to see it through. Hearty thanks go also to Martine Anglade for her cooperation, to my assistant Sylvie Auffret, and to Anne Fitamant-Peter, who followed this book every step of the way towards publication.

Françoise Lefébure wishes to thank Marie-Christine Caviglione for her help with styling the photographs.

Her thanks go also to all the shops and manufacturers who graciously supplied everything needed to show the recipes in the best light: L'Autre Côté (Avignon), Michel Biehn (Isle-sur-la-Sorgue), La Boutique du Moulin (Mougins), Le Cèdre Rouge (Avignon), Côté Cour (Isle-sur-la Sorgue), Gilbert Etiemble (antique tableware, at Opio), Jean Faucon (Apt), Mosaïque Gergino (Vallauris), Globe Trotter (Avignon), Jardin de Mougins (Mougins), Ombre et Soleil (Mougins), Spigo Toscano (Puy Sainte-Réparade), Bernard Pichon (Uzès), and Antony Pitot (Goult). Thanks also to: Anthéor, Augié Laribé, Casa Lopez, Etamine, Gunther Lambert, Habitat, Ilios, Le Jacquard Français, Quartz, Verrerie de Biot, Jean Vier, Villeroy et Boch, and Vincent Mit L'Ane.

Martine Anglade's thanks go to Michel Duhamel, Sylvie Auffret, and Annie Godefroy for the valued help.